I0148354

DREAM
TAKE
FLIGHT

An Unconventional Journey

A Shy Girl Breaks the Rules

LISA TURNER

Copyright © 2019, 2022, 2024 by **Lisa Turner**

All rights reserved. No part of this publication may be reproduced, distributed or transmitted in any form or by any means, without prior written permission.

Lisa Turner/Turner Creek Publishing
515 Barlow Fields Drive
Hayesville/NC 28904
www.lisaturnerbooks.com

This book is a memoir. It reflects the author's present recollections of experiences over time. Some names and characteristics have been changed, some events have been compressed or moved in time, and some dialogue has been recreated.

The book is designed to provide inspiration as well as entertainment to my readers. It is sold with the understanding that I am not trying to render psychological, legal, or any other kind of professional advice. The content of each chapter is the sole expression and opinion of its author. No warranties or guarantees are expressed or implied by the goal-setting procedures outlined in this book.

Enjoy!

Dream Take Flight/ Lisa Turner. — 3rd ed.
ISBN: 978-0-9970723-2-7 (Paperback)
ISBN: 978-0-9970723-4-1 (Hardcover)
ISBN: 978-0-9970723-3-4 (e-Book)]

Book Interior and E-book Design by Amit Dey (amitdey2528@gmail.com)

Free companion guides and bonus material for this book can be found at www.DreamTakeFlight.com

To Mom, who always said I could;
to Jerry, who always says I can.

*"We make a living by what we get, but we make
a life by what we give."*

~ Winston Churchill

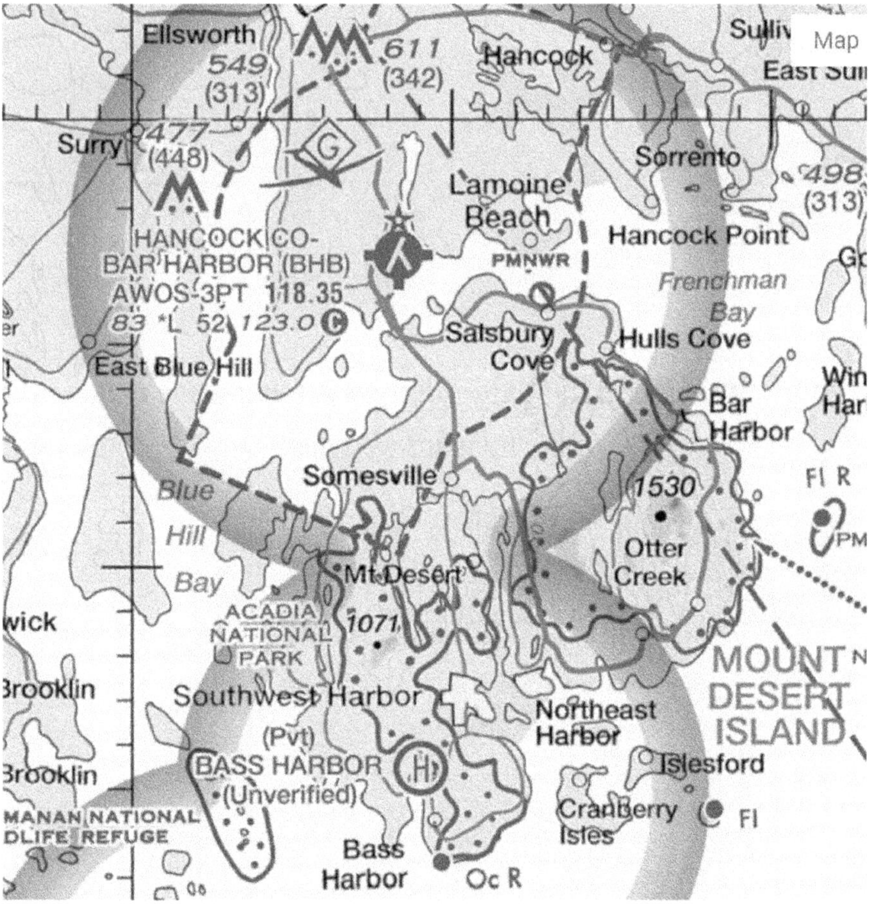

Map
Ellsworth
549
(313)
611
(342)
Hancock
Surry
477
(448)
Sorrento
Lamoine
Beach
Hancock Point
HANCOCK CO-
BAR HARBOR (BHB)
AWOS-3PT 118.35
83 *L 52 123.0
PMNWR
Frenchman
Bay
Salsbury
Cove
Hulls Cove
East Blue Hill
Bar
Harbor
Somesville
1530
Blue
Hill
Bay
Otter
Creek
Mt Desert
ACADIA
NATIONAL
PARK
1071
MOUNT
DESERT
ISLAND
Southwest Harbor
Northeast
Harbor
(Pvt)
BASS HARBOR
(Unverified)
Islesford
Cranberry
Isles
Bass
Harbor
Oc R

CONTENTS

FOREWORD

ANYONE WHO'S EVER HAD doubts about whether they can make their dreams come true should read this book. *Dream Take Flight* is a story about overcoming daunting odds to achieve the near impossible: A young girl in a difficult family situation, facing a scary world and uncertain future, makes up her mind that someday she will fly her own plane. It's not an easy path. On her own, she faces one challenge after another. But she perseveres, and in the end not only does she fly her own plane but also she actually builds it. Then she sets out on an epic solo flight. A tale of courage, iron will, and pure grit, Lisa Turner's journey from dream to reality does not disappoint. It's the great American story with a twist, and an inspiration to young people—especially young women—everywhere.

Granville N. Toogood is a best-selling author of six books, winner of the 2017 McGraw-Hill Classics Special Edition award, a former NBC Today Show News producer, Life Magazine writer, speaker, and top executive coach. His best-selling THE NEW ARTICULATE EXECUTIVE is standard issue in more than 100 business schools.

March 19, 2019, Ocean Ridge, Florida.

PREFACE

THIS BOOK IS FOR ANYONE who has ever set their sights on the improbable.

Since building and flying the Pulsar, I've wanted to write a story. I began writing snippets during my Pulsar cross country, and then a series of articles for *Kitplanes* magazine in the 1990s. The experience was so life changing that I kept writing stories until I had about 10 chapters. Then I wondered if anyone would really be interested, and the project fell into the cracks between careers.

In 2017, twenty years later, I picked it up again, not being able to forget the lessons or the spectacular excitement.

I realized that the Pulsar story wasn't complete without explaining to the reader why I built an airplane in my garage in the first place. This took me on a wild ride through my childhood years.

I have three reasons for writing this book.

The first is to get the memories on paper. The cathartic relief allowing these words to spill out onto the page provided both closure and appreciation.

The second is the hope that you – the reader – will read it and decide to do something you've always wanted to do. It doesn't have to be building and flying an airplane, it can be anything you really care about. To this end I've included chapters at the end of the book to serve as stepping-stones for your own journey.

The third reason is to celebrate an unconventional path for women of all ages. A tomboy at heart, I never understood why I couldn't take shop class, be a mechanic, or build an airplane.

Since I wrote the first article on building an airplane in *Kitplanes* magazine in 1996, I have had the opportunity through the Experimental Aircraft Association (EAA) to help other people build and fly their projects. The encouragement and joy that flows from helping others accomplish their goals will always be the reward that I seek in sharing the stories.

I hope *Dream Take Flight* gives you an insight, a chuckle, or a big dream to pursue.

PROLOGUE

Was the day starting out all wrong?

The sun's corona, still below the horizon, glowed a luminous yellow through a thick veil to the east. The forest canopy below my craft seemed alive as clouds parted and then reattached themselves to the treetops. Damp air snaked through the air vents as I held the control stick in a tight grip.

The instruments glowed in muted reds and greens on the panel, a measure of reassurance that would not last long.

I looked down at a pockmarked expanse of pine forest and glimmering pools. With alligators cruising through the ragged islands of tall grass and stagnant water, this would not be a comforting place for an emergency landing.

Tendrils of mist elongated and began to obscure the landscape below. Islands of dark cloud reached down from above. What had been a kernel of doubt now blossomed into a jagged chunk of fear as I observed the fast-moving darkness close in.

Trapped.

I took a deep breath and willed calm into my growing panic. I pushed the control stick forward, descending to 500 feet, trying to find a channel of visibility.

The sun materialized slowly in the east, a multicolor aura circling a bright yellow core. Fingers of peach-colored light reached out and touched the shiny white wings of the Pulsar.

What should I do?

The ground haze continued to grow, moving in patches, as the upper masses of cloud stood their ground. Technically I was still VFR (Visual Flight Rules) – having the ground in sight, one mile of visibility, and clear of clouds. Barely. I took in another gulping breath, feeling the sharp edges of failure.

In flight training they tell you that multiple small mistakes in judgment add up until you have a serious set of problems. In training I always vowed to not get myself into a dangerous situation.

Climb.

I pointed the nose of the little airplane up into a narrow channel of clear sky and applied power. I leveled off at 1,000 feet. I could no longer see the ground, except for holes scattered in the clouds. The silver sheen of the swamp pools reached up to my airplane in dancing beams, as if to draw me down and in.

Disappointment joined the knot of fear. The day I've dreamt about my whole life.

What am I going to do?

I banked my little craft to the right, changing course 180 degrees, heading back the way I had come, threading my way down through the gaps in the dark twisting cloud banks as rain began to splatter loudly on the canopy.

PART ONE

DREAM

"Life is either a daring adventure or nothing."

~ Helen Keller

1

DREAMS

THE NIGHT AIR SHIMMERED in mist and the pungent aroma of pine permeated the dampness. My bare feet sank into the emerald moss carpet of the forest, soft and lush. I spanned a moonlit cathedral clearing in six strides and re-entered the grove on a foot-worn path filled with wet leaves and spent pine needles.

Out of the corner of my eye I caught a glimpse of motion behind me. Twigs cracked. A rhythmic panting grew louder.

Faster. Run faster.

I dared a quick glance behind. Flashes of silver fur, oval sea-blue eyes, and ivory claws pounding the path, gaining on me as I broke out of the tree line, sprinting to the cliffs.

Go, go! Now!

I floated my arms out from my sides and caught the heavy air in a quick jerk. Lifting effortlessly on air wings, my body launched out over the silver-speckled granite cliff. The galloping tiger came to an abrupt halt just short of the cliff rim, disoriented. Pebbles and dirt fell from the turf edge, tumbling down the steep bank in slow motion. The sleek animal stood motionless at the edge and shook its head in confusion.

Lights in the valley twinkled like 10,000 chandeliers as I slid through the air on a wind fold. My small frame in a soft caress, my long hair swirled outwards. Air rushing now, faster and faster. Was I falling or flying?

Sudden panic stabbed at me as I looked down into the twilight. *I'm falling!*

I was much too far away from the small homes tucked into the valley. Now I was disconnected. Would my powers hold? What if I fell now?

Float like its water; just float, relax.

I took a deep breath. My heart was still pounding from the sprint through the forest. I cocked my body downward and caught the liquid air again with my hands, accelerating toward the tiny lights below.

I have control. I won't fall. I am an airplane.

Faster I went, the air buffeting my hair and flattening my shirt. Fly up! Up! I swooped upward and banked to the left. Then to the right.

Flying! I am flying!

Exhilaration displaced my fear and the breath of the planet flowed with mine as I glided down toward the gleaming lights of the valley. I raised my head back and moved my arms out flat against the airstream to slow myself. The ground was coming up fast.

Too fast! Control, control. Concentrate.

As my descent slowed, houses and neighborhoods came into clear relief. Which house? I was lost. No, I would find it. I always did. I floated along, slowing, looking for landmarks. Slow, float, slow. . . 50 feet above the trees, feeling the arms of the breeze, slow.

Euphoria surged, my powers holding. I recognized the streets, I knew the way to go.

I floated up deliberately, my arms treading air. Like a helicopter descending slowly to its landing pad, I lowered, concentrating. Energy consumed. My feet touched the wet grass. All of my weight was now on the ground. Suddenly I felt my 60-pound frame sink in to the Earth with toes spread. I shivered involuntarily, with the cold reaching up from the soles of my feet.

No one saw my early morning descent into the backyard of our modest split-level home. This is the way it always was. I wasn't sure why no one noticed me, but I was glad, because the concentration was enormous; distractions interfered with my powers.

"Lisa!" My mother's call was urgent through the open bedroom door. "It's time to get up for school."

I blinked my eyes open and shut them again.

"Ten minutes."

"No, Lese, come on, please get up."

"Ok, ok, I'm up. I'm up."

I stretched and thought about going back to sleep. Back to my flight. I loved the sensation of flying through the night air, with complete control. It was so real. When I dreamed I was flying, I really was flying. The exhilaration and the fear competed and were real. Escape. Go back to sleep. Dream and fly. You are the airplane.

"Lisa!"

"I'm up, Mom, I'm up."

She calls me Lese when she's relaxed, and Lisa when she's tense.

I threw the blanket back on the bed and sat up. I rubbed my eyes and ran my hands through my short blonde hair.

I hate school days.

The energy of my dream began to fade as I thought about school. Everything was completely out of step. Teachers were always upset with me. But today is Friday. Tomorrow is Saturday. Maybe I could live through today and get to tomorrow. How?

Develop a plan.

Standing up, I navigated a winding path though comic books, *Tom Swift* and the *Hardy Boys* mysteries, transistor radio parts, Twinkie wrappers, and an assortment of cardboard boxes to the closet. I gathered up some clothes from the closet floor and padded down the hall to the bathroom.

"Don't be afraid to take a big step. You can't cross a chasm in two small jumps."

~ David Lloyd George

2

ROCKET PILOT

I PULLED A CEREAL BOX off the kitchen shelf. Mom had placed a ceramic bowl and a pint of milk on the counter. She sat next to me in her pajamas, disheveled. I knew she would go back to bed after I left for school. She lit a cigarette and inhaled deeply.

"That thing smells awful."

"I know. I shouldn't do it. Don't ever do this, Lese," Mom shook her head.

"Mom, why can't girls be rocket pilots?" I asked.

"Who said you couldn't be a rocket pilot?" Mom said with a puzzled look.

"Neil."

"Who is Neil?"

"My boyfriend at school. We sit together in reading class and homeroom."

"Your boyfriend? What did Neil tell you?" Mom looked at me with a smile and a what-is-it-now look.

"That girls can't be rocket pilots because they might need to be rescued because they don't know how to work things," I replied.

Mom unsuccessfully suppressed a chuckle and then looked at me with a serious face. "Lisa, you can be anything you want to be. If you want to be a rocket pilot, then you can be a rocket pilot. Don't listen to anyone who tells you anything else. If you think you can't be something, then you won't even try. Both boys and girls, and grownups, have to be rescued from time to time; it doesn't have anything to do with whether you are a boy or girl."

Mom got off the bar stool unsteadily and moved over to me for a hug. She was so smart and she knew exactly what I was thinking all the time, which made it difficult to get away with anything. I craved the attention that she gave me.

"Ok, so I want to invent a rocket ship like Tom Swift's rocket and take off from the backyard. Or, even better, make a backpack for flying through the air." I wouldn't mention to Mom right now that actually I could FLY through the air all by MYSELF. But I would tell her, soon. We were best friends; I had to tell Mom everything, no matter what it was. Even when I was bad, she listened to me carefully before the admonishment came.

"Lese, you can do all those things but there's one thing you will need to do first."

"What do I need to do first?" I was so happy she was taking me seriously.

"School. You need to pay attention in school. You need to learn about physics and math, and the other details that making a rocket ship require. I know you love to read, but there's more to navigating life than just being able to read."

I knew my mother was right, but I didn't want to think about it. She was being gentle with me. I needed discipline, but Mom didn't have the heart to deliver it. She spoiled me.

She went on, now more sternly, "Yesterday the school administrator called me to say that you'd missed three days of school again with no written excuse. It caught me off guard, I didn't know where you were."

I exhaled. I didn't want to go to school. I hated the little skirt I had on with the tartan design and the white plastic belt. It was impossible to climb a tree in it. Usually I wore shorts underneath my dresses so I could get out of them quickly when school was out. Mom didn't know that I was skipping school. I would tell the teacher an excuse, I would make it up, and she would write it down in a notebook. I thought they would let it go.

What was I thinking?

Mom knew now. I was trapped. My face flushed and my stomach knotted up. I was going to have to tell her everything. But not now.

"Oh, Lese, your Dad called. He wants to see you next weekend."

The knot in my stomach got bigger and my face got hotter. I held my breath as my mother looked at me.

No, no.

"The last time I was with Dad his girlfriend was mean to me. She doesn't like me. She said you didn't dress me right. And then her dog tried to bite me. She said I was a . . . waif. What's a waif?"

Mom shook her head and looked at me. "You didn't tell me the dog tried to bite you."

"It wasn't as bad as Alexandra saying you that you don't take care of me. Please Mom, I don't want to go."

"Ok. I'll tell your Dad you don't want to go now. Maybe later."

"Good." I took a deep breath in relief.

"Ok, Rocket Pilot in Training, finish up your cereal and brush your teeth. You need to get going."

Change the subject.

"Mom, have you seen Eric?"

"No, I haven't, did he escape again?"

"Yup, he did. I think he got out of his cage the day before yesterday, because I went to feed him last night and he wasn't in there."

"Didn't you end up finding him on that rhododendron plant by the front window in the living room last time? I think he likes that plant." Mom came over to me. "We'll find Eric. Come on, get ready for school."

"Let me look for Eric."

"No, Lese, not now. When you get home. Please."

"Ok, ok." I picked up my book bag and went out the back door.

Eric was a chameleon. He was a gift from my brother Jeff. Why Jeff chose to do something so nice for his little sister was inexplicable. I made a terrarium for Eric, filled with bugs, worms, twigs, and moss. But every few months he escaped. We always found him on a plant. Eric was a lime green American chameleon, also known as a red-throated Anole. His end-to-end size was all of five inches, so he blended in perfectly with the plants.

"The nicest thing about not planning is that failure comes as a complete surprise rather than being preceded by a period of worry and depression."

~ Sir John Harvey-Jones

3

THE FORT

SUNLIGHT SIFTED THROUGH THE TREES in dancing patches on the footpath to the aqueduct. An autumn chill hung in the air, dew drops sparkling on the tips of leaves and silver orbs hanging from the boughs of pine trees. The same rich pine aroma of my flying dream forest enveloped me, and I drank it in gulps as I started running on the path. A stillness hung in the morning air like a spell. I heard my sneakered feet crunch the pine needles and remaining crisp fall leaves. I reached the aqueduct and made a right turn, towards Happy Hollow Elementary School.

The aqueduct, as everyone called it, was the water supply for the town. It was a wide grass path that could fit a truck. I rarely saw anyone walking it, and never in the morning when I went to school. I could have taken the school bus, but the bus trip was 20 minutes long with all its stops. The aqueduct was a straight shot, private, and fun.

The eight-minute walk brought me to the edge of the schoolyard. I stopped and looked through the trees at the red brick building. Children were lingering around the picnic tables and playground, waiting for the bell to begin the day.

The last two days I had stopped exactly like this and decided not to go into the schoolyard, but to go back home and play. If I entered school now, would they send me to the principal's office? What excuse would I use for the last two days? What had Mom told them on the phone?

I'll be in trouble. I'll have to go to the principal's office again. I'll have to stay after school again. I will have to write a message over and over again. The other children will laugh at me again.

I shifted my weight from one foot to the other and closed my eyes. I took a deep breath and looked back at the schoolyard.

I can't.

I turned around and walked the half mile back home. The farther away I got from Happy Hollow School the better I felt.

I returned through the backyard, the sunlight brighter and the air warmer. I quietly inched open the side door to the garage. I listened for activity. Nothing. My mother had gone back to bed. This is how it always was. She would stay up all night and then sleep until 3 pm.

Sometimes the family friend, Chuck, would come over late at night and drink with Mom. They would laugh and then they would fight. Last week I had awoken with a start hearing them shouting. Then a glass broke. A spike of fear went through me and my breathing became quick and short.

Get out. Get out of the house.

I tiptoed down the hall from my bedroom, shaking and shrinking against the wall, hoping they wouldn't notice me. I slipped past the kitchen door where Mom and Chuck were screaming at each other. Down the stairs, into the garage, I slipped out the side door.

I breathed a sigh of relief. *Get away. Run.*

I put the sneakers and jeans on that I had grabbed and ran down the street to the model homes under construction. I entered the second home, which was farther along than the others, and went upstairs to the bathroom. The home was still only framed, not yet ready for drywall, but the house wrap was on the outside. I climbed inside the tub and took another deep breath. The pounding of my heart was slowing. *It's ok; it's ok.*

I fell asleep.

An icy breeze woke me up. I looked around. Where was I? A slug of fear. Then I realized that I'd run from the house. I had no idea what time it was. I shivered. *I better get home!* I sat up straight in the tub. Moonlight was shining through the open window frame. I saw my dog, Smiley, get up from her sentinel position next to the tub.

"Smiley! How did you get here?" She cocked her head. "You followed me! Good girl!" She wagged her tail vigorously. A collie-shepard mix, she was a loyal companion. She was named after her habit of baring her teeth into a smile when she got excited.

I crawled out of the bathtub and made my way down the steps to the first floor and exited the open side door. It was eerily quiet, and no lights were showing in any of the neighbors' homes. Chuck's car was gone.

Good.

I went in the garage side door with Smiley and took my sneakers off, padding quietly back upstairs to my room. The kitchen was a mess. Passing mom's room, I saw that she was asleep. I entered my room and lay down on my bed, quickly falling asleep.

■ ⬳ ■

I shook my head now as I recalled the incident.

I hope he never comes back.

I walked through the garage and snuck down the hallway. Across from my brother's room was a clothes closet packed with coats and shirts. I slid past the clothing to a small square door in the wall under the landing of our compact split-level home. I got on my hands and knees and moved the two latch bolts outward and moved the door aside. After crawling inside, I placed the door back into position. I had mounted two latches on the inside, so it was a secure space and no one could break in.

My fort consisted of a six-foot by five-foot space, with another three feet extending back under the stairs. Piled in layers on the concrete floor were four blankets and two pillows that I propped up on one side to provide sitting comfort while reading.

Stacked along one wall in between the two-by-fours were sets of *Hardy Boys, Nancy Drew,* and *Tom Swift* hardback books, and three stacks of Superman comic books. A single 40-watt light bulb in a fixture hung bare from the four-foot-high ceiling.

In another corner were my catalogs and kit components - *Popular Mechanics,* the *Allied* catalog, *Edmund Scientific,* and *Boy's Life.* I would ask Mom for money so that I could send away for airplane model kits and electronics kits. She would give me ten cents and I would painstakingly print my name and address on the order form and tape the dime above it, fill out the front of an envelope, and wait patiently for the model brochure to arrive ten weeks later.

The comic books were creased and worn. I reached over to the stack and pulled out the one on the bottom. I propped up the pillows and leaned back, reading. I felt the cold coming through the blanket layers from the concrete floor. I needed to get another blanket or maybe some towels from the upstairs closet. Not now. I lay on my side, trying to get more comfortable.

I began reading, losing track of time.

Lisa

"It feels good to be lost in the right direction."

~ Anonymous

4

THE WICKED WITCH

I WAS STARTLED BY A loud staccato knock directly above my hideaway.

The front door. Uh oh.

I knew my mom was not going to wake up to answer the door. Her bedroom was upstairs and down the hallway. "Wait a minute!" I shouted from the crawlspace.

I crawled out the hatch and into the closet where I stood up and navigated through the clothing to the closet door. "I'm coming!" I shouted once more.

I ran up the short flight of stairs to the landing and opened the front door. A tall thin woman in a dark green dress with white piping trim at the shoulders stood holding a brown leather satchel. Her auburn hair was pulled up on the back of her head in a bun, making her face look stretched. I shrank back from the threshold.

Oh no! From the Principal's office!

But she also looked like someone else . . . The Wizard of Oz . . . the Wicked Witch of the West! In disguise!

"Are you Lisa Turner?" she uttered in a low, guttural voice, emphasizing YOU. "May I come in? Where is your mother?"

The witch-in-disguise glided through the doorway and on to the landing without waiting for me to answer. My heart was pounding. "I'll get my Mom, I'll get my Mom," was all I could utter. I ran up the stairs and down the hall to my mother's room as if being chased by a monster.

Bursting through the bedroom door I ran to my mother who was sound asleep. The clock by her bed indicated 12 noon.

"Mom, Mom, someone is here to see you from the school!"

Mom opened her eyes as I shook her shoulder urgently. "Ok, ok, give me a minute. Please go escort them to the living room. I'll be along in a few minutes."

I ran back down the hall. The wicked-witch-of-the-school stood on the landing, looking up. Yes, definitely she was looking more and more like the witch. A scowling, pinched face . . . about to yell . . .

"Uh, please come in, please come up to the living room and my mother will be out in a few minutes."

"Thank you." The woman walked up the stairs and followed me in to the living room.

"Have a seat, my mother will be right here."

At least my mother had taught me how to be polite in the face of adversity.

The woman chose a chair by the window and sat down, not saying a word. I didn't know whether to leave, stay where I was, or sit down. She wasn't saying anything more, so I stood uncomfortably, shifting from one foot to the other.

"Ah, let me check on my mom," I said in a whisper as I backed up slowly, expecting the wicked witch to fling a dart or spell of some sort. All the woman did was look out the window like a statue.

She's weird.

I retreated to the hallway where I inhaled deeply. Time slowed to a crawl, and it must have been at least four minutes before Mom came down the hall.

The woman stood as my mother entered the room.

"Mrs. Turner, I am Miss Baker, the truancy officer from the Happy Hollow Elementary School Principal's office. This is an official visit."

"Please have a seat, Miss Baker," my mother said courteously, with a smile, and sat down in the next chair.

How can Mom be so composed and polite? The wicked witch is right here in our living room.

"Would you like to speak privately or would you like Lisa to be present?" asked Mom.

"That's fine, she can stay here. In fact, it might be good for her to hear this," said the wicked witch.

My face was flushed. My throat was dry. I sat down on the edge of the chair but wished I could run down the hall to my room. Could I sneak away? Could I crawl under the chair? Would they notice?

"Are you aware, Mrs. Turner, that this is the third day that Lisa did not show up for school this week?" Mrs. Baker looked very serious and uttered this statement with venom. I shrank back in my seat.

Wow, am I in trouble!

Mom looked over at me with concern. "Lisa, I thought you were leaving for school this morning after breakfast? Didn't we talk about this?"

I tried to make myself disappear into the upholstery seat cushion.

"Did you come back home and go to your fort again?"

I bit my lower lip and lowered my head. I traced the outline of the trim on the upholstered chair arm.

I let Mom down. What am I going to do now?

"Miss Baker, I do understand that this is serious. Lisa is having difficulty with her school subjects for a variety of reasons. One of these is a lack of discipline and oversight from me. Another is having to repeat a grade and being teased by the other children. Another is perhaps an absent father."

Mom turned to me. "Lisa, you can see that this is troubling. School is important. I'd like you to take the school bus from now on and not walk to school. We'll talk more, ok?"

I nodded, still tongue-tied.

My mother continued, "Miss Baker, please tell Mr. Garner and Mr. Charles that Lisa will now be riding the school bus. Add her name to the ridership list and call me immediately if Lisa is missing."

"Mrs. Turner, I will be happy to tell the principal and administrator of your plan, and I think it is a very good idea. We have never been happy with the walk to school idea, especially with a child barely 12 years old and one on the small side, you never know what could happen." Miss Baker wrote furiously in a notebook she had pulled out of her satchel while she was talking.

I sighed and looked around nervously. Would the wicked witch never leave?

In my peripheral vision I spotted Eric, the chameleon, on the rhododendron plant. His bright lime green head was nodding up and down, up and down. He cocked his head toward the wicked witch, moving his angular jaw back and forth. He took a few quick steps on the large leaf and crouched.

Uh Oh.

Miss Baker began speaking again, but I wasn't listening.

"Alright then, but I will need . . . OH!!"

Eric had jumped directly onto the wicked witch's green dress with the white piping and blended right in. She jumped up, hopping on one foot and slapping at her dress.

"Get off, get off!" the wicked witch shrieked.

Poor Eric, oh no!

"Off, off, get off!" she shrieked as Eric went flying.

Miss Baker grabbed her satchel and ran to the stairs. "We will talk again," she shouted from the landing. We heard the door slam.

Mom and I both looked down at little Eric, who had somehow survived the awful encounter with the wicked witch and had hopped back on to the rhododendron leaf. He cocked his head to one side, then up and down.

We heard a car start and then roar up the street.

Mom looked back at me, trying very hard to be serious but with a twinkling in her eyes that couldn't be held captive.

We both burst out laughing at the same time.

"Do not fear the winds of adversity. Remember, a kite rises against the wind rather than with it."

~ Unknown

5

CAR TROUBLE

I AWOKE TO THE SOUND of the garage door moving noisily in its tracks. My room was directly over the garage. It was a loud, complaining noise on this early Saturday morning, breaking the soft morning chatter of the songbirds. Pale filtered sunlight began its dance on the far wall of my bedroom. The casement windows were both cracked open, the air cool and clean smelling with a hint of decaying leaves. Soon the neighbors would be mowing their lawns, further disrupting the morning calm.

I moved the blanket aside and stood up, the mist of dreams still clinging like tendrils.

A flying machine.

Walking over to the window in my bare feet, I climbed up on the wooden toy box under the window and looked out. My brother was pulling a Toro lawn mower out in to the driveway.

I smiled.

I have a plan.

Jeffrey fiddled with some cables on the machine and pushed a lever. He pulled a cord with a red handle and the engine made a scraping noise. He pulled the cord again, harder. The same noise. Then he pulled the lever back to where it was to begin with. Again he yanked on the cord and this time the engine rumbled to life unsteadily. I watched as he walked the mower to the edge of the lawn. He pulled another lever at the top of the handle, and the mower began moving across the lawn. I watched as my brother allowed the machine to roll across the carpet of lawn in neat, manicured rows. I inhaled the air with the earthy, cut grass smell.

Can I do that?

I went to the closet. Saturday! No school, just time to play. Time to put my plan together. I pushed the closet track door to the left as catalogs and model kit parts fell out onto the floor. The problem with my room organization was that I thought everything should be within reach. I had arranged a dual path through the room, with stuff on either side. I still couldn't find anything. I pulled on a bright blue t-shirt from the closet floor, a pair of long pants, and white cotton socks. Where were my sneakers? I walked across the room and picked up the left one and looked around the jumble. I found the mate under the bed.

At four feet nine inches tall and just over 70 pounds I thought I could accomplish anything. I delighted in running up to the doorjamb where Mom measured my height and marked it with the date.

I always figured out a way to reach things. Sometimes my plans didn't go well. The day I decided to wash my Mom's 1956 Lincoln Premier was one of those days. Just getting the garage door up was a challenge. To get the car out into the driveway for washing, I went to the front of the car, lodged myself between the front bumper and the wall, and pushed with my feet on the wall and my back on the bumper. I pushed and pushed, to no avail. Then I realized that the parking brake was set. I figured out how to release the brake. Then I tried again. This time the car began moving, very slowly, out into the driveway.

A 12-year-old has no concept of a 4,000-pound metal mass on a slope. I ran to the car door, jumped into the driver seat, and had the brake back on just before the car reached the street.

I was so pleased to have the car out. For the next hour and a half I washed and dried the entire car. I knew Mom would be surprised. After I washed the car, I realized that I didn't know how to get it back into the garage. This was a real dilemma. I could try to push it back in, but with the slope on the driveway, I doubted that I would be able to release the brake and then run to the back of the car to push it.

It's a surprise. I have to put the car back in the garage.

My second thought to get the car back in the garage was to find the keys, start the car, and drive it in to the garage. I considered that I didn't know how to drive a car, and even though I'd watched my mother and my brother very intently, I really did not know what all the controls did.

The day ended well, with my mother waking up to my search for her car keys as I rummaged around in her pocket book in her bedroom.

My attention turned back to the cool fall day outside my window and my brother walking with the mower up and down the yard. I needed to think this plan through all the way, unlike the car-washing project. I didn't want to get in trouble *again*.

Suddenly the mower shut off. Jeff was pulling the machine back into the garage. The garage door closed, and Jeff got into his car. The strange-looking Isetta with three wheels started, and Jeff was off up the street.

"Life is really simple, but we insist on making it complicated."

~ Confucius

6

THE LAWN MOWER

I PULLED THE MOWER OUT into the driveway and located it sideways so it wouldn't roll down the slope. I reached for the wadded-up piece of paper in my pocket with the directions I had written down.

I pulled my red wagon out and lined it up with the back of the mower. I took the wagon handle and placed it low on the back of the mower. I sat down next to the mower and tried to determine where to tie the handle. I wrapped a short section of white cotton rope around both mower handle-stabilizing tubes, bringing a section through the wagon handle. I did my best at a square knot, which I tied as a granny knot and then deliberately undid it, rerouting the rope under-over to make the square knot. I never could figure out why I couldn't tie the square knot first since every time I tried it, it turned out as a granny knot. Maybe it was because I was left-handed.

I tested my tandem arrangement by climbing in the wagon and kneeling. I grabbed the mower handle assembly at the top to see if I could turn it. There was no way of finding out until the wagon was under way. I would just have to test it.

A feeling of apprehension stopped me and I sat down in the wagon. Was there something I was missing? I was planning on riding down to the end of the street, a cul-de-sac, and coming back. Will the mower stay running? Will my wagon track it?

No, it will be fine.

I grabbed the pull cord and yanked. The cord wouldn't move at all. What was I doing wrong? I pulled harder. The cord moved out from the case about two inches. I pulled again. Three inches. When I watched my brother start the mower, it looked easy. Disappointment soaked my excitement. I sat down in the wagon.

"Lisa what are you doing?" came a voice from behind me. Startled, I turned to see Will, a friend who lived across the street.

"You scared me!" I said.

"What are you doing with that lawn mower?" Will said.

"Don't tell anyone, Will."

"How can I tell anyone if I don't know what you are doing?" Will was two years older than me, but with the same slim build as mine. His shock of blonde hair flopped across his forehead and stuck up straight on the top of his head looking like he just woke up. His bright blue eyes gazed out of a face full of freckles.

"I'm trying to start this thing."

"Uh oh." Will saw the red wagon. "You're gonna get in trouble with that."

"Don't tell!"

"I won't! But someone is going to see you for sure."

"Will, here, come on, I can't start it, the pull cord is stuck or something. What do you think is wrong with it?" I grabbed the pull cord and yanked. The cord came out two inches and stopped.

Will looked carefully at the choke lever, and switches. "Well, for one thing, if you had started it, you wouldn't have gone very far. The fuel selector is set to OFF."

"It's not in my notes. No wonder."

He moved the switch to ON. "Stand back," Will said as he struggled with the pull cord. It came all the way out and the engine turned over but did not start.

"Wow!" I exclaimed. "How did you do that?"

Will pulled the cord a second time, faster. The engine sounded like it was going to catch. On the third pull, the Toro roared to life. Will grinned and said something to me, but I couldn't hear him. Debris from under the mower was redistributing itself across the driveway.

"Thanks!" I shouted as I jumped in my wagon. I pushed the traction engage lever to the first stop, and the mower moved forward with a jerk, causing me to fall backwards into the wagon. I got back on my knees and grabbed the mower handle to steer. The rope went taut and away I went, down the driveway towards the street.

Will stood in the driveway, shaking his head in disbelief and shouting something I couldn't hear. The mower picked up speed on the driveway slope and I had just enough room to turn the Toro into the street.

My trepidation gave way to jubilance. I gave a shout, "Yay!" and looked down the street. The mower was chewing up leaves and small stones, spitting them out the discharge chute. Dust and debris spewed from the blade casings, filling the air behind me with a dust cloud.

I looked at the traction lever and moved it to "2." Now I was really flying down the road, toward the cul-de-sac, where I would have room to turn around. I forgot about the racket and flying pebbles as I felt the breeze in my hair and watched the landscape go by at four mph.

Success!

I heard shouting behind me over the roar of the mower. I looked back up the street and saw Mr. Hunter, a neighbor, come running down his driveway behind me. My mower-powered wagon wasn't fast enough to outrun Mr. Hunter. I thought about putting in more power to escape.

"Hey! Hey, hey," said Mr. Hunter as he caught up with me.

"Stop! Stop! Stop! He said. "Hey, hey, hey!" Mr. Hunter's eyes bulged and his mouth was wide open as he shouted at me.

I wondered if Mr. Hunter always said things in threes. I pulled the traction lever to stop. The mower's forward motion stopped so fast I fell forward in my wagon and nearly fell over into the street. I hit my knee hard on the side of the wagon and winced.

Mr. Hunter reached me and grabbed my arm and the mower handle. He looked at the handle and pushed the OFF button. The engine sputtered and died.

Oh gee, great, how am I going to get this thing started again.

"This is dangerous!" said Mr. Hunter. "Do your parents know where you are?" His eyes were wide with panic. His breath came in spurts as he blurted the words. I got the feeling he didn't go jogging very often.

I sat in my red wagon, quiet, my knee throbbing. I was speechless again. This is always what happened, I just couldn't figure out what to say or do when confronted with an angry adult.

Will came running down the street, stopping in front of us.

"Will, you need to help this little girl get back to her house with this."

Mr. Hunter turned back toward me.

"Are your parents home?"

"My Mom is home."

"Where is your dad?"

"I don't have a dad."

"What do you mean you don't have a dad?"

"He is not with us anymore."

"Oh, I'm sorry!"

"No, I mean he lives in the city, he left us to be with someone else."

"You mean he divorced your Mom."

"That's it."

"Ok, well, William can help you get this back home. This is not safe. See the blades under that cover?"

He pointed to the mower casing. "The blades are always going, and if the machine overturns and hits you, it would be a very bad accident. It could even kill you. Will you promise not to do this again?"

"Ok, I said. I looked down at the street and the areas of grass and debris scattered about.

Not.

I couldn't wait to get home, to get away, to stop being in trouble. My plan was perfect, except for Mr. Hunter having nothing else to do on a Saturday morning than to prevent a little girl from experimenting with machinery.

I got out of the wagon painfully, trying not to show I had bruised my knee. Will and I untied the wagon and he pushed the mower and I pulled the wagon back up the street to the house. Mr. Hunter stood in the middle of the street, watching us, shaking his head.

I hope he doesn't call Mom.

"Well, you got out of that pretty good," said Will.

"Yeah, well if Mr. Hunter had more interesting things to do inside his house instead of running out here to stop me it would have been better. I was just getting going. I was going to continue to the turnaround circle and the end of the street and then come back up this way."

"It was fun, huh?"

"Great! It was great! Will, we need to make a machine that runs with an engine but it's safe and you and I can fit in it and go exploring."

"Just buy a motorized cart, a go-cart, I've seen them," said Will, throwing his hands in the air. "You're making things too complicated."

"No. How am I going to buy a go-cart? They must be at least a hundred dollars. Second, what fun is that? The fun part is making it."

Will looked at me and laughed. His blue eyes danced with amusement.

We reached the driveway. I looked around to see if anyone was looking at us. The neighborhood was quiet. It looked like only Mr. Hunter had discovered my adventure. He was now gone from the street.

"Come over to my house, Lisa. Let's play in the fort after we put this back in your garage. Hopefully no one will know what you did."

"Me? You helped!"

"I was afraid you were going to say that."

We put the mower and the wagon back in the garage in the corner. I looked around. Except for the songbirds, the neighborhood was quiet, awaiting the hustle and bustle of weekend chores.

I sighed. Back to the drawing board.

"Start where you are. Use what you have.
Do what you can."

~ Arthur Ashe

7

RADIOS AND SPACESHIPS

THAT NIGHT AS I WAS FALLING asleep, I heard a car pull in the driveway. I knew it wasn't my brother because he was on a trip somewhere.

Probably just turning around.

There was a knock on the door and I heard my mother answering. I heard Chuck's voice.

Oh no.

I sat up.

Where can I hide.

I got out of bed and pressed my ear up to the wall.

"Heath, I had to come back to say I am sorry," I heard Chuck say.

"Chuck, it always ends in a fight. The last time was the worst. I can't see things getting any better. You're not moving in, and we're not getting married. Ever."

Mom's words were strong.

Good for you, Mom!

"I expected that. Ok, well, I'm sorry. I'm moving to Cleveland. Can we have one more drink together?"

"No. Chuck, I'm sorry. You have to leave. Now."

I heard Chuck mumbling something. The door opened and closed. I heard the car start and drive away. Everything was quiet. I opened the door to the hallway and looked out.

Mom was standing in the hall in a robe. I came out of the doorway and walked over to her.

"I was scared," I said.

Mom hugged me. "I know you were. I was too. Things will be fine, ok?" She held me by the shoulders and looked at me. A tear ran down her cheek. She hugged me again.

■ ⟶ ■

I immersed myself in catalogs and comic books when I didn't have a solution to life's problems. I loved playing with the older boys in the neighborhood, who were interested in the same things I was.

"If we are going to build a spaceship, we have to have a radio," I said to Will as we got off the school bus the next day. "I ordered a kit radio from a catalog. *Edmund Scientific*."

"Why do you need a radio?" asked Will.

"What if you are up there in space and get lost?" I replied.

"That does make sense."

"Plus, when you're bored going somewhere, you can listen to music. The AM band will reach a long way."

Will looked at me and shook his head. "You're the only girl I know who talks like that. My sisters all want to play house and make tiny sets of clothes for the dolls."

"Ick," I said, laughing. "I'm glad I don't have to do that."

"Me either. You're a lot more fun to play with."

We stopped in the street as I pulled out an *Edmund Scientific* catalog from my book bag.

"I didn't think you were supposed to bring those to school."

"I put it in the textbook in class and then I look like I'm reading the textbook."

"Then how do you learn anything?"

"Why do you think I'm having to repeat the grade?"

"I like you," said Will.

"I like you, too, Will."

"Do you want to get married and start a family?" asked the sandy-haired 14-year-old.

"No! That sounds awful."

Will burst into laughter.

I was finally allowed to enroll in junior high school. I think the elementary school was just trying to get rid of me. The school was "downtown" about three miles from the house. It was a different bus route and a different set of classmates. I was apprehensive.

The night before the first day of school Mom asked me if I understood where to get the bus and if I had everything I needed. I wasn't sure, but I said yes. I was hoping that she would take me to school on the first day.

"Mom, would you take me to school tomorrow?" I asked tentatively at dinner.

She looked at me with her "no" face, but there was more there that I couldn't decipher. A sadness; a sense of emptiness, and fear. The emotions swirled out and caught me by surprise.

"Lisa, I'm not feeling well. I'm not confident driving the car. I don't think it would be safe. I'm sorry to disappoint you. Will you be ok taking the school bus?"

I was shocked. I had always thought that my mother could do anything, and would; that she was ageless and made all the right decisions; and that she was always going to be there for me.

"Of course, Mom, of course, that will be fine." I tried to hide my disappointment. "Why don't you feel well?" I asked.

"Oh, it's nothing, I'm just tired, I'll be fine, please don't worry."

Mom opened the refrigerator and took out a bottle of Tawny Port. She poured six ounces into a tumbler.

"Want a taste?" She offered the bottle to me.

"No, no, Mom, that stuff is awful, you already asked me to taste it."

"Of course, you're right, Lese, I wasn't thinking."

As my mother walked unsteadily down the hall to her room, I felt a wave of confusion engulfed me. As I stood there in the kitchen, I felt helpless. For years Mom ordered grocery deliveries from S.S. Pierce and only left the house for doctor appointments. I thought this was normal.

It's not normal.

That night I went to sleep worried. Worried about starting a new school, worried about growing up, and worried about Mom.

My optimistic nature could not be suppressed for long. Although emotional tempests could wash over me, I always righted, like a small sailboat, and set off again.

Teachers in the new school took extra interest in me, probably because I had just spent two years trying to get through one grade. But finding myself in a class with 30 other students arranged "A to Z," frustrated me.

"How are you supposed to hear what she is saying?" I said to Tom Yaeger as we strained to hear Mrs. Wilson from the last row of desks in science class.

"Shh, you two!" exclaimed Mrs. Wilson, who could see us talking. She put her finger to her lips.

"Did she just say we will learn about the planets today? I couldn't hear."

"I guess we will need hearing aids!" said Tom in a loud voice.

As we laughed uproariously, Mrs. Wilson shouted, "I'll see you two after class."

"You must do the things you think you cannot do."

~ Eleanor Roosevelt

8

THE PROMISE

AS FALL TURNED TO WINTER my mother began to show more confusion in between her normally lucid and witty conversations with me.

"Lese, I can't find my checkbook, I saw a man come in to the house and remove it from the table over there."

"Really? What did the man look like? Did you recognize him?" I said, incredulous.

"Yes, actually I think it was Fred from the house up the street."

"I didn't know there was anyone named Fred up the street." I went over to Mom's writing desk and opened the second drawer. "Look, Mom, here is your checkbook!"

"Oh my goodness, he returned it! Are any checks gone?"

I opened the checkbook. Mom taught me how to write checks, and I sat with her every month to sort and pay the bills. "No, Mom, they are all here."

"Oh, ok, that's good then."

I replaced the checkbook in the drawer and wondered what to do. "Mom, what is Aunt Olive's phone number? Don't you think it would be nice if we visited with them next week?"

"Oh, Lese, you can go out with Olive and John. I'll stay here, I really don't want to go anywhere."

"Well, ok, that's fine, I'll call and see what their schedule is," I continued in as normal a voice as I could manage. I was worried. I didn't know what to make of Mom seeing things that weren't there and telling stories that clearly had no basis in fact.

Mom was my best friend. She was my confidante; she was my rock. She told funny stories; she was fun to be around; she treated me as an equal. She encouraged me to explore, to grow, to create, to persevere. She showed me how to write notes of appreciation, and she taught me how to shake hands properly.

We would practice the handshake, pretending we were well-to-do-people. "Ah yes, pleased to meet you Mr. Merriweather, how are you today?" my mother would say in an affected voice and a firm handshake. I would giggle and smile. "Don't have a dead-fish handshake, Lisa, it gives a poor impression," she would tell me. Then Mom held out the limp hand, and I would begin laughing uncontrollably.

Remembering the antics brought a smile to my face as I looked in the address book for the phone number. Then I composed myself and took a deep breath before picking up the phone.

Aunt Olive answered immediately.

"Hi, Aunt Olive this is Lisa."

"Oh Lisa, dear, how are you? How kind of you to call. It's been forever since we've seen you."

"I'm fine, do you want to visit?"

"Dear, we would love to see you. Would you like to go to a movie?"

"Yes, I would like that."

"I'll come get you," said Olive.

The next day my aunt came to the house to pick me up. I always enjoyed Aunt Olive. She was like Mom, someone you could confide in. I hopped in to the Volkswagen Beetle and we were off to the movies.

During our time together I described the confusion that Mom was showing. Olive pursed her lips and her expression grew serious.

"Instead of dropping you off, I will come into the house."

When we returned to the house several hours later, Olive came in and we walked down the hall to mom's bedroom. She was napping and got up unsteadily as we knocked and entered.

Olive and Mom embraced. Mom put on her robe and we went out to the kitchen. I could see the shock on my aunt's face as she looked at my mother.

"Can I get you something?" Mom asked Olive.

"No thanks. Heath, I think we need to get you some medical attention." Olive spoke matter-of-factly. "You're not looking well."

"I'll be fine, I'll be fine," said Mom, sitting unsteadily on a kitchen stool.

"Let me get you over to the doctor's office first thing in the morning, alright?"

Mom looked at Olive in resignation. "Ok," she said.

I was relieved.

The next day I left for school before Olive arrived. When I got home that afternoon, I asked Mom how things went. She was sitting in the kitchen with her Tawny Port.

"Dr. True is concerned about my liver," she said straightforwardly, "he wants to run some tests."

"I'm not sure the Tawny Port is helpful," I said

"No, it's not. It might be my last bottle of Port in a while."

I shook my head. "Whatever Dr. True says, you need to do. Find out what's wrong and fix it, right?"

I walked over to her and gave her a hug. She felt frail and shaky. "Mom. I'm telling you what you tell me when I'm sick. You're my best friend in the whole world, and I want you to get better fast. Ok?"

"Ok."

The next morning I was surprised to see Mom come into the kitchen as I was eating breakfast. Her appointment wasn't until 2 pm that afternoon.

"I wanted to see you off to school," she said.

I felt something catch in my chest. There was something wrong. I tried to get some air into my lungs.

What is happening?

"Olive is coming to pick me up. They are going to keep me overnight. I would like you to get off the bus at the Addens, Ok?"

Act normal.

"That's fine, Mom, it's just down the road from school. I like Aunt Olive and Uncle John." I gathered up my books, and we went down the stairs to the landing.

"It's just a few days." Mom looked at me. "Lisa, I need to tell you some things."

"I worry when you call me Lisa. What did I do now?"

"Oh, Lese." Mom smiled and shook her head. "Nothing, you're fine. I'm so pleased you're going to school every day now."

I set my books down on the stairs. I looked straight at Mom. The fatigue I was used to seeing was gone from her eyes. The frailty seemed gone. There was a strength in her demeanor that I had not seen in a long time. She reached out and enveloped me in an embrace. For a moment we were both quiet. She stepped away and rested her hands on my shoulders. I looked at her intently.

Her eyes glistened and I could sense the effort she was expending formulating her thoughts. It reminded me of our friend-to-friend, equal-to-equal talks.

"Don't forget your sense of humor. I am not talking about joking, but about balance and perspective. Having a good sense of humor means you won't take things too seriously and allows you to remain optimistic and make the best of whatever happens."

While I had heard my mother say this before, I was mystified that she would be here on the landing at 7 am saying this to me. I nodded as she went on, now more urgently.

"Lese, you know how I feel about your school work. School is going to be the key for you to do what you want in life. I know how you love your independence. School will show you how to master yourself, how to master your life."

A smile transformed into a quiet forcefulness. In all of our talks, I hadn't seen this fervency.

I took a deep breath. "I promise I will. I will do it for you. This time I really will."

"You know I've heard that before," Mom said, with a gentle laugh. The strange spell was broken. I exhaled, relieved.

"I love you," she said, smiling with her secret smile and the twinkling eyes that I adored. She was back to her regular self, I thought.

"I love you too, Mom. Tons and bunches." I picked up my books from the landing. I opened the door and then turned to look back. "See you in a few days, right?"

"A few days," she nodded. As I turned to leave, I didn't see the tear overflow the corner of her eye and travel down her cheek.

Mom left the door open and stood in the doorway, watching me walk down the driveway to the street. I turned to wave. Her paisley robe billowed in a brief breeze, and she pushed her flowing chestnut brown hair back from her face. I started up the street and then stopped to look back at the house. Mom stood framed in the doorway, watching me. I waved. She waved back.

That was the last time I saw her.

"Come back. Even as a shadow, even as a dream."

~ Euripides

9

THE RAFT

TWO DAYS AT THE ADDENS stretched to seven. The third day when my brother and sister showed up, I knew it was serious.

"I'd like to go visit Mom."

"Lisa, the hospital has a rule about children coming in to the special care unit," said my sister, 11 years my senior. Heather had gotten married the year before, and lived in Durham, North Carolina, with her husband, where they were both attending graduate school.

"I'll be sure to tell her that you are fine and thinking of her."

I was being a pest. Heather, the family matriarch, was making the decisions, and the rest of us were secretly glad that she took control, even if she was making it up as she went along.

"Well, I miss her."

"I'm sure you do, Lisa. We're doing everything we can to make her well, please be patient."

I couldn't figure out why the hospital wouldn't let children visit. Did children carry extra germs or something? I sighed and shook my head.

My brother Jeffrey walked in to the living room where Heather and I were sitting on the couch and sat down across from us in an overstuffed chair. He was attending Marlboro College in Marlboro, Vermont, and had arrived at the Adden's little cottage right after Heather.

Jeffrey was eight years my senior. I worshipped him because he had a train set and his own phonograph. Jeff also knew about cars. In groups he was witty and fun, making people laugh. And he'd given me Eric, the chameleon.

I adored Jeff's attention. To get it, I'd perform antics. When he was sitting quietly, I'd jump on him unexpectedly. I tried to wake him up from a nap once by pouring a glass of milk over him. I tried to play with his train set, but he locked the door.

"You're in trouble now, Lisa. Big trouble," Jeff would say. "Go make me 15 pieces of cinnamon toast."

"Ok," I said. I went to make the buttered cinnamon toast but ended up eating half of it myself before Jeff came into the kitchen.

Another time Jeff was playing darts. I really wanted to play, so he let me stand under the dartboard.

"Ok, stand really still. I'm going to put the darts in right above your head.

I stood still. Jeff threw the darts. I was hoping that his aim was good. It wasn't. A dart went into the air and then came down tip first, into my head, and stuck there. It didn't hurt, but I knew it was in my head, so I ran off before Jeff could grab it.

"Mom! Mom! Jeff threw a dart in my head!"

"What? He what? JEFFREY!" she shouted.

That was the end of the dart game. I guess you would have to say it was a normal brother-sister relationship.

My sister, on the other hand, was like a second mom, only much sterner. She knew everything; she could cook, she could sing and dance, she could entertain people and tell funny stories, she was always dressed up, and she would always know the answer to anything that you asked her. She was everything I wanted to be, except the cooking and dressing up parts.

"So Lisa, you're catching the bus right down the street here for school. Is school going ok?" Heather asked me.

"Uh huh."

Heather knew all about my poor performance in school and repeating several grades. It embarrassed me. I wanted her to be proud of me. Heather was already in graduate school, proving that she could do what Mom wanted me to do.

I could never think of things to say when we were together. Heather and Jeff seemed to have no trouble at all carrying on conversations. I was usually at a loss for words and would go quiet.

"Well I am glad that you got into junior high school Lisa. You almost didn't make it. Mom had to work hard to convince them you'd turn things around. You know if you don't improve, you're going to be stuck in the same grade again."

I heard my mother's words in my mind again. I felt my breathing catch, and my stomach felt empty. I didn't know how I was going to meet everyone's expectations. I had already been labeled a troublemaker at the new school.

They have no idea how hard it is.

The next afternoon on the walk back to the Addens from the bus stop I started thinking about what I would do when Mom came home from the hospital. If I could please my teachers, Mom would be pleased.

It was a bright, sun-drenched day, cool at 40 degrees. A raw breeze rolled through the bare tree branches. Leaves in the street, dry and brittle, rustled across the gray pavement. The smell of wood smoke drifted in and out of the wind as I walked, clutching my heavy book bag. I zipped up my navy-blue jacket but the wind still found entrances.

I had formed a plan during the day. Tonight I would write Mom, telling her what I had accomplished in the last few days of school. Every night I was sitting down at my cousin's desk upstairs at the Addens, opening my books and completing my assignments. I would give the note to Heather to take to the hospital. I knew Mom would be pleased and that would help her get well.

The breeze picked up and penetrated my jacket in waves as the color began draining from the sky. I shivered and hunched up my shoulders, walking faster down the lane to the little cottage in the woods.

When I arrived at the house ten minutes later, Heather came up to my room.

"We need to talk about something, Lisa."

"Ok."

Heather sat down on the bench at the foot of the bed and patted the space next to her.

I looked intently at Heather's face and suddenly I knew what she was going to say. I was on a raft on a river, not stopping, with nowhere to tie up, no way to get off. Hunger pangs in my stomach turned to painful little knots, expanding.

"Lisa, I am sorry to tell you this."

I squeezed my eyes shut. My twelve years of life experience was on fast forward. I held my breath.

"Mom is not coming home. The doctors did everything they could. She was very ill. She passed away peacefully this morning."

The raft bounced on river waves, rocks in a blur. I held on. I was being carried away, there was no stopping the swiftness of the water. Fear cascaded over me. I could not find my voice.

Heather put her arms around me and held me in a long hug. We both glided together down the river in swells and eddies. I wanted to cry but I couldn't.

"We have a lot of things to figure out." Heather held me at arm's length now and looked at me solemnly. Her eyes were full of tears and they streamed down her face. She took a deep breath.

"It's going to take some time. We'd like you to stay here with your aunt and uncle as we work through the details. Ok?"

I nodded but could not speak. The raft stopped bouncing and was moving swiftly on smoother water past a rocky cove. Hold on.

■ ⌐◦ ■

That night I lay in bed, feeling the ebb and flow of the raft in the river. The water was shallow and clear, rocks were smooth and the water drifted around the boulders in eddies and strong currents. I held on to a rope across the middle of the little raft, knowing there was nothing I could do to influence where I went. I was lost, nothing looked familiar. I felt empty. A thick wood passed by on the left, dark with mist.

"Lese! Over here!"

I looked up. The shore was close now on the right, and smooth black rocks guided my raft to a sandy beach. The sand was white and glistening. I got out of the raft and sat on the beach, trembling.

"Over here!"

I heard Mom's voice.

"Mom!"

"Don't worry, Lese, I'm with you. I'm here. It's ok."

"Mom I can't see you!"

"It's ok. I'm here. It's ok."

"I knew you weren't gone. I knew it."

"If opportunity doesn't knock, build a door."

~ Milton Berle

10

THE ENGLISH TEACHER

"WHAT'S your name?"

"Lisa. Lisa Turner."

"Where did you come from? I don't recall seeing you in 6th grade. I'm Mary Beth. Pleased to meet you." Mary Beth reached over and shook my outstretched hand. We were both in the second row of homeroom, the classroom where the day began.

"My Mom died, and I came here to stay with my Dad's brother and family."

"Oh no! Where's your Dad?"

"He's in Boston. He left when I was six."

"I can't believe that. It's awful. What did your Mom die of?"

"I'm not sure. She missed my Dad. I think she was sad."

The teacher walked in to the class with a large briefcase in one hand and a stack of papers in the other. "Hello everyone! Since it's the first day of school, I'll call names but after I learn who you are, I'll know if you're here or not," he announced.

I watched Mr. Shinebarger, the homeroom teacher, write his name with an artistic flourish on the board in perfectly formed cursive.

"Wow, look how he writes." I whispered.

Mary Beth looked up from her notebook. We both watched Mr. Shinebarger write on the blackboard. We were transfixed.

"How does he do that? That's not normal for a man, is it?" said Mary Beth.

"I don't think so. I hope he doesn't expect us to do that."

My first day at Alfred Almond Central School, in Almond, New York, was, as psychologist Morris Massey once said, "a significant emotional event." Everything was new. I was frightened and afraid that I would make a mistake, forget something I was supposed to do, or be embarrassed.

Everything had happened so quickly after mom died. I finished out the rest of the school year staying at the Addens' and threw myself into the schoolwork because of Mom. There was nothing else to do but try not to repeat more classes.

So here I was, in western New York, at my Dad's brother's family farm. Bob and Sue Turner had three children, one of them only a year my senior in age but vastly more grown up than me. She took me under her wing and helped me whenever she could. I'm sure she thought I was strange when I arrived. I realized later that she was, for her age, amazingly thoughtful and kind, having given up her room to a shared arrangement.

I knew that this was an opportunity; a time when I could begin with a clean slate. I resisted the temptation to sit in the back row, remembering a teacher's advice in Junior High: "Lisa, sit in the first or second row. Not only can you hear what is going on, you will be perceived as attentive by your teachers."

I need all the help I can get.

"Mr. Shinebarger is a new teacher here," said Mary Beth, bringing me back from my musings. "It's his first year."

"Like me."

"Yes, you are both new here – you will have to hang out together!"

We laughed. I took a good look at Mr. Shinebarger. He was about 30 years old, five foot ten inches tall, with a solid build. He had on a navy suit, a crisp white dress shirt, and a blue striped tie. He had a neatly trimmed haircut with light brown hair, and a face with deep set blue eyes – very blue eyes. And, most intriguing, a mystical sort of smile that teamed with his eyes to make you want to stare . . .

"Mr. Shinebarger is not just the homeroom teacher, he teaches English too," said Mary Beth.

"What? Oh, sorry, I wasn't paying attention."

"I said, he's our homeroom teacher, and he also teaches English."

"That's good. I love to read. *Tom Swift*, *Nancy Drew*, *The Hardy Boys*, and Superman comics!"

Mary Beth thought this was uproariously funny. "I don't think we're going to be reading those in 7th grade."

As Mr. Shinebarger spoke, he looked at me with a smile. It was a special smile, a secret smile. I felt embraced. His blue eyes sparkled and danced.

I was standing next to Mr. Shinebarger's desk in homeroom. I had stayed after school to come talk to Mr. Shinebarger. I wasn't sure what I was going to talk about, but I knew I wanted to meet and talk to him.

Staying after school was not easy logistically. There was only one school bus run, and my aunt and uncle's house was five miles from the school. So I decided to take up field hockey. That way, twice a week I could stay after school and talk to Mr. Shinebarger for 20 minutes before I was due out on the hockey field.

I was devious.

"I see your grades are coming up with the tutoring that your aunt is getting you – I expect you are pleased about that," said Mr. Shinebarger one afternoon.

"Finally, yeah. It's not easy."

"Most important things are not easy, Lisa."

Mr. Shinebarger gazed at me, and for a moment I couldn't think of anything to say. I just knew I wanted to keep standing next to his desk.

"Lisa, you are so quiet yet attentive in class. Is everything going ok?" Mr. Shinebarger gazed at me with concern.

As he looked at me, a flutter ran from my head to my toes and then back up.

What was that?

"Everything just scares me, is all."

"What scares you?" he asked.

"When you asked each of us to bring something from home and describe it to the class, how it worked, in front of everyone. Remember I froze up, and the kids laughed."

"But then you did well," said Mr. Shinebarger."

"But I was so frightened I couldn't think."

"Yes, you were nervous. But that's not unusual. What else scares you?"

I couldn't believe that Mr. Shinebarger was asking me these questions, and so gently, in such a quiet voice. "Two days ago in math class Mr. Smith asked each of us to go up to the blackboard–I mean GO UP TO THE BLACKBOARD–and write out the solution to the math problem. He called on ME. I totally forgot how to do the problem and then the class laughed at me because I was standing up there with a stupid look on my face and all I wanted to do was go back to my seat, which I did."

Mr. Shinebarger smiled his secret smile. The flutter bolt ripple did its dance again.

This is different.

"That must have been difficult for you. Do you realize that everyone has that same fear?"

"It doesn't seem like it."

"They do. I do. It will get easier every time. Don't think about yourself. Think about what you are giving to the other students."

Mr. Shinebarger looked at the giant school clock on the wall. "You need to get going. We can talk again if you like."

Again if I like? Oh, yes.

Another thrill ran from my chest to my feet and back. I looked straight at Mr. Shinebarger. "You can call me Lee. That is my nickname."

I had just made it up. I liked the sound of it. Lee. A tomboy name.

"Ok, Lee, I like that. When we are talking together one on one, you can call me Larry, ok?"

"Ok, Mr. ... Larry." We both laughed. "Thank you."

I played hockey with wild abandon. Maybe Larry would come out of his classroom and see me playing. I felt a thrill reverberate through my whole body again. I didn't know what it was, but I liked it.

When my aunt picked me up after practice, I was careful to not mention that I had just fallen in love with my 30-year-old English teacher. That night I fell asleep with a jumble of images playing in my head. Field hockey, English class, and my new best friend – Larry.

"Do What You Can With All You Have,
Wherever You Are."

~ Theodore Roosevelt

11

THE CRUSH

TWO DAYS LATER I WAS back at Larry's desk. His blue eyes radiated warmth as he gazed at me. I looked at him and the flutter bolt struck again. It felt like you just lost your balance going down a set of stairs and then have to grab the rail, a feeling of falling. I was enraptured.

I told Larry about my Mom and repeating two grades. I told him that my mother returned to me in my dreams and that I didn't feel that she was really gone.

"Lee, let's go back to our conversation Tuesday. You said that a lot of things scare you. Do you mind if I share some things with you?"

"Of course not, sure." I'd forgotten that I'd named myself Lee. I liked it.

"Here, have a seat and put your book bag down."

I sat down, enchanted.

"Some things are hard to explain, but I'll try. When we're only 13 years old, there are a lot of things that are happening that can be scary. You feel like you're in a boat that's not being steered sometimes."

How does he know?

Larry's special gaze reached out and held me captured. I took a breath.

"When this happens, you feel that things are happening to you that you can't control, right?"

I nodded.

"I want you to look at these situations differently."

I didn't know where this was going, but I wanted the conversation to continue for hours. I no longer cared about field hockey practice or anything else, only the words that Larry was saying so gently with great care three feet from me.

"Think about this. YOU are in control. How? By choosing, in the moment, how you will view something. If you decide to view it as positive, it will be positive. If you decide it's negative, then it will be negative. You're the one that decides. The only thing that you can truly control and influence in life is how you view things. It's a superpower. Most people don't realize they have it."

Larry's gaze reached out, mesmerizing. I sat there looking back at him, not sure I was absorbing what he was saying and not caring except for the tractor beam of attention that held me in its grip.

"That's number one. Number two is to take complete responsibility for the situations you find yourself in. If you are called up to the board to do a math problem, realize that every other student is scared FOR YOU because THEY don't want to be there. So what do you do? Decide to make it positive, decide to make the best of it, and the fear will fall away, leaving you at your best."

As I listened to Larry, I realized that he sounded a lot like my Mom.

"Is this making sense?" asked Larry, continuing to display that secret stunning smile.

"Well, sort of. Let me think about it. I have to go to field hockey now," I said softly, hating to interrupt the spell that had been cast.

"Ok. You know what?"

"What?" I gazed at Larry, not wanting to go. I hung on every word, every inflection, every move, hypnotized.

"Everything is going to be fine."

I felt breathless as a blissful happiness expanded in my chest, blotting out everything else in the room except Larry's gaze and secret smile.

■ ⟶ ■

That night falling asleep in a flourishing sense of wonder, I was transported to a world of spaceships, rockets, helicopters, and jetpacks.

I was seated in the cockpit of a flying car. The panel was brightly lighted, and a dozen gauges stretched from one side to the other. Switches lined the bottom of the panel. To the left was the ignition key. To the right were short levers for wing deployment.

At first, I was alone in the cockpit and going through a list of things to start the machine. As I began flipping switches in growing excitement, I realized that Larry was in the passenger seat.

Exhilarated, I turned to look at Larry. It seemed completely normal that he would be in the flying car with me. "How does this work," asked Larry, matter-of-factly.

"Ok, this is the control for speed." I reached for the lever and showed Larry. "To start it, you move this lever here," I said, reaching to the center of the instrument display and flipping a switch, "that starts the fuel, then ignition is here." I pointed to a key next to the fuel switch.

"I'll start it in a minute and show you. Then the most important part of this vehicle is the fold-out wing on each side. As you saw when we got in, you can't really see them in the sides. When you are ready to fly, then you just unlock them, and pull them out. There's a pin that secures them in their flying state so that they don't fold up in flight. That would not be good."

Larry was smiling at me. I was overjoyed. He looked like he didn't believe what I was saying. His charming secret smile reached out. I felt my breathing growing faster, but tried to be calm. A flutter.

"Do you understand how it works now?"

"I don't have a clue. A single clue," said Larry. "What would I know, I am an English teacher."

We laughed.

"I'm going to start it and show you. Put this harness on."

I reached up and got the harness that was secured behind us. As I passed it over to Larry, our fingertips touched, and a thrill went through my hand to my heart.

"A flying car is simple, really, it's just a car with wings, and controls for the ailerons, and a horizontal tail control, and you have to have a two-way radio to talk to the people on the ground, of course. . ." I desperately wanted to reach over and hug Larry but resisted. I turned the key in the ignition. The engine started quickly and loped a little and then smoothed out.

"So you see, right now, this is a car, and it drives like a car," I said as I moved the throttle forward and the craft began moving across the school parking lot.

"What do you think?"

"Goodness, I am amazed, Lee."

Suddenly the engine began to run roughly, with strange whining noise that I could not identify. What was wrong?

"Lisa! You're going to be late for school!" I awoke to the sound of an alarm next to my bed and my cousin looking at me from across the room.

"Who is Larry?" she asked.

*"Being courageous does not mean never being scared;
it means acting as you know you must even though
you are undeniably afraid."*

~ Archbishop Desmond Tutu

12

TRADING PLACES

I WALKED UP TO THE TEACHER'S DESK at the beginning of study hall.

"May I please get a pass to go to the Guidance Office?"

Miss Devlin looked up from her book over a pair of wire-framed glasses with a scowl. "What for?"

"I need to talk to Mr. Sterling about my classes."

"Alright," said Miss. Devlin. "Thirty minutes?"

"Yes, please." I picked up the approval slip and put it in my pocket. Students were not allowed in the hallways during classes without a reason.

I walked to the school guidance counselor's office and stood in the doorway. It was close to lunchtime, and the administrators were gone. The guidance counselor, Mr. Sterling, was at his desk to the right of the entrance. I waited for him to look up.

"Can I help you?" he said.

I entered the office and stopped in front of the desk. Paper piles were arranged neatly across the front of the desk and the rest of the space was filled with pens, paperclips, calendars, and books.

"Oh, you're the new student here aren't you? What is your name?"

"Lisa Turner," I said.

"Sue Turner's daughter?"

"Um, stepdaughter."

"Stepdaughter? Ok. How can I help you?"

I had thought up this plan to talk to the guidance counselor about my classes but now, in the office, I was not feeling as brave as I had when I wrote down my plan in private.

Go ahead, you thought it up, go ahead.

"Uh, I would like to take the shop class. Can I add the shop class to my schedule, Mr. Sterling?"

Mr. Sterling put his pen down on the desk and leaned back in his chair. The old wooden chair creaked as he shifted his weight. The springs squeaked in strain.

A little oil would help that awful noise. He probably doesn't notice it.

Mr. Sterling cocked his head and looked perplexed. "Are you saying you want to take the boy's shop class?"

"Yes." I felt like I was jumping over a cliff. I had gone too far. Why was I here? What was I thinking? Will Mr. Sterling get mad at me? Will he tell my teachers that I am a troublemaker?

"Hmm," he muttered, leaning even farther back in his chair. The springs complained again as he rotated slightly. I watched as Mr. Sterling pursed his lips and then began tapping the end of his pen on the chair arm. He removed his glasses and rubbed the bridge of his nose.

I felt my nerve slipping away, my confidence turning to mush.

"Here, Lisa, sit down a minute." Mr. Sterling waved to the polished wood chair in front of his desk. I sat down. I was half the size of the chair and tried not to be awkward as I sat in it. I placed my books in my lap and began fiddling with the book strap.

Now I am trapped.

I looked at Mr. Sterling.

"I've never had a girl ask to take shop class. This sets a precedent. I'll have to bring this up with Mr. Cliquinnoi, the school principal. Don't you like your home economics class?"

I pushed my book strap across the top of my textbooks. I took a deep breath.

Lese, you thought this up. Now is your chance. Just say what you're thinking.

"It's not that I don't like home economics. It's that I want to learn mechanics, and woodworking, and how to use tools. Those things are interesting; I'm sure the cooking and sewing are going to be useful, but I'll never learn about engines in home economics."

Mr. Sterling made a sound between a snort and a chuckle and then frowned and rubbed his temple. He picked his pen up off the desk and started tapping it on the blotter.

"Well, if I can get Mr. Cliquinnoi to agree . . . you'd still need to take home economics in addition to the shop class. I don't know what your grade average is, but I'll look it up. You've got to maintain a B average or I can't let you use a study hall to attend shop."

"My grade average is a B now – 86 – I'll give it more attention – I'll make sure it does not slip."

"Lisa, let me look into this, and I'll talk to Mr. C. I'll let you know what we decide, ok? I also need to talk to the shop teacher, Mr. Gerace. Don't get your hopes up, but I will do what I can."

How could I not get my hopes up?

Mr. Sterling got up from his creaking wood chair with some effort and placed the pen back on the desk. He extended his large bony hand, and I reached out to grasp it. His grip was light and short. I think he thought he would crush my 13-year-old hand. My mother would have judged Mr. Sterling's handshake deficient.

"Thank you," I said as I turned to leave in relief. I held out the hall pass that Mr. Sterling would have to initial. Rules. He gave me back the pass, and I started out. I stopped at the door and summoned up some of the courage that was flowing back in.

"Mr. Sterling, can I ask another question?"

Mr. Sterling was just settling back in his chair. He turned to look at me. "What would that be?"

"Can boys take home economics?"

I saw just a trace of a smile on Mr. Sterling's face for the first time. "There you go again, Lisa, asking a question I never got before."

"Well, I mean, I was just wondering. I'm sure that the boys might be needing some of the skills the girls are learning – I mean, not making dresses, but the cooking and sewing would be useful."

Now Mr. Sterling was actually smiling at me. I wasn't sure if he was inwardly making fun of me. I had a chance to make it into shop class, and that's all I cared about. I felt excited and relieved. I had put a plan together and summoned the confidence to talk to Mr. Sterling. Mr. Sterling was the second most important person in the school administration. And now he was going to talk to the most important person – the principal.

"Thank you," I said as I turned to go. I had already used up 20 minutes of my study hall and I needed to ponder Plan B if Plan A didn't work.

■ ━━ ■

Several days later Mr. Gerace, the science teacher and also the shop teacher, walked up to my desk in biology just before the class began.

Mr. Gerace had a round, friendly face. He placed his palms on my desk and looked at me. "I don't know how you did it, but you got yourself into my shop class. This is a first. A girl in shop class." He smiled.

My jaw dropped. "Are you serious?" I knew Mr. Gerace to have a good sense of humor, and I hoped he wasn't kidding with me.

"You bet I'm serious. Class is at 2 pm Tuesdays and Wednesdays, I hear they are letting you out of study hall as long as your grades hold up."

I could scarcely pay attention as Mr. Gerace began the lecture. I had gotten myself into shop class.

See what a little perseverance can do?

PART TWO

BUILD

"I realized early on that success was tied to not giving up. If you simply didn't give up you would outlast the people who came in on the bus with you."

~ Harrison Ford

13

THE BICYCLE APPRENTICE

I WALKED THROUGH THE OPEN door to the bicycle shop and past dozens of brand-new bicycles hanging in the window and lined up along the wall.

"Can I help you?" a voice said from a desk behind the counter.

"My name is Lisa Turner. I have an appointment with you today at 2 pm for a job interview?"

A portly man with a round face and beard stubble looked up from the desk with a frown.

"Oh jeez, I didn't think they would send a girl." The man got up from his chair and extended a grease-stained hand toward me. I gripped it. Firm.

"Here, have a seat." The man pointed to a chair at the side of his desk, and I walked around the counter and sat down.

I looked around the shop. There were bicycle parts everywhere; hanging from the ceiling, bolted to walls, in bins and boxes, and shelf upon shelf of items, each one peeking out from its box so you could see what it was. The corkboard behind the desk was overfull with papers and pictures stapled and tacked everywhere. The desk was piled with invoices and work orders, calendars, and several greasy bicycle chains on a towel. The backdoor was open, and a breeze smelling of palmetto and palm mixed with oil, tires, and grease wafted from back to front.

"What did you say your name was?" The man looked at me with a confused expression.

"Lisa, Lisa Turner. My nickname is Lese, like car lease."

"My name is Robert. Pleased to meet you." Robert extended his greasy hand again, another strong squeeze.

"That's a good handshake, girl, you look like you are strong," said Robert. "Do you know anything about bicycles or am I going to have to teach you everything?"

"I work on my own bicycle."

"That's what they all say," said Robert. "Are you strong, can you lift boxes and things? We aren't going to have time around here to help you with things, you will have to do everything the rest of us do here."

"Sure, I can do it," I said confidently, although I wasn't sure exactly what I was going to be lifting.

"Are you married?"

"No."

"Good."

"You're not going to get me in trouble working alongside my mechanics, are you?"

"I get along well with the guys," I replied.

"That's what I mean. One of my guys is married, you will have to be careful."

"I'll be careful." I wasn't sure what Robert meant.

"Ok." Robert looked at my resume and application for the first time. "Jeez, you got a college degree in English? What the hell are you doing here?"

I knew this question could come up, but I wasn't prepared for Robert's phrasing. "I took a teaching job in the public schools and it wasn't what I thought it would be. I moved here to Florida to try other things."

Robert seemed to think this was ok. "I couldn't teach school," he said, "Tough, tough job and crazy kids nowadays."

I felt myself getting nervous, thinking this opportunity might slip away. I needed the employment and was excited about doing something I loved – tinker with bicycles, for pay?

"Well I'm sure being a teacher pays more than working on bicycles, even if it is tough," said Robert.

I cleared my throat. "Which would you rather have, doing something you don't like but are earning the money, or do something you do like and just get by?"

"Earn the money."

I saw the beginnings of a smile on Robert's creased and weathered face.

"I see here that since you got out of college and came to Florida you've been working construction on a high-rise in Deerfield Beach?"

"Yes, I was a trim carpenter."

"Why did you quit that?"

"All the trim was done. I saw your ad."

"Ok, look, I'll tell you what. I really need someone reliable, someone who will show up for work day after day, on time. Lord knows there have been enough guys come through here totally unreliable. Just up and gone; no call, no nothing. It's not as if I didn't pay them a good wage. Plus, I need to train you. I need you to be a fast learner. If I am going to train you, then you have to stick around and produce for me. You can't just up and quit after a few months. Can you do that?" Robert looked at me quizzically, rubbing the stubble on his chin.

"Yes, I can. I am very reliable," I said. Although Robert seemed a little odd, I could picture myself learning about bicycle mechanics from him. His shop, Boca Raton Cyclery, was highly regarded and my friends thought it was the best shop between Boca Raton and Boynton Beach.

Robert shuffled some papers around on his cramped desk and pulled out the rest of the information sheets from the employment agency. "Okay, how about you start as an apprentice mechanic at $2.25 an hour. After two weeks I'll evaluate your work and if I think you can handle the job, I'll give it to you permanent. OK?"

I didn't need to think about it. "Yes! Thank you, great."

"When can you start?"

"Tomorrow?"

"Good. 7:30 am sharp. Now remember, don't get either of my guys in trouble. Guys are guys you know; they get distracted easily. Did anyone ever tell you that you're built like a brick shithouse?"

"A what?"

"Okay, hey, that's a compliment, girl. It just means you are, uh, you are attractive. That's what that means, attractive. I just don't want my guys getting involved with you outside the mechanics. The job that has to be done here, you know what I mean? Justin, who is my best mechanic, has a wacko wife, and she's jealous of everything he does. If you mess with him, she'll come here and kill you. I really mean it, she'll kill you."

"I won't come on to your guys, I promise."

This was turning into one of the strangest job interviews I had ever had. But I wanted the job, and I was confident that I could be a bicycle mechanic and not bother the guys. In fact, I enjoyed being around men and thought that they respected me for not being a tease.

I showed up for work the next morning. Robert introduced me to his mechanics, and for the next 16 months we all got along fabulously. I learned an entirely new set of vocabulary words that had never even been mentioned in college. I learned how to rebuild a bicycle from the frame up, how to quote repairs, how to choose and adjust the tools of the trade, and how to sell bicycles to customers. And the wacko wife never came after me.

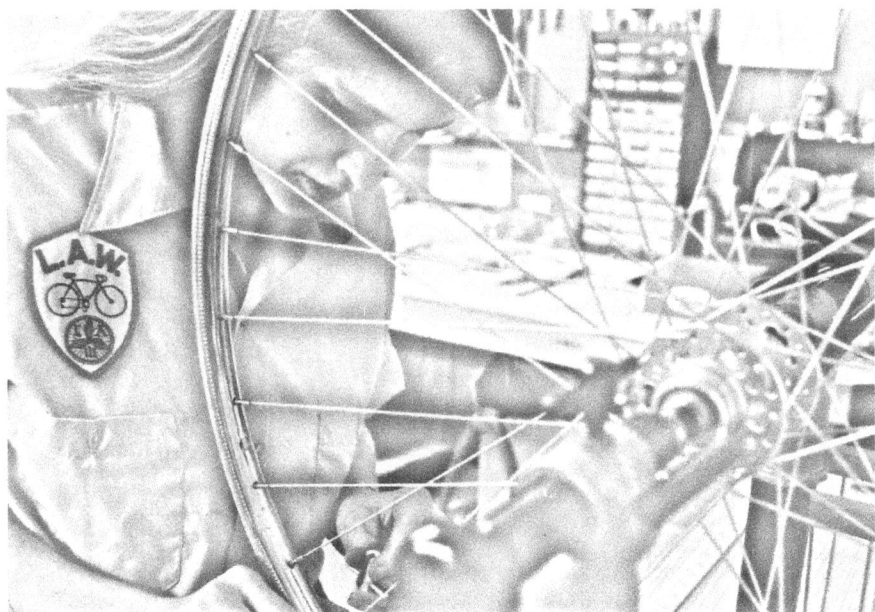

"It is not because things are difficult that we do not dare; it is because we do not dare that they are difficult."

~ Seneca

14

THE BANK

THE NINETY-DEGREE AIR shimmered in layers on the sidewalk as I left the even hotter interior of the Honda Civic. One of these days I should save up for an air-conditioned car, I thought to myself. South Florida in July was brutal.

Rivulets of sweat ran down my face as I climbed the broad marble steps of the bank. Clutching a file folder in my right hand, I opened the large glass door. As a blast of cool air hit my face, I exhaled in relief.

"May I help you?" A woman in her mid-thirties with long brown hair looked up from the desk across from the teller windows.

"Yes, please. I'd like to talk to someone about a loan."

"Business or personal?"

"Ah, business, but the business doesn't exist yet. I'm starting a business and I need capital." A drip of sweat from my cheek hit the file folder I was holding and ran to the corner, dripping once on to the white carpet.

The woman looked at me with disapproval. "Hmm. No business yet. Ok, well, have a seat here." She motioned to one of the chairs in front of her desk. "It looks like it's hot out there."

"Whew, is it ever." I sat down.

"I'm Susan," the woman said, as she leaned toward me and shook my hand. She didn't really want to shake my hand, but it was part of her job, I thought to myself. Her hand was limp, and she kept her hand cupped so that it encountered minimal contact.

How odd. Mom would not have approved. Worse than the dead fish shake.

"Welcome to Barnett Bank. Do you have an account with us?"

"Yes, I do."

"Account number?"

I read it off to her and she entered it into the computer.

"Ok, what are you thinking about for a loan?

"I need about $3,000."

I see you only have $650 in the bank. What are you going to use as collateral? Do you have any property?

"I don't have any collateral." *If I already had a lot of stuff, why would I be here at the bank trying to get more stuff?*

"Ok. Married?"

"No."

"Alimony?"

"No."

"Co-signer?"

"No."

Susan pursed her lips several times and squinted at her workstation. Then she adjusted her reading glasses downward on her nose and looked at me. "Surely you know the bank has rules about loans. It's all about risk. Banks hate risk. I thought I could get around the rule that says you have to be in business for three years before you would qualify for something . . . but I'm not able to turn this in your favor. I'm really sorry. We value you as a Barnett Bank customer. I can't approve you for a loan right now."

I wasn't sure what to say. If a person already has a business that was making money, why would they need more money from a bank? I was beginning to feel in over my head. Reaching too high.

"Don't give up," said a voice in my head. I was startled. It sounded like my mother.

"Hello?" Susan was looking at me intently.

"Oh, yes, I'm sorry. I was thinking of something. Well, ok, I appreciate you taking the time." I reached for my file folder, the blue color now stained with several fresh streaks of salt-infused sweat.

I reached out to shake Susan's petite, unresponsive hand. "Let me reassemble my plan and I'll be back to see you, ok?"

"Absolutely fine, good luck." Susan emphasized *good luck*. It was obvious she couldn't wait for me to leave and invite some big shot over with lots of money who wanted a bank loan even though they didn't need it.

I exhaled as I walked away from the desk across the sea of white carpet. I was relieved to be out of the encounter, and disappointed to have not understood the rules of the game.

The summer heat hit me and covered me like a blanket as I walked outside. I opened the car door and entered an oven, so hot the brief contact with the ignition switch metal scorched my fingers. "Yikes," I said aloud as I cranked down both windows.

Moving off into traffic and a weak ocean breeze, I felt confused and puzzled.

"Don't give up," said Mom.

■ ⟷ ■

Just as I flipped the stained blue file folder on the table in my one-room apartment the phone rang.

"Hello."

"Lisa, this is Heather. Do you want to come over for dinner tonight? How did the trip to the bank go?"

"Sis, that would be great. I'll tell you when I see you."

"The greatest mistake you can make in life is to be continually fearing you will make one."

~ Elbert Hubbard

15

THE LOAN

"SO, YOU WERE UNSUCCESSFUL?" My sister's husband Persifor – everyone called him Perky – greeted me from the living room as I came through the front door. A tall, slim man in his 60s, he moved as someone much younger and spryer.

"Oh, yeah, I'm so bummed out. I had all my materials and screwed up my confidence for nothing. What was I thinking? What I don't understand is that banks only lend to people who don't need a loan. How crazy is that? I'll be right back Perk, let me see what I can do for Heather."

"Good idea. She's fixing swordfish. I can't wait to hear," said Perky.

I walked into the kitchen and helped Heather load the plates. "That smells wonderful. You're amazing, I don't know how you do this," I said.

"Spend some time in the kitchen and you could do it, too, Lisa."

"Why spend time in a kitchen when you could be building or fixing something?" Sis looked at me and shook her head, like I'd done something bad.

"If you had a family to take care of, you'd have to be in the kitchen."

"That's why I don't have a family," I said.

"You're incorrigible." Heather looked at me with a stern face but a hint of a smile broke though.

"I know." I poured out a cold beer that Perky had retrieved from the refrigerator and sat down.

"Lese, I'm sure it's disappointing," said Perky. "But there's more than one way to set your sail. How about going back to the bank tomorrow with me?"

Heather looked up in surprise.

"Perk, you know I'm trying to make my own way," I said.

"I know. But part of wisdom is knowing when to ask for help."

"I guess. What are you suggesting? I got turned down today."

"You didn't actually turn anything in, though, right? The entry person who is supposed to find a reason why you shouldn't have a loan caught you. It doesn't count. Let's talk to someone who can understand your background."

Going out the front door that night after dinner I realized I'd forgotten part of my bank folder. I moved back into the living room to retrieve it. I overheard Heather talking in the dining room.

"Persifor, you are going too far with the bank help with Lisa. She needs to make her own way. I don't like the idea of her starting this business. I just don't see how she is going to become self-sufficient fast enough without finding a regular – professional – paying job."

I listened, motionless, knowing I shouldn't. I started backing up slowly towards the door but then stopped.

"Darling, settle down. She wants to start a business. Let her learn how to make her own way."

"I think it's a mistake," said Heather.

"Why don't you tell her that? She's your sister," said Perky.

"No, no, I don't want to interfere."

I heard Heather picking up plates. She sat the plates down noisily on the countertop in the kitchen. "And you shouldn't either."

I heard Perky get up from his chair and make a harrumph noise, and I backed silently out of the living room and out the front door.

"It's not who you think you are that holds you back;
it's who you think you're not."

~ Anonymous

16

IT'S WHO YOU KNOW

PERKY PARKED THE SILVER HONDA Accord across from Barnett Bank in a tight space on the bustling Atlantic Avenue in Delray Beach.

"Do you have all your paperwork?"

"Yes." I had moved the business overview from the sweat-stained blue folder to a fresh green folder. Maybe the color would help.

"I spoke with Brian last night, he is anxious to meet you and find out about your business plans."

"Well Perk, without your introduction, I doubt that Mr. Pfeiffler would have taken my call."

We moved from the comfort of the air-conditioned car to the mid-morning heat of the summer day, building as the sun rose in the sky.

Persifor Frazer III had lived in south Florida for more than 40 years. In 1951 Perky started his own clothing retail business next to the bank we were walking toward now.

"Perky, when did you sell Mark, Fore, and Strike?" I asked.

"Only two years ago. After you get your business loan, you'll see how much work a business can be."

"Heather said your customers included Marilyn Monroe and James Cagney. Is that true?"

"Yes, lots of celebrities from Palm Beach and New York. They put their pants on one side at a time, just like us, Lese."

"I guess if you love it, then it doesn't matter how much work it is, right?" I said.

"So right you are."

Perky was dressed in a casual Lily print shirt, khaki trousers, and espadrilles without socks, considered a casual sort of elegance in south Florida. His demeanor created a gentlemanly aura to him, bringing attention and respect.

We walked up the marble steps to the bank and eased through the heavy glass doors. I remembered my encounter the day before as the blast of air conditioning hit us.

"Brian's office is over here, to the right." Perky led the way noiselessly on the thick carpeting into an alcove. The brunette who intercepted me yesterday looked up from her desk with a flash of recognition. A disapproving gaze followed us across the lobby.

In the alcove across from the bank president's office, we met a woman in her forties with blonde hair tied up behind her head in a bun. "Perky, so good to see you! You can go on in."

"Perky."

Brian Pfeiffler spoke in a loud deep voice and stood up from his desk. "Ah, this is Miss Turner?"

The bank president was tall, slim, and impeccably dressed. He reached a large hand out to mine. His handshake was firm and strong.

"That's what I love to see – a good strong handshake! It tells you a lot about a person," he said in a booming voice.

Mom was right.

"Have a seat, have a seat," said Brian, motioning to the large stuffed chairs in front of his desk.

"So, you're here for a business loan?"

"Yes, sir, I have some information." I held up the green folder.

"Don't worry about that. What I want you to tell me, from your memory, is what your business is going to be, why you are starting it, who your customers are going to be, and how you are going to be successful." Brian leaned back in his chair and folded his hands together behind his head.

I felt a rush of anxiety. I looked over at Perky, who nodded at me. I looked down at my folder, collected my thoughts, and looked back up at Brian.

"I worked as an apprentice for 18 months at Boca Cyclery. I enjoyed the work. It included a little of everything, from bicycle component overhaul to tune-ups, and I was the service writer for customers bringing their bikes in. I watched how the owner ran the business. He was very customer centric.

"I want to open my own bicycle shop. I know I can deliver service as good as Boca Cyclery at less cost. There's a stretch of Federal Highway between Delray Beach and Boynton Beach with a few low-rent buildings that I could choose from. The nearest bike shop will be downtown Delray - at least five miles away – and with being right on the main highway, I would get a lot of exposure."

Brian looked at me with great interest. He placed his palms on his desk and leaned forward. "How will you differentiate yourself from the other bike shops?" he asked.

"Customer service and price. I don't mind working long hours or thinking up services that no one else offers. For example, all the shops close early on Christmas. That means customers have to come get the new bikes for the children in the middle of the day – making their day even more complicated. I'll stay open until 11 pm, when they can come get the bikes after the kids are in bed."

Brian nodded. "So tell me, what is your first-year projected budget and income?"

"Startup expenses of $3,000, monthly expenses of $3,200, which includes parts, inventory, rent, electric, a loan payment and my salary. Income the first year estimated at $35,000, leaving a first-year loss of $3,400." I paused a moment.

Brian nodded and Perky was smiling.

"I figured break even the second year, and a net profit of $10,000 the third year."

"And you have all that in your folder?" asked Brian, as he reached across the desk to accept my clean green file folder.

"Yes." I took a deep breath.

Brian cleared his throat as he read through my spreadsheet. "Lisa, here's some advice. You did a good job on these projections, but you're on the low side."

"Low side?"

"Yes. Most startups are cash strapped. You've got here that you need only $3,000 from the bank."

"I didn't know if I would be able to get a loan, so I kept it as low as I could," I said.

Brian looked at Perky and then over at me. "Let's make your loan $6,000."

I was stunned. In 1975, the median family income was less than $12,000 a year. Minimum wage was $2.10 an hour. The average business rent was $200 a month.

"Lisa, I see here that you graduated Washington College with a degree in English with a teaching certification. Wouldn't it be a lot easier to just go teach English?"

Another one.

"I really want to be a mechanic."

"I'll have the paperwork ready for you to sign and funds moved to a business account first thing tomorrow morning."

"The future belongs to those who believe in the beauty of their dreams."

~ Eleanor Roosevelt

17

THE PLASTIC CHAIR PLACE

"I GUESS IT'S WHO you know!" I gave Perky a hug as we walked down the steps from the bank.

"Don't forget I worked with Brian for 20 years, Lese. I knew once he met you all would be fine. He's a good judge of character."

"I don't know how to thank you, Perk. Hey how about free bicycle maintenance."

"No, no, I'll be paying for it. You can't afford to give things away."

"Well, I'm just overwhelmed. This is a dream come true."

"Lese, just because you graduated college on a certain career path doesn't mean you have to follow it. I liked your answer to Brian about wanting to be a mechanic. You may find out that there are other things you want to do. When I started Mark, Fore, and Strike my family thought I was crazy. You have to believe in yourself."

"You are so easy to talk to."

"I am happy to listen, Lese. Your sister and I are so pleased you decided to move to our corner of the world. You are just starting out.

It's important not to let anyone else crush your dreams, whatever they are."

I was exhilarated. I hadn't met anyone quite like Persifor Frazer III. I could talk to Perky about anything. I was finding this true of many men I met. They would bypass game playing and say what they were thinking.

Should I share my dream?

I looked back at Perky. "I have lots of things on my list. One of them is from a recurring dream I have."

"A dream of?"

"Flying. A dream of flying."

"An airplane you mean?"

"Sort of. I just put my arms out and take off. I can fly over fields and valleys and houses. It's totally exhilarating. I don't need an airplane. For the longest time I would have this dream and actually feel that it was happening, that it was real. But I'd wake up, and logically I realized that it was not possible."

"I've had a dream about flying, but I was in an airplane," Perky said.

"How about a jetpack? Or some kind of contraption you could strap on?"

Perky parked the Honda in front of the restaurant we called "the plastic chair place," on the beachfront in Delray. "Come on, let's have lunch and celebrate. I want to hear more about the flying dream."

We walked up the steps and picked a table, hearing a shout. "Perky! Hey Perky!" shouted a man at one of the other tables.

"Mike! What serendipity. I want to introduce you to Lisa Turner, my sister-in-law, who wants to build a flying machine."

"Sit down with me, I haven't ordered yet," Mike said. He pulled a chair out for me.

"Lese, Mike is the flight instructor at Pompano Beach Airpark."

Mike reached out a burly hand. "Pleased to meet you Lisa, Mike Cross."

I felt giddy. It was like playing hooky. Perky was so easy to talk to. And when I thought about flying, the exhilaration was palpable. I hadn't told anyone about my dream except Mom years ago. Now Perky knew, and he didn't think I was crazy. And now I was sitting next to a flight instructor.

"Tell Mike about your flying machine," said Perky. Both men looked at me while I spilled out my enthusiasm. "It's a dream. Anti-gravity. I just lift off and glide. Over houses, over fields, over streets and forest."

"Ah, the flying dream," said Mike. I have it too."

"You know what I'm saying? Really? I haven't told anyone."

"I think you are a future pilot."

"Yes, I would love to be a pilot. There's only one problem."

"Ok, I know what you are going to say. You are just out of college with financial obligations. That happened to all of us. But if you have the flying dream, then you have to become a pilot," said Mike, waving his arms in excitement.

"Tell us about your flying machine, what will you build after you become a pilot?" asked Perky.

"You won't think I'm nuts?"

"You're nuts already, it doesn't matter," Perky said with a smile. Mike and I laughed.

"The problem with a jetpack is protection from the elements. You really need something around you for protection. But it would be super light and super small so that you have lots of maneuverability and visibility," I said as I replicated Mike's habit of moving his arms in the air.

Between the excitement of the bank and these two men lavishing so much attention on me, I was babbling. I stood up. "I'll be right back," I said as I headed to the restroom.

When I came back Mike and Perky were deep in discussion.

"Ok, we have it figured out," said Perky.

"Figured out what?" I asked.

"If you are going to build a flying machine, you need to get some pilot experience." Perky looked at Mike, who nodded. "Be at the Pompano Airpark at 8 am sharp tomorrow morning."

"Who, me?" I asked.

"Yes, you."

I pinched myself.

"I believe that if one always looked at the skies, one would end up with wings."

~ Gustave Flaubert

18

AIRPLANES

I PULLED UP TO THE small FBO building at Pompano Airpark and left the windows down on the car. It was a beautiful summer day, the sun beginning to heat the landscape. I went into the airport office. Several plate-glass windows looked out onto the airport ramps and runways. I went up to the counter. "Mike Cross, please."

"He's taxiing up now," said the young man.

I looked out the window to see a red and white Piper Cherokee PA-28-140 arrive at a set of tie-downs. Mike was with a student. I felt excitement building, just looking at the airplanes, but wondered if I could learn to fly one.

They got out of the aircraft and didn't worry about the tie-downs. Would Mike take me to the same airplane or would we go into the classroom?

They came inside, carrying maps. Mike looked happy to see me and reached his hand out. "Let me introduce you to Greg." Mike looked at his student, who turned to me with a handshake.

"Hi, Greg. Were you getting a lesson?" I asked.

"Yes," Greg replied, "this was my third lesson, it's great!"

Both men looked warm, their faces flushed.

"I guess you need to turn the air conditioning up in the plane, right?" I said.

Both men thought this was hilarious.

"Well, in a minute you'll see how good the air conditioning is," said Mike. "It's called climb to altitude."

"See you later, Mike, next week same?"

"Sure, 7 am is good. C'mon Lisa, let's fly!"

I thought there would be more to it than just walking to the airplane and getting in, but that's what it was.

"We preflighted this morning, I will show you that next lesson, let's just get going, it's going to be a hot day."

Mike showed me where to step on the wing and I moved over and into the left seat. I looked at the instrument panel and felt excitement grow, mixed with some anxiety. I took a deep breath and let it out slowly.

"Neat, huh?" said Mike

"I love it. But I don't have a clue what anything is. My flying dream isn't this complicated."

"You will. Let's just have fun today and then we'll start learning protocol in a few days."

Mike started the aircraft, leaving his door open. A breeze blew in from the prop. "No air conditioning. Too expensive and adds too much weight. Same reason it's not in your Civic."

Now I understood the laughter at my comment earlier.

"Ok, I want you to watch everything I do. Put your feet lightly on the rudder pedals, feel what I am doing. Watch the yoke. Just relax."

The apprehension gave way to exhilaration as we taxied across the ramp. Mike picked up the radio microphone and began talking to someone. It sounded like gobbledygook to me.

I hope I don't have to do that.

At the end of the taxiway we stopped and Mike did a run-up. All I could do was look out at the runway. I was mesmerized. As we took the runway and Mike applied power he said, "Hold your yoke and get a feel for this as I fly it."

"Ok."

In 30 seconds we were off the ground, pointed towards the clouds. A few minutes later we were level. "You have the airplane!" Mike shouted.

"What?" Between the engine roar and the wind I could hardly hear what he was saying.

"You have the airplane. Put your feet on the rudder pedals and your hands back on the yoke. Have some fun."

"Point the airplane over there," Mike said, as he pointed to the right. I turned the yoke as he added some power. Soon we were straight and level at 3,500 feet in the Pompano flight training area. I looked down at the square fields and tiny fences. Tiny cars. Tiny buildings.

Like the dream.

"Make a turn. Push in a little left rudder and turn the yoke." I couldn't believe Mike was letting me fly. I had no idea what I was doing. I turned the yoke to the left. The airplane turned to the left and descended.

"That's good. Good. Pull back a little."

I played. This was amazing.

"Time to go back," Mike said.

"What? It's only been a few minutes!" I exclaimed.

"It's been 45 minutes."

More gobbledygook on the radio, and then the runway appeared in the windshield. Mike made the landing look like the aircraft was on rails. I couldn't wait for the next lesson.

"Many a trip continues long after movement in time and space have ceased."

~ John Steinbeck

19

DREAM TAKE FLIGHT

OVER THE NEXT TEN DAYS I showed up every morning at Pompano Air Park when Mike was working. With the preparations to open the bicycle shop, I had the ability to move things around on my schedule. I knew that once I opened my business, it would consume all of my time.

One day I asked Brent, the man behind the FBO service counter, what I owed.

"Nothing yet."

"How could it be nothing yet? I've had 8 lessons," I asked.

"Uh, wait a minute, let me look. Someone is paying for your lessons."

"What?"

"Somebody named Persifor."

Perky.

Mike walked in to the office.

"Mike, hey, how many lessons are we doing?"

"Your brother-in-law told me that you should solo."

"Solo? Wow. That will take a while. I didn't realize Perky was paying for this."

"That's Perky. Anyway, you just might surprise yourself," replied Mike. "Come on, let's go."

We went out to the practice area for every lesson, doing turns, stalls, emergency procedures, slips, and glides. Soon Mike was letting me take off and climb to the training area. "Just don't make me talk on that gobbledygook radio." I said one day.

"Aha! That reminds me, let's practice the radio."

"That was smart of me to bring it up. I can't understand what they are saying. How can you expect me to fly and talk at the same time?"

Mike smiled.

After pattern work, I was starting to feel comfortable landing the airplane. As the kinesthetics worked into my muscle memory it got easier to gauge the landing height and speed of the aircraft.

"Every day I want you to try to replicate what I am doing so you can do it yourself," he said.

As we came in to land one day, Mike continued to hold the yoke and operate the throttle as I felt his operation of the controls.

"Ok, you do it," said Mike.

The landing was smooth as we flew down the runway, inches from the pavement, then touching on the mains and holding the nose off, waiting for speed to bleed off before applying the brakes.

"You just landed it," said Mike.

"I did not, you landed it," I replied.

"Nope. I took the pressure off. Nice job."

■　＿＿＿　■

My sister invited me to dinner one night during my lessons. I couldn't stop babbling. "It's just, well, I can't describe it, it's like anti-gravity and then landing there's this equilibrium between flying and touching down, and the times you squeak the pavement you feel this thrill and excitement and there's no other feeling like it! Perky, this is a door into another wonderful world. Thank you."

"I have a feeling you will solo soon."

"Solo? I only have 10 hours in my logbook so far, Perk."

Perky had a strange secret smile on his face, and Heather gave me a hug. "I'm proud of you, Lisa," she whispered in my ear.

Wow. Perky won her over.

The next day dawned clear and calm and felt a little cooler. I preflighted the Cherokee, and Mike came out of the FBO. "Preflight?" asked Mike.

"I was talking to Perky last night. He thinks I'll solo soon. Ha! I have a long way to go."

Mike smiled and walked behind me as I preflighted the Cherokee.

"You do know that Perky is an accomplished pilot?" Mike asked.

"Heather told me he was a pilot in the war."

"Yes. Perk joined the U.S. Army Air Corps in 1941 and went to West Point. He went to mechanic school, bomb school, and then pilot training, and even flew training missions with Jimmy Stewart."

"You're kidding," I said.

"He trained in Sebring and Avon Park, and ended up flying B-17s during the war. He was trained as a pilot, gunner, and bombardier. He survived a ditching and a parachuting out of a bullet-ridden B-17 and made it back somehow, amazing. He received the Distinguished Flying Cross." Mike stopped talking suddenly. I could see the emotion on his face.

"I grew up with Perk. I know all the stories. The amazing thing is that they are true."

"Well that explains why he's so appreciative of life and everything in it now," I said.

"Ok, let's go. I'm getting sentimental." Mike took a deep breath, and we got into the airplane. Mike called Ground. I took the controls and taxied out to the ramp.

"What do you say we do some touch and goes?" said Mike.

"You handle the radio," I asked Mike.

"No, no, here you tell them." Mike handed me the microphone.

"No, stop! I can't!" I froze. Talk on the radio? What was I going to say?

Mike took the microphone. Here, like this. "Pompano Tower, Piper Cherokee five-seven-three-five-two would like to stay in the pattern for touch and goes."

"Cherokee Three-five-two, cleared for takeoff one five. Report each downwind mid field, Pompano."

"See, that's not so bad, is it?" said Mike. "On the next circuit you try it, ok?"

My dread of talking on the radio was finally overcome by my delight with flying, and I took the microphone and screwed up my courage. If I was going to be a pilot, I was going to have to talk on the radio.

"Say you're a student pilot, and they will speak slower," said Mike.

On the following circuit I took the mike. "Pompano Tower, Cherokee three five two, student pilot, would like to do a touch and go."

"Cherokee Three-five-two, cleared for touch and go one five. Report downwind mid field, Pompano."

"Not so bad, huh?" said Mike.

"Awful!" I screwed up my face and Mike laughed.

I practiced on the next circuit and didn't feel any better about it, but the controllers were talking slower and more clearly for me, which was a help.

Downwind on the fourth circuit, Mike picked up the radio. "Pompano Tower, Three-five-two will be full stop."

"Three-five-two, full stop on 5, Pompano."

As we pulled off, Mike keyed the microphone. "Pompano Tower, three-five-two will do two solo touch and goes and one to full stop."

My eyes were wide with astonishment and I stared at Mike.

"Lisa, listen. Go do three takeoffs and landings. Have a blast." He opened the door and jumped out on to the pavement before I could argue.

No, no, don't go.

I didn't know what to do. I was totally and completely surprised. I felt a rush of excitement, and a constriction in the back of my throat. I looked at Mike, now standing on the tarmac with his flight bag. He pulled out a hand-held radio. "Go, go, go! Good luck!" he mouthed, over the sound of the engine and prop.

I reached for the radio mike in my sweaty right hand. "Pompano, Cherokee three-five-two STUDENT PILOT would like to taxi to 5, would like to stay in the pattern for two touch and goes."

"Three-five-two, taxi to 5, takeoff approved when ready."

"Three-five-two taxi to 5 takeoff approved when ready," I repeated.

I could stop right now, tell Mike I wasn't ready to solo . . . or I could take off.

I taxied to 5 and lined up. My heart was beating as fast as a hummingbird's wings. It was a very quiet morning on the airport and there was no traffic.

What am I doing?

I applied power. The PA-28 lifted off early and fast and climbed much faster than I was used to. Of course, I thought to myself, the 200-pound instructor isn't here, and I am 124 pounds.

A mixture of anxiety and anticipation filled my lungs.

I'm in an airplane by myself.

I turned downwind and realized I was high and fast. I reduced the power slightly and tried to settle down. I took a deep breath and scanned my instruments.

"Pompano Tower, three-five-two student pilot reporting midfield for touch and go 5."

"Three-five-two, cleared for touch and go, 5."

Reduce throttle. Still too fast. Turning Base. One notch of flaps. Too high! Too fast!

"Pompano Tower, three-five-two requests go around," I said.

"Three-five-two go around approved, report midfield downwind for 5. You're doing fine."

I'm doing fine? The Tower thinks I'm doing fine? I'd never heard that before.

Full power, flaps up. I flew down the runway at 75 feet and saw Mike do a thumbs-up signal.

He thinks it's ok? It was a screw-up.

Concentrate. Speed, altitude, compensate for Mike not being in the airplane. But pretend he is here with you. What would he say?

Turning downwind things felt much better. Watch speed, check surroundings, call the Tower. Reduce speed. Flaps. Turn to the runway. Be gentle, measured. Deep breath. Ok.

The runway unfolded like a carpet. Over the fence, speed 80 knots, hold it just off the pavement, a little backpressure, wait. A squeak as the tires kissed the pavement. Wait for the nose wheel. Keep a little backpressure on the yoke. Wait.

"Go again!" I shouted to myself in the cockpit in excitement, steadily applying throttle and holding the rudder straight as the airplane rolled down the centerline and took off again. I felt like I was in the surf on the beach, and a huge wave came up and over me, washing energy and buoyancy over me. Elation rocked my body, the fear evaporating into the air.

In my peripheral vision I could see Mike standing on the taxiway next to his flight bag, grinning, with another thumbs-up.

I did two more touch and goes and then taxied over to Mike. He grabbed his bag and hopped back in the airplane. I was dripping with sweat, and as happy as I'd ever been in my life. I couldn't think of anything to say and must have had the silliest of expressions on my face. I wiped another drip of sweat from my forehead. I exhaled deeply.

"Congratulations!" came booming over the radio speaker from the Tower.

"Lisa, that was great! Here, thank the Tower." Mike passed me the microphone.

I grabbed the radio. "Thank you!"

"Contact Ground, point-niner. Have a great day."

We taxied back to the FBO.

"Do I have to get out of the airplane?" I asked Mike.

"Yeah, I have another lesson to give. But first let's take your picture next to the airplane and I want to sign your logbook."

I was in the clouds.

Thank you Perky

PARKING

TURNERS
BICYCLES
MO PEDS

R.F. SOWREY

"To open a business is very easy; to keep it open is very difficult."

~ Chinese proverb

20

THE BICYCLE SHOP

A SEDAN PULLED OFF NORTH Federal Highway in Delray Beach and followed a short, tree-lined lane to the small cottage. A bicycle was half in and half out of the car's trunk, a rope securing the handlebars to the trunk latch. The car pulled into one of the spaces next to the bicycle rack filled with rentals. It was a warm spring day, the sunlight floated through the thick canopy of pine and cedar.

"Good. I need a few more repairs this week," I said to myself. Tim, my helper, had Wednesdays off.

I walked from the work area out into the showroom and past the large plate-glass window. Two bicycles hung from the ceiling, and a row of six ten-speed bicycles angled out from the glass. On the other side of the showroom four bicycles adorned with repair tags awaited their owners.

I walked out the door and over to the car to help the driver.

"I got it, I got," the man said, struggling with the rope.

"Here let me help," I said as I tried to figure out the knot. It wasn't a square knot, but the nylon came loose in my hands as I manipulated the material. I lifted the three-speed cruiser out of the trunk and walked it in to the shop.

"Gee, thanks."

"No problem. It's what I do." I smiled at the man, who was in his 60s or 70s I gauged, looking at his portly stature and sun-weathered hands and face.

"I need to get this bicycle fixed for my daughter. I accidently ran over it backing out of the garage. Boy, am I in trouble." He shook his head and pursed his lips nervously. "Where is the owner?"

"I'm the owner."

"You're the owner?" The man looked confused. "Ok, then, where is the mechanic?"

"I'm the mechanic."

"You're the mechanic?" The man looked like he had just dialed a wrong number. "You're the owner and the mechanic? Are you sure?"

"I'm sure. I'm the mechanic; this is my bike shop. I'm Lisa." I offered my hand.

"I'm Ed."

Ed gripped my hand lightly and carefully. "I'm sorry, I didn't mean to indicate that I was surprised that, uh, you're a young woman, it's just unusual, you know."

"No problem, Ed. Let's figure out what your daughter's bike needs. Workload is light right now so I can get it done right away."

"That's wonderful," said Ed, looking relieved and still confused.

■ ⟶ ■

I thought back to how I arrived in this little building set back from the highway. The great excitement of my first solo flight nearly overwhelmed my business plans. I could become homeless and bum around the airport, hoping for rides, or I could execute my bicycle shop plan. When I asked about being a line girl, the airport manager said, "What? What is that?"

"Isn't that the same thing as a line boy? I replied.

"You're not a boy."

My face turned red and I didn't know how to reply. Most of the time I thought I was too shy, but at times I just blurted out what I was thinking and then felt embarrassed about it. If I'd had more courage, more grit, I would have continued to challenge the airport manager about why girls couldn't do what line boys do. I wasn't really sure what a line boy did, but I was sure that I could do it.

I left the FBO embarrassed and disappointed. I resolved to develop more courage. I just wasn't sure where to begin.

Once I opened the small bike shop and customers began to stream in I felt more comfortable. But there was something missing. I was out of step with my long-range plan. I didn't know what it was.

"So you think you can get this done today?" said Ed.

"Oh, sorry, I was thinking of something . . . yes, of course, I need to fix the front wheel, repair the tire, and realign the handlebars." I scribbled on a repair ticket. "Come back at 5 today?"

"Good, see you then."

I carried the bike in to the back of the shop and began dissembling the wheel and tire. I loved working on bicycles. Just add a motor . . .

Wait. I got it. Airplanes. That's what I should be working on. Airplanes.

Airplanes.

I was fortunate to have started the bike shop at the same time the bicycle and moped boom began in the mid-seventies. I ended up renting, repairing, and selling both. I went to night school for two-stroke engine repair.

In the third year I broke even and began to make money. I worked six days a week to do it. I began to save money and put it back into the shop, but I had a bad habit of buying tools and gadgets, reducing what I had left over.

I decided to tune up cars. I went to night school to learn automotive tune-up. I was always the only woman in class. I enjoyed the attention from the men. All of my friends were men. I still had trouble communicating with other women. I assumed that it was because I hadn't been trained to lure the opposite sex when I was growing up. In my opinion, this was ok, and even a good thing. I was completely accepted by the guys. In fact, many of them would confide in me.

"You're easy to talk to, and don't play games," said Tim one day when we were crushed with work at the shop and working side by side. "You listen. When I come to work every day I know who I'm going to be with. Consistency."

"Thanks, Tim. It's just me. I enjoy men. I don't want to be one, I just like being with them."

"That's a good sign," said Tim as he went back to packing headset bearings.

It was wild. Here's a guy who was talking to a girl like she was a guy, with trust and without fear. I loved it.

"So, Tim, how come you haven't invited me out to dinner?"

"Because you're my boss, and you could probably beat me up if I tried anything."

"Right answer!"

We looked at each other and laughed. We knew we could tease each other. It was so comfortable and I was glad to have a competent mechanic working for me. I unclipped the bike stand arms and lowered the repaired bike to the floor. I began polishing the metal.

"That's why people like us. We clean the bikes too!"

"It's what I would want," I said.

"So what do you want to be when you grow up?" Tim gave out a hearty laugh.

"That's the problem, Tim, seriously, I don't know. I think there's something I'm missing. I'd like to be working on airplanes, and fly. And own an airplane. Best of all would be to make a custom airplane. Or a jet pack, or a helicopter, or something to get off the ground in."

Tim was quiet, and I looked over at him as he adjusted a headset bearing.

"Ok, you sell me the shop and you go back to school."

"Deal."

"Men are disturbed not by things, but by the views which they take of things."

~ Epictetus, Philosopher

21

IN THE PATTERN

I LIFTED OFF AND GLIDED over the rooftops of the houses; over the lake, higher into the night mist. Higher and higher, I leveled off at about 500 feet where I could explore the landscape and revel in the euphoria I always experienced when I glided and swooped without effort. I floated along, enjoying the sensations of the slippery airstream.

I hear an airplane.

I woke up and looked around my little bedroom, neat as a pin. The neatness was rebellion against my earlier life of messiness. Now organization was a handhold for me in feeling in control. Sunlight played on the wall and reminded me of the childhood days when I would wake up, not knowing what set of troubles I would land in that day.

Here I was organized, employed, and single in the cookie-cutter house I had just bought on the small lake after my three-year marriage ended. After I sold my bicycle shop, I returned to school to learn engineering. I got a job as an electronics technician at a manufacturing firm in Boca Raton.

One day while we were working on power supplies a fellow tech turned to me and said, "You do realize that the company will pay for you to go to night school for anything you want."

"Anything?" I asked.

"Well, it has to be technical or leadership, not cooking or something."

"That's a relief. I've made a point of not learning how to do anything functional in a kitchen."

The tech thought this was uproarious.

So, I went to night school. After two years I had a Masters in Business. In the last class, the instructor suggested we continue on and get a doctorate. "It's only another three years of night school," he said. The students looked around in disbelief.

"He's crazy, who in their right mind would do that?"

I signed up.

I heard the airplane again. I went over to the window and looked out. I saw a small plane at about 700 feet fly over.

Sightseeing?

As I got ready to start the day, I heard the engine again.

Why am I hearing so many airplanes?

Now all I could think about was airplanes. This must be a signal.

I had plans to do yard work on this beautiful Saturday. But maybe . . . I should find a map. I dug around in my desk. There were boxes still piled up from my move. I opened the box labeled "desk files" and removed the folder that said Maps.

Lantana. I unfolded the Boynton Beach map and found my street. Less than a mile and a half from my house, as the crow flies, was an airport. I looked at the detail. It had three runways and no control tower.

It's a signal.

Working full time, I always assumed that I didn't have time to do anything else. My career was everything to me. But should it be? I sat down in the kitchen with a cup of coffee and began thinking about how I could learn to fly.

Are you so busy that you don't have time to fly? I asked myself. Are you afraid you'll fail? Are you afraid you'll be pulled away from your current career? Is that so bad? Can I afford to fly? It's been 20 years since I soloed. Start fresh. I looked at the neat list I'd made for planting chores this weekend.

I heard another airplane fly over the house. I picked up the chores list and dropped it in the trash. I grabbed my car keys and went to the garage.

The Lantana airport was off a major road, and had a quaint, old-style terminal building with a breezeway. The place reminded me of a TGI Fridays, with all the airplane models and memorabilia hung from ceilings and arranged along walls. I introduced myself to the man behind the counter, named Rick. "Is there a flight school here?" I asked.

"Of course. First door on your right. Lantana Flight School. The Madisons own it. Been in business for a long time. They even have a female flight instructor."

"Thanks." I replied.

"Good luck."

I walked out of the FBO into the breezeway, turned left, then right down a porch area with doors. "Lantana Flight School" – first on the right. I walked in.

A young woman looked up behind the counter. Brown hair reached her shoulders. "Can I help you?" She brushed the bangs from her eyes.

"Do you offer flight instruction?"

"Absolutely. Is it for you?"

"Yes, for me."

"I'm Ellen, one of the instructors, hi." She stood up and reached her hand out over the counter to grip my hand. "When can you start?"

"I can learn on weekends, right?"

"Of course. It's a little busy on weekends, but we will fit it in. Just let me know so I can put it in the book."

"Next available?"

"As soon as Lois comes back to hold the fort here, we can go now. Here, have a seat and fill out this info sheet."

Go now?

I sat down. I wasn't completely sure I wanted to begin so fast. I felt I was floating in river rapids again, not sure what would be around the corner, but knowing it was also inevitable. I starting filling out the student information sheet.

"How often can you take lessons?" Ellen flipped her brown curls backwards over her shoulder.

"I work full time at Sensormatic Electronics in Boca. About 55 hours a week, so I only have the weekends for flying. But it's doable, if I stick to the schedule, right?"

"Of course!" Ellen exuded enthusiasm. I liked her.

A man and woman came through the front door. They were in their late sixties.

"We're back." They looked at me and said hi. What can we do for you? Is Ellen helping you? We own Madison Flight School."

"We're all set, yes, Lisa wants to learn how to fly."

"Great." said the man. "Do you want me to take it or you?" He looked at Ellen.

"I'll take it, Tom, I'll take it."

"You've been taking on a lot of students, Ellen. Don't get overwhelmed."

"Ellen can handle it." Lois walked around the counter and sat down at the computer terminal.

"Lisa, let's go flying." Ellen had keys in her hand and we headed out the door.

"That was awkward," I said to Ellen.

"Yeah. I'm sorry. You walked in at the right time. More and more students are asking for me, and I think Tom is upset about it."

"Have you been in a small plane before?" Ellen opened the left-hand door of the red and white Cessna 152.

I thought back twenty years to the Piper Cherokee 140.

"Yes." Ten lessons twenty years ago . . . would I remember anything? Why not start from scratch and not be as nervous.

"Let's start at the beginning."

"Good," I replied.

Good.

■ ⌐—⌐ ■

The view out the high-winged Cessna was very different from the Piper Cherokee, and I liked it. "You can see a lot with the wings up there," I said to Ellen.

"The problem with that is it's hard to see any aircraft above you, and when landing you don't get as much ground effect," Ellen said.

"Watch me while I do the preflight. We'll spend more time on it the next lesson, I want to get you in the air." It reminded me of Mike, my previous instructor. They want to get you hooked.

No problem. I'm already hooked.

Once inside the 152, I realized how small the cockpit was. Ellen and I were shoulder to shoulder without our jackets on. It most certainly seemed smaller than the Piper cockpit. "Wow, this is tight. How does this compare to the Piper Cherokee cockpit?" I said.

"The 140 or 151? Smaller."

"Yeah, so how do the guys fly in this?"

"They just jam in. It's a trainer. Most students move on to the 172. More room. But more expensive."

The case of nerves I carried into almost every social situation began to ebb slowly as I became more interested in the airplane.

Ellen pointed out the controls as she began taxiing the 152 out of the ramp area and down a taxiway.

"No tower?" I asked.

"No, no tower here, but we're nestled in Palm Beach airspace, so eventually we have to talk to ATC. What we do here is make announcements on the radio so others in the vicinity know what we are doing."

I thought back to my intense fear talking on the radio. Can I get over that now? Have to.

After a run-up with checks and a final look at base leg for traffic, Ellen keyed the mic. "Lantana Traffic, Cessna four-oh-five taking off runway three-three, departing to the west."

The 152 roared down the runway and took off quickly. The sensation was exhilarating, the view magical.

Nearly twenty years later. What took me so long? Is this the missing piece?

'We all live under the same sky, but we don't all have the same horizon.'

~ Konrad Adenauer

22

THE FLIGHT TEST

E LLEN WAS PATIENT BUT stern. I wanted to please her and worked hard at my training. In the beginning many of the motor skills felt familiar but then as the training accelerated, I found myself in uncharted territory. I spent all of my non-work time immersed in flying and ground school. My flying dreams returned. A good sign. I felt like a slow learner, but I persisted. On one cross country I couldn't identify the airport I was supposed to land at, panicked, and flew back. I was embarrassed and discouraged.

"I'm glad you told me, Lese. Most students don't tell me when they turn around. Hey, you're not alone. Keep working at it, ok?"

"Ok. But I really feel stupid."

"Enough of that. Let's chart you another cross country."

Less than four months from the day I walked into the flight school it was time for my flight test. I was paralyzed with apprehension just thinking about it.

"Come on, Lese, you fly with me, you can fly with the FAA."

"Oh, no! The stories I've heard. I've got a dreadful case of nerves."

"Everyone does, you'll do fine. Don't psych yourself out."

"Easy for you to say!" I was psyching myself out.

The day arrived. I walked in to the flight office hyperventilating.

"Stop that!" Ellen looked at me. What's the worst thing? You can always take it over, it's not like he will ban you from being a pilot."

"Are you Lisa Turner?" A tall lanky man with close cropped salt and pepper hair walked out of the training room in the back of the office. "Check ride?"

"Yes, yes, I am Lisa." We shook hands.

"Bill, Bill Yates. Come on back, we'll do the ground portion first."

I'd studied hard, and Ellen had briefed me on the components of the oral tests. Bill asked me the questions in a monotone. I wondered if he was a cyborg.

"Ok. Let's fly. Go preflight 405, I'll be right out."

"Ok."

I walked out of the training room and collected the keys for the 152. Ellen raised her eyebrows at me in inquiry.

"It went well, I think."

"Good," replied Ellen. "Calm down."

I left the office and preflighted the airplane. I felt the anxiety ramp up. I was far more comfortable on the book knowledge than I was on my flying ability. And I was just making it worse by allowing my nerves to take over my brain.

I checked the topped fuel tanks one more time and untied the ropes. I noticed that the wind was picking up. I looked toward the west, where the skies were darkening. I felt knots forming in the bottom of my stomach. Would the weather hold or not? I took a deep breath and looked westward again. Am I imagining it? I had an odd feeling of foreboding.

You're making this up.

Bill came out of the office. "Are we all set?" He stepped up on the wing struts and looked in the fuel tanks on both wings.

"I checked them."

"You never know. I always make sure."

I felt my stomach tighten more and my throat go dry as we buckled in. Hope I can talk, I thought to myself.

"Let's head west," said Bill.

"Ok."

"What? I can't hear you. Speak up," shouted Bill.

"Ok!" I croaked. I'd lost my voice. How would I talk on the radio? I was beginning to feel sick to my stomach.

After an uneventful takeoff I headed west from the airport. This was one of the few ways to get out of Lantana without going through controlled airspace. I felt some relief wash over me as I realized we'd be going to the training area and not into controlled airspace.

Bill wasn't talking. He sat rigid in the right seat, looking straight out. I struggled to swallow my fear.

Cyborg.

"Climb to 2,500."

"Climb to 2,500," I repeated.

"Demonstrate a power-off stall."

I was comfortable with the exercise because I'd practiced it so many times. As the stall horn went off, I put the nose down and added power. Out of the corner of my eye I saw dark sky moving toward us. A few large rain drops hit the windshield. A typical south Florida thunderstorm. They were unpredictable and dangerous to small aircraft.

"Now let's do a 60-degree turn," said Bill.

"Bill, look over there. It doesn't look good." I pointed to the advancing vertical mass moving toward us.

"Do you want to go back to the airport?" He said it as if I was chickening out, as if I wasn't strong enough to continue the test.

"I think we should," I replied.

There's no other choice. It's a safety issue.

"Ok, your choice. Go." Bill was unreadable.

I turned the Cessna around and headed back to the airport, but it was too late. The winds and rain caught up with the little craft as if a hand was reaching out and grabbing control of the airplane. I expected Bill to take over the controls at any moment but he was unmoving in the passenger seat.

Bill finally spoke. "Do a straight in, we need to get on the ground fast. Don't use flaps."

"Lantana Traffic, Cessna Four Zero Five two miles inbound, will be straight in on nine, Lantana."

The 152 rocked and bounced in the air currents as we approached the runway, and it was all I could do to keep the airplane straight. I'd never been in a situation where it was this rough. The visibility had dropped to almost nothing as we crossed the threshold. Hard rain streaked the windshield and thunder reverberated through the air with bright flashes of light. The clot of fear in my stomach gave way to survival instinct as I did everything I could to control the airplane and not crash into the ground. I couldn't believe that the examiner was still hands off the controls.

The airplane was pushed up and down in tight quick movements as we came in over the pavement and then the tires squealed as we hit the runway hard. The nosewheel came down with a bump as I wrestled with the controls.

"Jesus, you're trying to kill me!" shouted Bill.

I felt like an arrow had gone through my gut.

I've failed.

The wind and rain were now full force, the nearby windsock straight out. The little plane rocked and vibrated as we taxied to the flight school ramp.

"Tie the plane down tight!" shouted Bill, exiting the plane and running into the flight office.

I sat there in shock and embarrassment. The rain was beating on the windshield, and lightning flashed across the field followed by a deafening clap of thunder. I took a gulp of air and then exhaled.

What if I'd followed Bill's instructions and continued the test? We could have crashed.

I shut down the engine and opened the door. The wind nearly tore it out of my grasp. I spent time with the tie-down ropes, and kept getting blown into the airplane as I worked to make sure every line was tight. By the time I walked into the flight office, I looked like I'd jumped into a pool with my clothes on.

"Here she is. Here she is. She tried to kill me!" Bill looked at Ellen and Lois.

"Oh come on Bill, I saw that landing, any pilot would have trouble with those gusts, it was a great landing given the conditions," Ellen said.

"Reschedule." Bill walked out the office door.

I slumped down in the seat next to the door, dripping.

"You're a mess," said Ellen, as she handed me a towel. "Hey, listen. This isn't a failure. He didn't pink slip you. It's just a reschedule."

"What? I thought I'd failed! That was awful. I'm quitting. This is too much."

"No," said Ellen, gently. "Don't quit. That's Bill. He's not that personable. Get past that. I think he does it on purpose to test students. Don't let it get to you. He did admit to me that you handled the airplane admirably given the conditions."

"He did? Really? Ellen, are you making this up? He told me that I was trying to kill him. Jeez."

"He has a strange sense of humor."

"I guess so!"

"I'll reschedule your check ride. Let's you and me spend some dual time next week to make sure you're totally comfortable."

I was still in distress and feeling I would just not come back. I'd give Ellen a call and say that's it. I can't do this. Sorry. I took a deep breath and pushed my wet hair out of my eyes. "I'll think about it."

As I looked out the window, the vicious wind and rain stopped and the sun came out as if someone had flipped a switch.

"When fears are grounded, dreams take flight."

~ Anon

23

SECOND CHANCE

I SPENT SEVERAL WEEKS with flight instructors. Ellen suggested that I ask Tom to take me out, since he was about the size of Bill, and I'd have a good sense of how the airplane would handle.

"Can you get me a different FAA examiner?" I asked Ellen.

Ellen laughed. "No, not unless you want to wait for Bill to retire."

I shook my head. "I can't believe how nervous I am."

"Lese, listen. All new pilots go through this. It's normal. A fifth of student pilots don't pass the first time and have to re-do the whole thing. You didn't get pink slipped, so it means that what you demonstrated already was ok."

"Right. Thunderstorm landings. I can't help feeling scared."

Ellen looked at me with serious eyes and went on. "You _can_ help it. You _can_ decide how to view it. You're sabotaging yourself, telling yourself that you can't do it. If you keep doing that, then it will become a self-fulfilling prophecy, and the bad things you think might happen will happen. You'll create them. You've got to change your mindset and get some confidence."

"But how do I do that?"

"Lese, you're a very enthusiastic and positive person, right?"

"Right."

"So, think about this. You love to fly. You dream about flying. You've trained hard. You've completed your cross-countries. You're a thoughtful pilot. So change your mindset. Think, I'm a good pilot, I'm not going to make up catastrophes, I can do this, and I'm confident I can do this."

"Have you thought about being a psychologist? I asked Ellen.

Ellen laughed. "That's good to know in case I lose my instructor job." She looked at Lois.

"When is the check ride?"

"Next week. Let's go fly again."

The day came. I woke up with a feeling of queasiness. The fear of failure grew like a mass in my stomach as I got ready to go to the airport. I felt lightheaded and worried.

Oh great. I'm sick on my flight test day.

It was a beautiful morning at the airport. I'd taken the day off work, telling everyone that I had appointments. No one knew I was retaking my flight test, not even Perky, who had given me encouragement similar to Ellen's.

I walked into the office, trying to banish the misgivings from my mind.

"Ok! Great day for a check ride," exclaimed Ellen.

"Ok. I'm barely under control," I said.

"Good and bad news, Lese," said Ellen.

Good. The examiner can't make it.

"Bill is running late. He'll be here at 10 instead of 9:30."

My heart sank. More time to amass anxiety.

"Go on out and preflight, and then I'll occupy your mind waiting here in the office," said Ellen.

I took the keys and went out to the airplane. I spent a long time checking everything. I thought about how durable the airplane was. Students manhandle it every day and it still stays in one piece.

If I had my own airplane, I would keep it in tiptop shape.

My own airplane. Could I have my own airplane? I'd always assumed I'd rent one.

My own airplane.

A vision of trips in my own airplane appeared. I was giving someone a ride. Perky. I knew my own airplane inside out. I was confident. I'd passed my check ride. As I kept daydreaming I saw Larry, my middle school homeroom teacher, in the airplane. The flying car! I laughed.

I can do it.

I went back into the office.

"I can't check anything else unless I take it apart," I said to Ellen. I looked at the clock. It was 9:45.

My own airplane.

The door opened and in swung Bill.

"You're early," said Ellen.

"Yup, got through early on the last test. I had to pink slip a student. Awful."

The chunk of fear in my stomach came back. Could I control it?

"Bill! You're so mean!" Ellen threw her hair back over her should and laughed.

Ellen was completely unfazed by this cruel man. Had she even ridden with him, I thought. He's like Jekyll and Hyde.

"Ok, well, is the student ready?" Bill looked at me.

"Yes, yes, ready."

"You're not going to kill me this time, are you?"

"Ellen is right. He has a mean streak.

"I'll try not to," I blurted out.

"Hey, that's funny! C'mon let's go," he said. Ellen was shaking her head at Bill in disapproval.

We went out to the airplane. As Bill checked the gas levels in the tanks, I stood at the aircraft door, rocking from foot to foot. We got in the airplane and I picked up the checklist. I took a deep breath.

My own airplane.

I started the Cessna and taxied out to Runway 33.

"Take me to Boca Raton Airport," said Bill, in a commanding tone.

"Got it."

I can do it.

My hands were trembling but my stomach knots began to untangle. We stopped at the runway run-up area and I checked the instruments and controls. The winds were calm as I lined up on the runway. I pushed the throttle in and the Cessna gathered speed and lifted off. My spirits lifted with the airplane, and we left the pattern to the south.

"Before we get to Boca, let's climb to 3,500."

"Three thousand five hundred." I added power and the plane reached altitude.

Bill looked at his notebook. "Hmm, already did stall, cross-wind landings...." Bill was mumbling things I couldn't hear.

"Sorry, I can't hear you, Bill."

"I'm talking to myself," Bill said loudly. "Do a 60-degree turn for me please."

I entered the steep turn, applying some power and watching my altitude. After one 360-degree turn, I prepared to flatten it.

"No, wait, I have the airplane," said Bill as he pushed the 152 over even farther in the turn and added power.

I was shocked. Ellen had told me, if the examiner ever takes over the controls, you've failed big time. I felt a mixture of deflation and disappointment flood into my lungs.

"See? You do another one now," said Bill. "You have the airplane."

In surprise I took the controls back and tried to do a turn exactly like Bill. It seemed to me that it was steeper than 60 degrees. After 360 degrees, I brought the craft back to straight and level.

"Good!" shouted Bill. I looked over to see if I'd heard him correctly. What I thought might have been a partial smile was quickly gone and replaced with a blank stare out the window.

"Oops, engine failure!" Bill now shouted, pulling the throttle out to idle.

I went through my checklist by heart and said the items aloud. "Best glide...check fuel...emergency landing spot... see that golf course right there to our left? We will land there if we don't get the engine back."

My own airplane.

I lined up with the fairway. Two golfers looked up in horror as they saw the little blue-and-white Cessna drifting down slowly 400 feet above them. They began pointing and gesturing, and then they ran for their golf carts in panic.

Is he going to make me really land here? We can't do that.

"Ok, power!" said Bill, and I moved the throttle forward with relief. The airplane gained speed and I climbed out to 1,000 feet. The Boca Raton airport was off to our right.

"Let's land at Boca."

I took a deep breath as my confidence continued to grow. I made my calls to traffic and lined up on final.

"Oh shoot! I dropped my pencil!" I heard Bill say, as I saw him fling his pencil across to my feet.

What in the world is he doing?

Then Ellen's words came to me. "At some point in the check ride Bill will try to distract you, or give you vertigo to see how you handle it."

"Can you get my pencil? It fell at your feet," asked Bill.

I looked out at my position for landing. We had plenty of altitude and the airplane was stable. "Sure." I reached down to my feet without actually looking so I wouldn't get disoriented. I felt the pencil in my fingers and brought it up, handing it to Bill. I wanted to make a wisecrack but thought better of it.

I passed over the threshold and came over the runway. Glide, glide, nose up a little, slowing, the tires met the pavement with a small squeak just as the stall horn went off. Keep control . . . nose down . . . deep breath.

"Ok, let's go again," said Bill.

I retracted the flaps and added power.

"Climb to 4,500. Let's go to Palm Beach and land," he said.

Class C airspace!

I inhaled and held my breath, trying to hold back the apprehension that had flooded back in.

After reaching altitude, Bill asked me to perform a few more maneuvers. I couldn't stop thinking about Palm Beach. I'd need to talk to Approach first, then the tower. I had practiced it in my mind, and was now replaying it. I had the instructions on my clipboard. I took a look at that now. Bill went back to his tight-lipped cyborg self, staring ahead. As I looked at the radio frequencies and instructions, I began to feel the anxiety drain.

Your own airplane.

As we were coming up on Lantana, I started to enter the Approach frequency in the radio. Bill reached over and brushed away my hand. "No, that was just a test, let's go back to Lantana."

Relief flooded my senses as I made calls to Lantana traffic. I landed the Cessna, trying not to over think it. It was a completely different experience than the first landing I'd made with Bill. I taxied over to the flight school.

"I'll see you inside," Bill said gruffly, and he left the airplane.

The man is inscrutable.

I sat in the airplane as the tightness in my breathing melted away and an airy lightness replaced it. I felt completely different, as if I had been transported to a different dimension. I went through my shutdown checklist and climbed out of the airplane.

I entered the office, afraid of what I might hear. I thought I'd done well, but Bill was a wildcard. For all I knew, he could have thought my performance was awful. And he'd taken control of the airplane in my 60-degree turn maneuver.

Whatever it is, it's ok.

Bill and Ellen were in the corner, talking and looking at paperwork. When I shut the door, Bill looked up. "Congratulations, pilot. I'm glad you didn't try to kill me this time."

A brief smile flashed across his craggy face and then it was gone.

"Only those who risk going too far can possibly find out how far one can go."

~ T.S. Eliot

24

THE PHONE CALL

I SAT AT THE KITCHEN TABLE with a 3-x-5 index card with my Dad's phone number on it. It was dog-eared and wrinkled from taking it out of my pocket and then putting it back in my pocket over and over again.

I was thinking of a lot of other things I could be doing right now. Maybe I'll go outside and mow. I looked at the piece of paper for the tenth time and sighed. Heather had asked me why I wanted Dad's phone number.

"You've never wanted to call Dad before. Why now?"

"I want to tell him I got my pilot's license," I said.

Heather went to her address book and looked it up. She wrote it on a card and passed it to me.

"I'm sensing there's more to this than just telling him about your pilot's license."

"No, that's it," I lied.

"Well, tell him we all said hi, and tell him I hope he can come visit us in Maine next year."

I picked up the phone number one more time and looked at it. San Antonio, Texas. I closed my eyes and exhaled. Then I picked up the phone.

Maybe he won't answer.

"Hello."

"Dad?"

"Lisa?"

"What a surprise! Is there something wrong?"

"No, no, I'm calling to tell you about something . . . I got my pilot's license."

"Lisa, good for you. Heather told me you were taking flight lessons. That's a great achievement."

My case of nerves retreated slightly as Dad's words came confidently across the line.

"How is everything else, Lisa?" he asked.

"Fine, fine, the job is good, I enjoy the work, I'm in a good community with the new house, and the divorce trauma is fading."

"I know about divorce trauma. I'm sorry you had to go through that. You're doing the right thing to get on with your life, Lisa. I am so pleased that you called."

Tension crept into the back of my shoulders. "Dad, I have something to ask you."

"Yes?"

I couldn't remember the last time I had called my Dad. While I had seen him numerous times since he left when I was a child, we did not have a developed relationship. It wasn't because we didn't care about it, or hadn't tried; it was just awkward and neither of us knew where to begin emotionally.

I went on, "After I got my pilot's license last week, I wanted to rent a plane and visit Bob and Sue in the Keys. I thought that would be a lot of fun. But after talking to the flight school, and calculating the cost for an airplane, I was shocked. Just renting a Cessna 152 was too much for me. I guess I should have thought about that. A pilot without a plane!"

"Well, you'll have to set your sights lower then," said Dad matter-of-factly. "Keep saving your money and fly locally."

I took a shallow breath. "Dad, wait, there's something I want to tell you, but I don't know where to start." My voice felt stuck and my brain scrambled to make order out of what I wanted to say.

I shouldn't have called.

"Go ahead Lisa, I'm listening."

I took a breath. "I'm going to build an airplane for myself."

"What? Say that again?"

"Dad, I've had a dream about flying my whole life. When I moved to this house, I realized I'm right in the pattern for aircraft landing and taking off at the airport. The more I fly the more I love it. Somehow I've got to get an airplane."

"What does Heather think of that?"

"I haven't told her."

Silence.

I forged ahead. "The price of the older airplanes is about what a fuselage kit would be. The old airplanes are like jalopies; you have to spend money on them, nothing is new, and they are hard to see out of. I have a dream and that dream is to build and fly a brand-new craft with everything I want in it."

There was complete silence at the other end of the line.

"Dad?"

Maybe I didn't say that right. It makes it sound like I want a Ferrari.

"Lisa? A kit airplane? You mean an airplane that fits a whole person in it? Not a model? I've never heard of this apart from engineers experimenting with aircraft, or hobbyists experimenting with aircraft. How would you find an engine for it? It sounds dangerous, it really does."

I launched out again, the excitement of my idea blotting out the anxiety. "Dad, it's not that bad. There are dozens of kit plane manufacturers out there who have tested designs and have aircraft flying. The one I am looking at has more than 200 completed kits flying."

"The one you are looking at?" Dad cleared his throat. "How would you afford a kit airplane if you can't afford a Cessna?"

Dad hit a nerve. I didn't know how I was going to afford the kit. But I knew the kit—one of three that I had researched—would wind up in my garage within the next three months. I just knew it. I would figure out a way.

"I have a plan. I'll get the fuselage first, then the wings. Then the rest of the surfaces. Then I'll order the firewall forward kit. Then I'll design and make the panel. It will take years to construct."

"My goodness, Lisa. How can you plan something like this and hold down a full-time job? Heather says you have reached a manager position and are putting in 10 to 12 hours a day."

"The weekends, Dad, the weekends. It will take a while is all."

"I guess so. I don't know what to say, Lisa. I am trying to discourage you, but at the same time you know I care about what you want to do. I am sorry we haven't spent time together. I am so glad that you called; I don't want to spoil it for you. But I am concerned. Heather says you can be impulsive, impetuous."

I felt the void between us and so much yearned to close it, to talk, to listen, to explain that everything was ok, to have a relationship. Almost 40 years had passed since Dad left the family. I had no rancor or bitterness now, there was nothing that would have changed what had happened.

"Dad, one of the airplane kits on my list is built in San Antonio."

"There's an aircraft kit manufacturer here? What's their name?"

"Aero Designs."

"Aero Designs. Haven't heard of them. San Antonio is a big city with sprawling suburbs," said Dad.

"I'm coming there to test fly it, to see if I like it."

"Lisa, you're serious, aren't you?" Dad said in a gravelly voice.

"Yes. I've narrowed my choices to three aircraft, and Aero Designs has passed all of my criteria. I want to tour the factory and then fly the airplane."

"When are you coming? Will you come stay with us?"

The magic words.

"Yes, yes, thank you, that would be great, we will have a chance to visit," I said.

"Yes, we will. Lisa, I may try to talk you out of building a kit airplane, but one there's one thing you can count on."

"Yes, Dad?"

"I love you."

"I love you, too, Dad."

"Let me know what your plans are."

"I will."

I hung up the phone and exhaled deeply with a loud sigh. I closed my eyes and felt the bunched-up index card in my hand. I'd made even more of a mess of it while I was on the phone.

Maybe you're getting some guts.

"You have brains in your head. You have feet in your shoes. You can steer yourself any direction you choose. You're on your own, and you know what you know. And you are the one who'll decide where you go."

~ Dr. Seuss

25

THE PULSAR FACTORY

"I'LL BE FLYING INTO the San Antonio airport on Delta, arriving at 11:10 am," I said to Bob.

"I'll be there to pick you up. We'll go to the factory for a tour, and then we'll go to the Bulverde airport for a flight."

A flight!

Bob Kromer was the multi-talented sales person for Aero Designs. From test pilot to marketing guru, Bob worked with a talented group of Pulsar factory engineers, including the creative John Hutson, and Mark Brown who designed the Pulsar. Earlier in the month at the Sun 'n Fun Fly-In Pulsar booth, Bob sensed my seriousness for the aircraft and sent a follow-up letter to me with a hefty discount attached. Smart. Reducing my choices to three kits, Bob's letter prompted me to test fly the Pulsar first. My intent was to visit the factories of all three kit manufacturers and fly the planes before making the decision.

Bob was waiting for me outside the airport, and I hopped into the passenger seat with my backpack.

"Good flight?" said Bob.

"Yes, the big silver tube. Smooth and fast."

"Your Dad lives here in San Antonio? How often do you visit?"

"First time actually. Dad left the family when I was small, so we haven't spent a lot of time together. I'm looking forward to it tonight."

"After your Pulsar flight I'll be happy to drop you off there."

"Thanks, that would be great."

We arrived at the factory and Bob introduced me to associates. I noticed all the Pulsar photos pasted to the wall.

"How many kits are flying?" I asked Bob.

"More than 200 now."

"That's a good sign."

Bob took me through every area of the factory. From the fiberglass mold enclaves to the kitting area; everything was clean, neat, and efficient. Employees were friendly and attentive.

"This one, serial number 463, could be in your garage in three weeks," said Bob with a wide grin. He pointed to a fuselage that was going into a crate with lots of labeled boxes piled up beside it.

"Oh stop! I'm supposed to be making a logical decision here, Bob. I haven't been to the other kit manufacturers yet, and you are tugging at my emotions."

Bob grinned. "Let's go fly one."

In less than 15 minutes we pulled up to a t-hangar at the small, single strip, non-towered airport. Bob opened the hangar door, and we looked in on the Pulsar demo plane. The two-seat composite airplane was white with a red stripe. Bob grabbed the wood propeller at the root and pulled it out into the sunshine.

The Lexan canopy and composite smooth lines with an impeccable paint job made the small airplane look futuristic, like something out of *Popular Mechanics*. I'd seen one at the Oshkosh fly-in, but somehow that one didn't look this beguiling.

"This is one of the first kits to get the Rotax 912 engine instead of the 582," said Bob, as he took his tool kit out of the car and began removing engine cover screws with an electric screwdriver. "Let's look everything over and then we'll hop in."

The engine installation was neat and compact. It didn't look like any of the engines I'd worked on in my classes. It looked like a simple, modern engine installation in . . . an airplane.

Bob slid into the pilot seat. "Step up on to the wing, step into the seat, sit on the back of the seat and slide in."

As I eased into the passenger seat, I felt like I was getting into a tiny jet fighter. I looked at Bob. "Kind of a tight fit for you, but perfect for me!" I exclaimed.

"It's actually not bad. One of our Pulsar pilots is six foot three inches and weighs 235 pounds and he was able to design his seating so it was fine. The cabin is about 38 inches wide but the clear canopy makes it look bigger."

"Clear," Bob shouted, as he pulled out the choke and turned the key. The engine sprang to life, and Bob pushed in the choke slowly as the engine got smoothed out.

"Amazingly quiet," I said through the intercom. "And these headsets are great. None of my instructors used headsets in training. No wonder I couldn't hear anything."

"Old school," said Bob. "The schools didn't want to spend money on intercoms." Bob waited for the oil temperature to come up and then pushed the throttle up slowly to get a slow taxi, using a bit of braking to steer. When we reached the end of the taxiway, we stopped and Bob ran through a checklist. I was amazed at the visibility from the small plane.

"Ready?" asked Bob.

"You bet!"

We taxied onto the runway and Bob made his announcements. There was no other traffic in sight. Bob slowly applied throttle until it was full stop. The Pulsar gathered speed quickly as it tracked perfectly down the centerline. Before we even got a fourth of the way down the 2,800-foot strip the Pulsar was in the air and we began a fast ascent.

Exhilaration seemed to replace the blood in my veins as we climbed. Bob looked over at me and my mouth was hanging open in amazement. I realized that this was the smallest, fastest airplane I'd ever been in.

Bob grinned broadly as we leveled off on downwind and exited the pattern. "I don't need to ask what you think, I can see it on your face," he said.

"I didn't realize you could really turn yourself into a bird!"

We climbed to 5,500 feet and leveled off. "Here," Bob said, taking his hand off the center stick. "It takes very little input."

"You sure?"

"Yeah, go."

I gripped the stick and simply tried to keep the Pulsar level and flat. It felt stable and didn't stray. I began a slow turn to the right, adding a little elevator. The craft tracked perfectly and felt intuitive.

I marveled at the view outside the expansive canopy. Fields of crops stretched to the horizon in the clear air. The comparison between this airplane and the Cessna 152 or Piper Cherokee I'd trained in was like the difference between driving a station wagon and driving a Porsche.

We did tight turns, slow flight, and then a stall. Bob did the first stall and then handed it to me. I gradually pulled power as we mushed along at 58 mph, nose slightly up. At 48 mph I felt the stick lose life and felt air bubbling over the wings. The craft stayed level as I kept equal pressure on the rudder pedals. Bob nodded as

I applied power and put the nose down. Life immediately flowed back into the control stick and we were back to 150 mph in a flash.

"Your airplane," I said to Bob. Trickles of sweat ran down my back as the adrenaline surged. I'd been transported to another world. We returned to Bulverde and entered the pattern at 1,700 feet. "How do you slow this thing to land?" I questioned Bob. "It's slippery isn't it? I worry about that."

"Ok, watch. The key is pulling power. Yes, the airplane is slick, but it's predictable." Bob pulled most of the power out, and the Pulsar began to slow. "Get it under 80 mph for flaps." Bob pulled half flaps and then turned to base. "Then the rest," he said as he pulled the flap handle all the way to 30 degrees.

We stabilized at 70 mph. "I try for sixty-five over the fence, then you have the option of bleeding the speed a little more or putting on a tad bit of power." Bob flew above the threshold as if he were going to stay two feet off the pavement. He raised the nose ever so slightly and the mains chirped. "Hold the nose off as long as you can; the gear is not tough like the trainers."

After the nose wheel kissed the pavement, Bob applied some brake. Then he flipped the clip on the canopy and slid it forward half way. A welcome breeze entered the cockpit. We taxied back to the hangar. I shook my head as Bob shut off the engine. I lifted my headset off.

I looked at Bob and he looked at me. We both had wild broad grins. I shook my head.

"What do you think?"

"Where do I sign?"

The other two airplane kits on my list never had a chance.

*"The past cannot be changed. The future is yet
in your power."*

~ Unknown

26

MEETING DAD

"I THINK I KNOW EXACTLY where your Dad lives," said Bob as we drove back into San Antonio. "This address is the New Braunfels section." I snapped out of my euphoric reverie about the Pulsar and suddenly felt a slug of anxiety. Bob seemed to read my mind. "Are you worried about what your Dad will say?"

"Yes, I am."

"I hope the visit goes well."

"I know one thing. Nothing will change my mind about the Pulsar. I feel like a little kid at Christmas."

"Ok, I think it's right here," said Bob as he viewed addresses and pulled into a circular drive.

"You know your way around, Bob. Thanks so much."

We pulled up to the apartment. I shouldered my pack and shook Bob's hand. "Get that kit crated!"

"Here, I have a construction manual for you ahead of the kit. Bedtime reading!"

"But it will keep me up all night." I said as I shut the car door.

I headed up the walkway, taking a couple of deep breaths. Dad opened the front door before I had a chance to knock. He took my pack and waved a thanks to Bob. Dad closed the door and gave me a bear hug. He smiled happily, his eyes shining as he looked at me. "It's so good to see you, Lisa. I am so glad you came."

My nerves at being in a strange place and meeting Dad were counter balanced by my flight experience at Bulverde. I couldn't stop feeling the speed and freedom of the little airplane. Now as I felt Dad's embrace, I thought things might work out.

Dad placed the pack by the stairs. He motioned me into the living room. Pauline, Dad's third wife, came out of the kitchen and gave me an awkward hug. Pauline seemed more introverted than I was, and I thought in that moment that she was even more uncomfortable than I.

"I hope it's ok that I came, Pauline," I said as she backed away, looking serious.

"Oh yes, of course, your Dad is thrilled," she said, without expression.

Dad didn't seem to be listening to Pauline as he led me over to the seating area. "Here, come sit down. I imagine you've had a long day!"

"Yes, a long day. Palm Beach to San Antonio, a factory tour, and a flight in a kit aircraft."

"I will leave you two to visiting. We have dinner reservations for 7 pm," Pauline said as she disappeared into another room.

"Pauline is shy?"

"Yes, quite. Don't take it personally. Ok, tell me about the Pulsar."

"Ok, I won't take it personally. Quite a change from Alexandra, Dad. Exact opposite personalities."

"You're right. It's a relief."

"It's a relief for both of us, then," I replied.

I looked at Dad. I was surprised that I felt such equanimity talking to him now, after so many years. He was a handsome man, with deep-set blue eyes, salt-and-pepper hair graying at the temples, and a tall physique without heaviness. He looked great for 79. He still ran his own company, Project Control, a firm that saved owners money during commercial construction by coordinating and reviewing tasks between the architect and the builder.

"So, tell me about this kit airplane you want, Lisa."

"Dad, I know this sounds wild, but when I was small, I'd have dreams about spreading out my arms and flying over the hills and valleys. They were so real, I thought it was actually happening. Being in this little airplane today was as close to this free-flight experience as I've ever had. And it was real!"

Dad smiled as he listened to me. He could see the excitement as I waved my arms and talked about the flight.

"Lisa, don't get me wrong on this–I can appreciate your excitement and enthusiasm. I love that about you. But you've gone into uncharted territory with this airplane. It sounds like they are going to send you a box of parts and expect you to be able to assemble it."

"Uh, that's about right."

Dad's expression turned serious. I envisioned him talking to a building owner. "You're making a mistake here," I heard his voice in my mind.

"What level of aeromechanical engineering and assembly do you have to do so it doesn't kill you on the first flight?" asked Dad.

I closed my eyes and then opened them, looking at Dad, who was looking intently at me. I had forgotten what my next line of attack would be.

Your own airplane.

"Dad, there are 200 of these airplanes flying. The factory people know what they are doing. I will be very careful assembling it, and I will get an advisor. It's a no-cost service that the EAA provides."

"EAA?"

"Experimental Aircraft Association. They support the building and flying of experimental airplanes by providing education and a community of advisors." I was grabbing at things I could do or say to convince Dad that the activity was entirely safe.

"You know your sister isn't excited about it, either."

"I have mechanical ability from running the bike shop. And I've got a two-year degree in engineering. And I'm very safety conscious." I paused a moment to catch my breath. "I have to build this airplane."

Dad looked at me the way a parent would look at an adolescent. The expressions crossing his face went from concern to puzzlement to resignation and finally to a reluctant smile.

"Lisa, this means so much that you came to see me. You could have chosen to not communicate at all. I'm doing the typical parent thing of being concerned. I just want you to be as safe as possible."

"Right, I understand." I didn't really understand, but my nature was to be non-confrontational and smooth things over when they got my stomach churning. I was a Pollyanna wuss when it came to confrontation. One thing I did know. The Pulsar would show up at my doorstep in three weeks.

"Ok, enough lecturing. I think your mind is made up." Dad looked at me with an "OK, I give up" look.

"Yes, it is."

"Ok, well, I tried," said Dad. "It's probably safer than a motorcycle."

I better not tell Dad about the motorcycle.

"Ok, Lisa, I am a reluctant participant. Let's go to dinner and celebrate your kit airplane." The smile was warm and broad. Dad reached over and held my hand. "Promise me you will be careful."

"I promise, Dad. I promise."

Pauline entered the room. "We should be going, reservations are for 7 pm."

I'd lost track of time. I took a deep breath and looked at Dad. He squeezed my hand and stood up. "You know I love you." His eyes sparkled in intensity as he looked at me.

Pauline finally smiled.

"All you need is the plan, the road map, and the courage to press on to your destination."

~ Earl Nightingale

27

AIRPLANE PARTS

"I'M LEAVING at four today."

"Well it IS Friday. I doubt there will be much happening after lunch," said Carl.

"In that case, maybe I should leave at three."

Carl and I sat at a lunchroom table in the cafeteria at Sensormatic Electronics Corporation. Carl was a line engineer, and I managed the plant's training department. The bustle of employees grew louder around us as people filed in.

Carl arranged his silverware and looked up. "What's going on? You seem unusually happy today."

"Remember, it's Friday, and . . ."

"Hey Lese!" We were interrupted by Judy, the plant nurse, who came up to the table. "May I join you two?"

"Have a seat," I replied.

Judy sat down. "I have an ulterior motive. The golf league is starting back up and I need at least one more person. Maybe both of you?"

Carl shook his head. "No way. Thursday afternoons and Saturdays are consumed with little league and chores."

Judy looked at me and then at her notebook. "Ok, I'll add Lisa Turner...."

"Wait! Wait," I waved at Judy. "I know I said I was interested, but I have a new project coming up. Nights and weekends."

"No, your new project will be learning golf. What in the world could be more fun than golf?" said Judy.

"An airplane."

"An airplane?" said Judy.

Carl stopped eating and looked up.

"Well, an airplane kit. The truck is arriving tomorrow morning from the factory," I replied.

"What? Like a remote-control airplane that you fly off your lawn?" said Carl.

"No, an airplane that you put together in your garage and then put people in it and fly wherever you want." I smiled brightly.

"You look like a Cheshire cat. Stop that. You're pulling our legs. No one in their right mind would make an airplane in their garage and then test it with people," said Judy.

Carl looked perplexed. "You're serious, aren't you? If this is for real, then it's a whole lot more fun than golf."

"Carl!" Judy said in a stern nurse voice with a snarky smile.

"I'm serious. The truck arrives tomorrow and I have to finish getting the garage ready," I said.

Judy shook her head. "You're crazy. You are really crazy. I know you're joking with me. Ok, I'll find another golf partner."

Judy dug into her bacon sandwich, shaking her head.

Carl looked at me. "Leave at three."

I nodded.

Satisfaction washed over me the next morning as I looked over the interior of the garage. I was ready.

Tools hung on a pegboard above a ten-foot-long workbench arranged on four Craftsman toolboxes. When I sold my bicycle shop, I made a deal to take many of my personal tools. I remember the Snap-on tool truck arriving at the shop for the first time.

"May I speak to the owner," said the man with a friendly smile.

"I'm it," I replied.

A trace of surprise crossed the man's brow as he reached out to grasp my hand in a very solid handshake that I returned in kind.

"Ah, a good sign, the strong grip," he said to me. "John Giordano, pleased to meet you."

"Lisa, Lisa Turner," I replied.

"Need any tools?"

"Always need tools! Even when I don't!"

"Now that's what I like to hear," said John with a broad smile. "Come see what's on my truck."

"Are you the guy my mother warned me about who asks you if you want candy?"

John laughed as I followed him to the truck.

"This is better than candy. This is better than walking into a hardware store," I said.

There's nothing quite like a Snap-on tool truck and a charge account. Looking over the shiny assortment on the pegboard now, I shook my head thinking about my weakness for tools, machinery, and gadgets. To my left was a rough pine cabinet that I'd constructed, with dozens of cubby-hole shelves waiting for labels and parts.

"Come on, truck," I said to myself.

■ ⤛ ■

About 8:15 Sunday morning I heard the rumble of a diesel engine and the screech of air brakes outside. I dropped the spoon in the half full cereal bowl and ran out the front door.

I was surprised to see the size of the truck. So were my neighbors.

"What in the world?" Next-door neighbor Ben shouted after the rig passed his driveway and came to a stop with a loud screech. "Is this your airplane? I thought you were kidding."

"It's in boxes," I shouted.

The driver shut off the engine.

"That's better," said Ben. "Look, the thing takes up the whole street."

"Good thing it's Sunday."

The driver walked up to us. "Lisa?"

"That's me."

"Did the office tell you I don't have a lift gate?"

"A what?"

"A lift gate. It's a platform that helps unload heavy boxes."

"No. What are we going to do?"

"I have some time this morning, I'll help," said Ben. "Can we unload some of the boxes right in the truck?"

"I don't see why not, I have the time," said the driver.

"I'm sure not going to send you away," I replied. "Thanks, guys."

We spent the morning unloading boxes and crates, breaking open the largest crates that contained the fuselage pieces and hand carrying them to slings in the garage. We strapped the wing spars and skins to the garage ceiling where I'd mounted heavy lag screws and straps.

By 11 am the delivery truck had rumbled off, leaving peace and quiet along the small street once again. The birds resumed their song.

"Thanks Ben, that would have taken all day if not for you."

"No problem. It was fun. Now I want to see you put it all together."

I closed the garage door and took a deep breath, looking around inside. Surrounded by crates and parts, a feeling of overwhelm poked lightly at my jubilance. What had I done?

*"Don't be pushed by your problems.
Be led by your dreams."*

~ Ralph Waldo Emerson

28

SUNDAY DRIVERS

IN THE WEEK THAT FOLLOWED all I could think about at work was getting back home to the garage. In the early morning hours as I planned out each workday, I devised a schedule to give me as much time as possible at home. While I didn't want to compromise my employment, for the first time in a long time I felt there was something else that was as important as my career. How to shave 60 hours a week on the job to 45?

Monday night after work I parked the car in the driveway and went straight to the garage. I hadn't been dreaming. There really was a kit airplane filling the space.

I looked at all the crates. I had no idea what was in each box. I opened the first notebook and the pack of documentation from the kit. All of this paperwork would comprise my aircraft flight manual and build logs. While waiting for the kit, I'd studied up on what I needed to do to make the process go as smoothly as possible.

I looked down at the floor. I'd covered it with low pile carpet and then placed a 6-mil sheet of plastic over it. My plan was to wait until the plastic became dirty and full of fiberglass bits and pieces and then change it out for new. I'd done the same thing to the workbench.

My two cats, Kanga and Roo, discovered me in the garage and came in, delighted to have an unexplored play area. They began mapping the territory while I lined up my plans.

I worked on one box at a time, laying out all the bags, boxes, and loose pieces on the floor as I cross checked the inventory list. As I uncrated large items, such as the Lexan, I decided to take them into the house and store them under the stairs and in the living room. I wasn't prone to entertaining, so filling up the house with airplane parts would not be an embarrassment. In fact, having all the parts and pieces inside the house gave me a thrill every time I looked at them.

My day job went smoothly for the week, and I was able to stick to my nightly schedule. By Thursday night I'd unloaded and labeled nearly everything. After breakfast Friday I glanced into the dining room and living room before leaving for work. Wheel pants, landing gear, sheets of Lexan, foam ribs, fuselage halves for the engine compartment, and a spinner and prop were tucked in next to the furniture. Another electric thrill from head to feet. Airplane parts!

"I have all weekend!" I said to Kanga. He looked up briefly from his breakfast bowl and gave a gargled meow.

"Frank told me your airplane kit arrived," said Carl, leaning in to my office Friday morning.

"Yes!" I replied. "Can you believe it? I really have an entire airplane in little pieces sitting in the garage. And in the living room, dining room, and closets."

"No, I can't believe it. Plus, you're a girl. I actually think you're making the whole thing up." Carl's eyes gleamed as he pursed his lips in a gentle smile.

"Oops, you're onto me. Don't tell anyone, ok?"

Carl chuckled. "So, seriously, how long do you think it is going to take you to build?"

"I've been wondering that myself. The marketing literature says 800 hours. I read in *Kitplanes* you should always double whatever time they put in the sales video."

"It's going to be tough only having the weekends. I want to hear progress reports every Monday."

"You got it. I am going to drive you crazy by forcing you to look at airplane pictures."

"That's ok. It's way better than looking at baby pictures."

"They are baby pictures."

"My kind of baby," said Carl, nodding.

Since I lived in Florida, it was easy to work with the garage door open on the weekends. Even in December and January there were many balmy days that invited the warm Florida sea breezes in through windows and doors. There was only one problem leaving the door open while I worked.

Sunday drivers.

As I leaned over the fuselage one day, measuring for the seatback bulkhead, I heard a car come down the quiet street. The white Buick slowed to a crawl as a man in his 70s tried to get a look at what was happening in the garage. The car passed, and then came around the circle again, this time stopping and parking in the street.

"What is that?" the man said, stopping in the middle of the driveway.

"I'm building an airplane."

"May I come in and look at it?"

"Sure. Come on in."

Oh shoot. Why'd I leave the door up.

The man walked in slowly, looking at the fuselage and wing sections.

"By gosh, you're right, it's a real airplane. Is this a kit?"

"It is a kit."

"Who else is working on this?"

"Just me."

The man looked puzzled and then smiled. "Well, that's just great. I'm glad to see a woman with this kind of project. It's unusual, you know. It sure looks like you have your work cut out for you. Tell me about the plane."

"It's a Pulsar XP, a composite aircraft that will seat two and cruise at 145 miles per hour on 80 horsepower."

"Really? I'm amazed. I've never seen or heard of anything like this."

"It burns less than five gallons per hour, and it runs on auto gas."

"Auto gas? Do you land the airplane in the street and taxi up to a pump?" The man began to laugh.

Out in the street came a voice. "Peter! Peter! We have to get going!"

The man looked back at the parked car. "That's my wife. She doesn't care about airplanes. I wish she did."

"Feel free to invite her in to look," I said, against my best wishes.

"No, that's ok. I might come back though and look at your progress. Would that be alright?"

"Sure, of course," I said.

Well, maybe.

"I'm Peter Ross," the man said as he reached out to shake my hand.

"Pleased." His grip was solid.

I went back in to the garage and closed the door. I took a deep breath. I was fighting wanting to be completely alone and wanting to share the excitement with others.

I need to work on my social skills.

I opened the door into the house knowing the cats would be on the other side, waiting to come in to my new playground.

"Hey guys, come on in!"

My thoughts of social inadequacy evaporated as I picked up my tape measure again to work on the bulkheads.

"Keep your eyes on the stars, and your feet on the ground."

~ Theodore Roosevelt

29

HOW TO BUILD AN AIRPLANE

"SO HOW DO YOU KNOW what goes where?"
Gus, my closest friend, looked around the garage in disbelief. I laughed.

"I've seen you re-locate palm trees in your yard and work on your car, but I've never seen anyone build an airplane by themselves. Are you sure you don't want help?" asked Gus.

"Well, I'll need help at some stages – like installing the wings, and the engine . . . well, actually maybe not, I need to get a rolling hoist."

"You know you can ask if you need it."

"I really like working by myself. I am not sure why. It gives me a sense of control, I guess."

"When you finish will you take me flying?" asked Gus

"Are you serious?"

"Yes, I'm serious. There's only one thing I will need."

I looked at Gus. In his early 30s, he looked much older. Landscape work in the blazing Florida sun had given his face and arms a leathery texture. A shock of dark brown hair was partially covered by the bandanna he wore to help keep sweat out of his eyes while he worked. His thick beard was neatly trimmed. Gus stood five feet, six and a half inches tall, exactly my own height; his build was slim, tight, and muscled at 125 pounds, almost to the pound of my own weight. We could exchange clothes. His eyes danced with fun as he spoke.

"One thing, just one thing," Gus said.

I gave Gus a questioning look. "Yes?"

"A six-pack of beer. I'll need to drink a six before you take me flying."

"Oh come on Gus, that's crazy. You won't know where you are!"

"That's my point."

I shook my head. "Ok, Perky will be my first passenger because he gave me flying lessons; you will be my second. Good?"

"Let me think about whether I can do it sober or not."

"Well, you've got some time to decide." I waved my hand over the boxes and bins.

As I fell into a routine on the weekends, I opened the garage door for about four hours in the middle of the day, knowing I'd draw attention. It wasn't as busy as I thought it would be...until the day I rolled the fuselage shell, now on the main gear, out into the driveway. I'd place the tail in a sling and block the mains. Everyone driving, walking, or rollerblading by would stop to either find out what it was or check progress.

My shyness began to fade around the airplane. I wasn't sure why, but the overflow of excitement when visitors showed up made it easier. At least a dozen people, including the first visitor, Peter, stopped by every few weeks to check progress.

I had just put the door up when Perky drove up and parked. He looked intently into the garage as he walked up the driveway. "The project is really moving!" he said.

"Thanks to you! I wouldn't be working on an airplane if you hadn't infected me with the aviation bug."

"No, you were already infected. I just brought it out."

"You should bring Heather out here when you come by."

"You know Heather. She takes on the activities of six people. I don't know how she does everything. Besides, I think she worries about you and this airplane."

"You'll never achieve anything without taking some risk."

"She thinks it is a big risk."

"Think I could convince her otherwise?"

"Probably not."

"Well, not much I can do about that. But it bothers me."

"Keep on Lese, keep on. You can't let others dictate what you pursue."

"But I care what people think. Especially family."

"I'm sure you do. But you can't let it stop you."

"Easy to say, hard to do."

"Show me what you got done this week."

We walked over to the fuselage. I had tacked in the bulkheads, cut from sheets of foam core reinforced composite sheets.

I showed Perky my schedule. "Every week I pore through the assembly manuals and estimate how long a task will take. Then I make a list of the tasks, with the times. I make them small enough so that I can check them off when I've completed them, and it makes me feel like I am making progress."

"I see you've got the vertical tail assembly this weekend," he said as he pointed to the two halves of the tail spread out on the sawhorses.

"Right, it comes in two pre-molded foam core composite halves, I need to make the radio antenna out of a specific length copper strip, glass it in with a diode, and then mate and glass the halves. Then, since it takes 24 hours to reach strength, I'll bond the tail to the fuselage the next day."

Perky nodded and smiled. "Will the FAA come and do interim inspections?"

"No, they only verify at the end that you've done the work yourself, go over the logs and paperwork, and tell you to go test it. You can actually sign it off yourself in the logbook."

"How can that be safe?"

"They figure you are putting your own little pink body into the plane for the test flights, and you'll care enough to perform the safety checks before you fly."

"That's a surprise. Not everyone is thorough, and not everyone understands what can go wrong."

"That's why I have a technical counselor visiting the project, and I'll get all the eyes I can looking at it when I get out to the airport."

"I learn something new every time I come out here! Gotta run."

Perky got in his convertible roadster and drove off, waving.

■ ⟷ ■

The following week my EAA technical counselor (TC) arrived to introduce himself. I knew that I had a lot to learn, and I hoped the TC would help me keep my mistakes to a minimum.

As Don inspected my first glass joints in the seatback bulkhead, he harrumphed. "Your cutout clearance is perfect, but let me show you something. Get me some four-inch practice cloth."

We went over to the bench. I rolled out about ten inches of cloth.

"Mix up a small batch of epoxy," said Don.

I reached for a mixing cup and pulled the lever on the epoxy pump. The special pump mixed the resin and the hardener in the exact ratio straight into the cup. "What a timesaver," I said as I mixed the clear liquids with a flat stick. With the strip of fiberglass cloth on a piece of plastic I awaited Don's instructions.

"You do this half, I'll do the other half," said Don.

I brushed on the epoxy, letting it soak in. Don took the cup and brushed his side. Instead of saturating the cloth, he put two light coats on. Gradually the liquid absorbed. He reached for the heat gun and ran it over the cloth.

"See how your side has a lot of liquid on it?"

"Yes. A ton."

"Extra liquid adds weight. It will work fine in the airplane, but there are better ways to add weight if that's what you want. Like bricks."

"Bricks?"

"Yeah, make it light to start out. If you need weight later, add bricks."

"Ok! I get it. I'm making it too heavy. I began to laugh, realizing Don was making a joke. "I need to lighten up – literally! Bricks, right."

Don grinned. "The idea is to be precise on the epoxy and only use what you need to saturate, but not oversaturate, the cloth. It should just turn translucent, and you can use some heat to help it. Make sense?"

"Yes! I got it."

"Good work. I'll come by next month? I'll bring the bricks," said Don with a smile.

"No!" I replied, "Bring the bricks at the end, when I'll need them," I said as I made a scowling face at him.

Months went by, and I came to love the routine of nightly planning and anticipating the enjoyment I was getting working on the plane. All the things that had been hobbies – woodworking, metalworking, assembly, construction, and electronics were there in the airplane. I usually had three or four tracks of assembly going at one time. This made it easy to switch gears when one track wasn't going well.

When I was stumped, I'd call John Hutson, the go-to guy at the factory in San Antonio. He was always there, even on Sundays.

"John, you need to get a life. What are you doing at the factory today? It's Sunday."

"I know. I can't help it."

"Sounds familiar. During the week I can't wait to get out of work and come home to the airplane."

"How's it going?"

"I made a mistake measuring the flaps attachment to the wing by about half an inch. I can't believe it. It's already drilled and riveted. I didn't catch it until I looked and saw the gap."

"Everything is repairable." replied John. "Just drill the rivets out and start over. It's a lot of work, but it's the only avenue. The attachment rail is strong enough to handle the extra holes. No one will see it once they're filled and painted."

"I can't believe I did that."

"You don't want to hear this, but you'll make plenty more mistakes before you're in the air."

"As long as it's BEFORE I'm in the air," I said.

*"The Pessimist Sees Difficulty In Every Opportunity.
The Optimist Sees Opportunity In Every Difficulty."*

~ Winston Churchill

30

MISTAKES

A S I PASSED THE 1,000-hour build mark, I began to wonder how long the project would take. I had decided to not build the basic VFR Pulsar, instead wanting to add instrument flight rules (IFR) capability and detailed bells and whistles that were not called for in the manuals. With every addition, I'd call the factory for advice.

The instrument panel was one of my biggest challenges and ended up taking more time than I'd anticipated. The wiring for the panel was complex, and I spent a large amount of time making circuit diagrams. I spent about four months building and wiring the panel and installing the airframe electrical harnesses. I loved the detail; the time flew by.

Because the brakes were not strong enough (reported by builders who were already flying), I upgraded to the next larger Matco disc brakes. I also designed and fabricated toe brake extensions to fit inside the hollow heel brake levers to add more leverage.

"Don't pay attention to hours," other builders told me. But I realized it was taking far more time than I thought it would. I wondered if I was slow or just a perfectionist. There were more than a few times when I would decide to do a job over if it was not to my liking. I worked on the bearing for the control stick for six hours to get it smooth without any slop. It just had to be right.

One Saturday night I was working on the landing gear seal on the belly of the fuselage. The landing gear had already been bolted to structure, but the fuselage area between and around the fiberglass landing gear legs had to be glassed and sealed with a foam core composite piece.

With the fuselage rotated upside down in the slings and the legs up in the air I spent hours installing the seal and glassing it in. I finished it up with some lightweight fiberglass cloth and stood back. I was pleased.

By now I had the wings complete except for the top skins, and they were set up vertically on the other side of the garage area. I was able to just fit my Lincoln Mercury Cougar in next to the wings with the fuselage on the other side.

"Kanga, Roo, come on," I said to the feline aircraft advisors. I turned off the light and closed and locked the garage door.

Upstairs and in bed, I read ahead in the Pulsar manual. I would read sections over and over again. Exhausted, I turned off the light.

BAM! A loud report, like canon, came from the garage below me with such force that I jumped straight out of bed and turned the light back on. "What?" I shouted. Kanga and Roo, frightened, ran out of the bedroom and down the hall.

I ran down the stairs in my underwear. Whatever it was, I wanted to find out fast, not even thinking there could be any danger. My mind raced as I unlocked the door to the garage and flipped on the light.

"No!" I shouted out.

The upside-down fuselage had rotated in the slings. The landing gear leg on the wall side had performed a 180-degree arc, with the fiberglass stub end crashing to a stop through the sheet metal of the Cougar fender, just forward of the windshield. My jaw dropped as I stared in silence at the gear leg embedded in the car.

Then I noticed that the composite panel that I had so carefully glassed into the fuselage underbody was now lying in pieces on the floor next to the other gear leg, which had penetrated the plastic.

I realized that the epoxy was still setting up. What should I do? There was only one thing I could do. Start over, and start over quickly, right now, before the epoxy made it impossible to reinstall.

I ran upstairs and threw on a pair of jeans and a t-shirt and returned to the garage. The cats refused to emerge from the study, but I didn't have time to console them.

Trying not to look at the hole in the car fender, I worked quickly but carefully to reposition the fuselage in the sling. I secured the gear leg on the wall side, which is what I should have done to begin with. I peeled the glass off the composite strips and began to refit the panel.

At 1:30 in the morning I stood back and inspected my work. Pleased with the fit and finish, I once again turned off the light and headed upstairs, purposefully not looking at the car. There was nothing I could do about it. The cats had gotten over their trauma and were back on the bed.

I wish I was a cat?

I fell into bed, dreaming of loud crashes.

One Sunday night I'd just completed installing the end plates for the wing tanks. After cleaning the tanks one more time, I followed the directions for the plates. Each plate had a vent and an outlet where the fuel hose would hook up inside the fuselage. The pickup had to be on the bottom of the tank so that it would deliver as much gas as possible when the fuel level got low. The job was tedious and involved coating the plates with a strong black epoxy, called Proseal. It set up fast.

I stood back from my work around 10 pm and admired the neat fit. Then I cleaned up and went upstairs to bed.

As I lay in bed, I began thinking about the orientation of the plates. I did have the wings facing up when I installed the plates? I began to feel uncomfortable, second-guessing if I'd done it right or not.

A few minutes later I sat up straight and turned on the light. I padded down to the garage and turned on the lights. With no frightening crashes, the cats followed me downstairs, wondering what I was up to.

I entered the garage and turned on the light. I looked at the wings and my heart sank. They were both upside down during the end plate seal. The plates were oriented exactly 180 degrees wrong. How had I managed to do that? I had a 50/50 chance of getting it right . . . and I thought I had triple checked the orientation.

I realized it would be a sleepless night as I ran upstairs to throw on work clothes. Back in the garage, I backed out the screws from the nut plates and worked to free the plates without damaging them from the tank ends. By now the sealant was almost cured and presented a nearly impenetrable film between the plate and the mating surface of the wing tank cavity.

Kanga and Roo thought this new schedule was dandy. They batted balled up pieces of paper to each other over and over most of the night and then fell asleep cradled together as I put on some music to soothe me through the plate removal.

It took days to clean the tanks and the plates so that I could begin again. I wrote in the log, "builder error time = 22 hours." I remembered John Hutson's words about there being plenty of builder mistakes – you just had to catch them before they caught you.

Like a child unable to wind down after a long day of excitement, I always fell into bed over-excited. I'd read ahead in the instruction manual and look over the plans for the two hundredth time. Then I'd turn out the light and begin a set of dreams. Once again capturing the sensation of the Pulsar taking off from the Bulverde field, now I was in the pilot seat with no one else in the little airplane.

The 80-horsepower engine, with less than 875 pounds to lift, jumped off the runway. I had to be smooth and careful, there was so much power. In this dream somehow, I was also aware that I was dreaming. Observing my excitement at the takeoff power, I wondered if the real thing would feel the same way.

Entering the endless expanse of the blue sky dotted with cream-colored clouds, the airplane seemed to get smaller as it cocooned around my physical frame, powering me faster and steeper into the boundless space. The machine silently disappeared as I now flew effortlessly between clouds, slowing to float through the landscape. The planet's horizon appeared, with multicolor strata stretching ahead for as far as I could see. I drank in the spectacle in awe, having the realization that the flow was continuous and everything was connected.

Looking down at the earth's surface, now miles away, only quietude and an awareness unfettered by inner talk filled my consciousness.

"I think this is a dream," I said out loud and matter-of-factly to myself. "I have to return."

The multicolor fireworks dissolved and suddenly I was back in my Pulsar, on final approach to a runway that appeared to be miles wide with no end in sight. The Pulsar landed smoothly and quietly, and I let speed bleed off, trying to identify where I was.

This is how she will fly, I thought, as I reached over to silence the morning alarm.

"Everything is hard before it is easy."

~ Goethe

31

LEARN BY DOING

"I'M GOING TO MAKE a few circuits so you can see what I do. Then you fly them."

Greg completed a run-up check on the ramp and added power as we taxied out to the runway. Greg was the organizer for the Pulsar builder's group. We were meeting for the weekend in Lawrence, Kansas. More than 12 Pulsars had flown in for workshops and camaraderie. I enjoyed being with the all-male group, finding their discussions intriguing. I was in my element and enjoyed the attention.

Now, at 3 pm, things had quieted down at the small rural airport.

"Greg, I really appreciate this. I wouldn't know how else to learn enough for my first flight."

"No problem. I live for this." Greg lined up on 15, a 5,700-foot runway. "Ok. Feet on the rudder pedals, keep things straight. Just be light on the controls feeling what I am doing. Add full power slowly, this baby is quick."

Greg's Pulsar had the 65-horsepower, two-stroke Rotax. It was a reliable engine that took up very little space. But it was a full 15 horsepower short of what I was putting in my own Pulsar. Add two people and full tanks, and I expected that Greg's airplane would be sluggish. To my surprise, the craft picked up speed quickly and lifted off much sooner than I anticipated.

"Wow!" I shouted into the intercom. "That's amazing."

Greg nodded. We turned crosswind and then downwind. I watched Greg intently, getting ready to fly the airplane myself. Two circuits later, we lined up again.

"Ok, have fun. I'll make your calls so you can concentrate. Let me know what power settings you want."

Since I was in the passenger seat, it felt a little awkward using my left hand on the stick, but I would have to get the hang of it for training. Once again the craft accelerated rapidly, and the wheels lifted off sooner than I thought they would. I felt the airplane accelerate as we turned downwind.

"Pull to 4,200 rpm," I asked. The plane felt comfortable but quick. I realized I'd have to be very careful in my own Pulsar. I set up on final and tried to maintain a steady rate of descent. I was nervous as the craft started sinking. "Add a little power."

"I was just going to do that," said Greg.

My body felt hot and sweat ran down the inside of my shirt. Nervous anticipation had replaced the giddy excitement.

"Good, you're good, hold steady over the fence, about 65 mph. I'd rather you carry a little speed than to be going too slow," said Greg calmly.

I forgot about my fast heartbeat and concentrated on holding the Pulsar slightly nose up as we crossed the threshold. Suddenly I thought the airplane was trying to climb again, and I put the nose down slightly.

"No, no!" Greg shouted.

In a panic, I raised the nose, and the Pulsar aimed up into the sky.

"Go around! Go around!" Greg put in full power and we jumped back into the air.

"Oh God, I am sorry!" I shouted. I felt embarrassed and frightened. I'd almost crashed Greg's Pulsar.

Greg made position calls and then was quiet until we turned downwind.

"Do you want to take over and go back?" I asked.

"No, Lisa you're going to learn how to fly this airplane. Sorry I got a little excited."

"Well, I guess so. I almost took out your landing gear. Are you sure you want me to try again?"

"Absolutely, yes."

I turned to look straight at Greg to see if he was serious.

Greg turned and patted me on the shoulder. "Every pilot goes through this."

I was amazed at his patience. We turned final, and I lined up the Pulsar for the runway.

"Pretend you are going to fly exactly 12 inches over the runway the length of the runway and not land. Hold the nose a tiny bit up from level. The plane will land itself."

We crossed the threshold at 65 mph. I lightened my grip on the stick and didn't overreact this time as I imagined flying just off the surface as the speed bled down to 60. The Pulsar landed squarely and softly on both mains as I held the nose wheel off as the plane slowed, allowing it to lower itself.

"YEAH!" shouted Greg. "How was THAT!" He turned to smile at me, a big grin.

"Whew." I let a chunk of air out of my lungs in relief.

"We're going to do that again!" Greg applied power, and the Pulsar jumped off the runway.

That night at dinner I was charged.

"Here's to a newly minted Pulsar pilot!" shouted Greg, reaching out to clink beer mugs.

"Thanks to your patience," I said as I took a drink.

"Fine, that was fine. You're not going to know how to do that until you try it and then practice it."

Falling into bed that night exhausted, I couldn't wait to return home to my own Pulsar. All night long I dreamed about takeoffs and landings.

"Successful design is not the achievement of perfection but the minimization and accommodation of imperfection."

~ Henry Petroski

32

THE ENGINE START

I KEPT TO MY SCHEDULE, realizing that I might get into the air before the end of the year. The thought of it gave me that flutter thrill.

The tasks, however, became much more complex and time consuming. Although I'd designed and diagrammed the electrical system, the final assembly and hookups required painstaking detail.

The surface of the foam core composite, or the "skin" of the airplane, had to be filled before paint could be applied. The builders group warned me about this.

"What could be so bad about filling?" I said to Brad, a fellow builder, at one of the fly-ins. He had finished his Pulsar earlier in the year and had flown it to Kansas.

He began to laugh. "Nothing, that's the problem. Take and open a can of Smooth Prime. Brush it on a six-inch by six-inch portion of the skin. Let it dry. Now gently sand that area. No big deal, right? Put on another coat of Smooth Prime. Dry. Sand. Smooth Prime.

Dry. Sand. Inspect. Any voids? Mix up some epoxy and spread that over the area. Dry. Spray on a dark guide coat. Sand. Don't sand through all the layers!"

Brad went on, his hands up in the air, making the motions of sanding, painting, sanding, then back up in the air. A crowd had gathered, watching.

"No big deal. The only problem is that it takes forever. I mean forever. The answer is, it's easy; but it's painfully time consuming. And you'll look at areas you thought were done and realize you need another coat. That's what's so bad about filling the pinholes. There are no shortcuts."

I nodded. "Ok. No shortcuts. But every hour you do that it will be closer to flying."

"Nice thought. Until you keep seeing areas that have to be perfected. Then you think it's a trick someone thought up to drive you crazy. People come up with shortcuts and different materials. You should stick with Super Fil and Smooth Prime. It takes a little longer. Your airplane will look great. But you'll hate pinhole filling and consider a simple tube and fabric for your next airplane."

"I don't think so."

"We'll see. Maybe we should bet."

"That my next airplane will be tube and fabric? No way."

Brad smiled. Little did I know then that years later Brad would win that bet.

"Are you going to paint it yourself?" he asked.

"No, I decided that learning how to paint on my first airplane would be a mistake. I'm taking it to a pro with a booth."

"Good idea. I wish I'd done that. Every time I look at my airplane now I can see the thin and thick places. And I ended up making it pretty heavy. Tell your guy to go multiple light coats. It's not a car."

"You can always add bricks," I said under my breath.

"Bricks, huh? Did you say bricks?"

"I'm sorry," I smiled. "Sort of an inside joke. My tech counselor was watching how I saturated the fiberglass strips early on and suggested if I wanted a heavy airplane I could add bricks later. Sounds like filling is a similar opportunity."

The guys laughed and someone refilled our beer mugs.

I wasn't laughing now as I began another area of filling on the Pulsar. It was all I could do to remain patient throughout the process. Brad had been right about the psychology of filling.

Finally the craft was ready for paint. I enlisted my friends Gus and John to help me trailer the fuselage and wings to the paint shop in West Palm Beach. I was acting like a mother with a child. "Be careful! Don't dent anything!"

We got strange looks as we drove slowly up Congress Avenue. "That sort of looks like a futuristic airplane," said one man at a stoplight.

"It is," I replied.

At the paint shop in a different light we identified areas that still needed some filling. I went to work on it again and after a few days we were ready for paint. I'd laid out the stripes.

"Want to have a go?" said Charlie, holding the spray gun.

"No, this is all yours. This way I can blame you if I don't like it."

"Ha! I get it. Smart-ass girl. You'll love it!"

"I know I will." We laughed in unison, and I retreated from the booth. Charlie closed the door with a thud and I heard the filtration system turn on. He was in a head-to-toe suit with an air supply. I felt relieved realizing I'd made the right decision on the work.

Four days later, the ride home on the trailer was even more nerve wracking than the trip up. The airplane was stunningly beautiful now, with electric blue stripes on the fuselage, tail, and wings.

"Be careful! Be careful!" I found myself shouting over and over until I was hoarse. Back in the garage safely, I was on the home stretch. My excitement grew stronger every day that I was closer to flying.

■ ⬎ ■

"Thanks for coming to the engine start party," I said to Gus.

"Engine start? I wouldn't miss this for anything. Looks like you're ready."

"I followed the checklist but you never know. I'm trying to leave as few things as possible to chance," I replied.

"This is a party? Where's the food and liquor?"

"No beer until it actually starts."

"You're cruel." Gus said.

The plane was positioned half in and half out of the garage, with the tail almost in to the yard. I'd set a red 2.5-gallon jug of premium filtered auto gas on a stool at the level of the wings.

"What's the plan? What will you do if the plane takes off through the garage and you can't stop it? It will end up in your living room," said Gus, looking at the setup.

"Right. That's why I will rope the tail to a tree," I said as I headed over to the palm tree closest to the tail and began to tie some knots.

It was early evening in the quiet little neighborhood and I'd warned the homeowners closest to me that I was going to start the engine for the first time. Now they were in the street, watching. As Gus and I made final preparations, passersby were intrigued, and we'd attracted about 12 onlookers.

"Wow. I hope this goes well," said Gus to me quietly. "Look at all these people."

"Didn't I tell you this was a party? I put the nose into the garage so we can make sure no one gets near the prop. That would be bad. And you need to be very careful."

"I will be."

I climbed the stepladder and got into the airplane. The crowd got quiet. I thought that when this moment came I'd be nervous, and I hadn't anticipated onlookers. But I was completely fixated on double-checking every single item on the checklist I had in my hand.

"Gas supply hooked up."

"Check."

"Electrical hooked up."

"Check."

"Oil primed."

"Check."

I read off the rest of my list. I couldn't find anything that wasn't in order.

"CLEAR PROP!" I shouted. I turned the ignition key. The little engine began turning over vigorously. The prop rotated once, twice, three times.

Fuel pressure good. No oil pressure.

I turned the ignition to off. "I'm not getting oil pressure."

"I don't think there was enough time to get the pressure up. Try it again. Remember, there's very little oil inside the engine."

"But I primed it. I'm just nervous."

"Sure."

"CLEAR PROP!" I shouted. I turned the ignition key again, willing the engine to start. Two prop revolutions and the engine burst into noisy life, running unevenly. Oil pressure – yes! I began pushing the choke in slowly, and the engine began to even out. Over the din I heard a cheer go up from the crowd behind me. I pushed the throttle in slightly and looked at the engine monitor. Temps were coming up. Pressures were good. After a few more minutes, I shut the engine down and, as the geared Rotax does when it turns off, it shuddered to an instant stop.

"First engine start!" shouted Gus. "Great!"

I looked out into the darkness of the driveway and saw at least 15 people. They came up the driveway awkwardly, like a scene out of a zombie movie.

"It's not that loud," said Don, my neighbor from across the street. "Gosh, you could fly it from your driveway, right?" he laughed. "I don't think there's anything in the homeowner regulations that say you can't have an airplane in your driveway."

"Yeah," I said, "but I'd end up taking out all the mailboxes when I take off down the street."

I laughed a laugh of relief and began extricating myself from the cockpit.

Gus held my hand as I stepped out of the cockpit and onto the stepladder.

"Probably the only time I'll pilot an airplane without wings attached," I said.

"I hope," said Gus. "Can I have my beer now?"

*"Centuries and centuries and only in the present
do things happen."*

~ Jorge Luis Borges

33

THE AIRPORT

"**I**'M LOOKING FOR someone to share a hangar. Do you know anyone?"

Rick, behind the FBO counter, waited for a lull answering calls from incoming aircraft. "Hmm. It's pretty hard to find hangar space these days. And it's expensive. Can you tie it down outside?"

"Oh, goodness, no, it's brand new."

"All the better, it's brand new."

"No, I need a hangar. I don't want it outside." The thought of keeping the Pulsar out on the ramp would be like leaving your suede recliner out in the backyard.

"Go over to Palm Beach Aircraft and talk to Dave. He knows everything that's happening on the field and he might be able to help you."

"Thanks Rick, I will."

I drove out on the ramp and parked next to Dave's large hangar. It was packed with a King Air, a Waco YMF-5, two Cessna 172s, a 152, a Beech Bonanza, and a Cub. I went into the office. Dave had a good reputation on the field and was fair and knowledgeable. He was also known for picking competent mechanics to work for him. We shook hands. Before I could speak up, Dave asked me about the Pulsar.

"Funny you should ask. It's ready to be trailered out here for final assembly and testing."

"That's quite something, Lisa, it's only been a couple years, right?"

"Twenty months."

"Yeah, with you working full time and all, I'm amazed. How can I help you?"

"I'm looking to share a hangar with someone. Any ideas?"

Dave got up and looked at the airport hangar map on the wall and stroked his chin.

"Wingspan?"

"Twenty-five."

"Length?"

"Nineteen and a half."

"Height of tail?"

"Six point three."

"Hmm. Lisa, the field is full up, I don't know anyone who has any space."

"Shoot, I guess I'll have to get a really good cover for it and get a tie down."

"Wait a minute. Let's walk out into the hangar."

We walked into the hangar. Mechanics were working on the King Air and the Bonanza. "Look at this side corner here. I bet your Pulsar would nestle next to this Waco. It doesn't go out often, and your Pulsar won't need a tug it's so light. I can't guarantee you can have the space long term, but let's see how it works out. What do you think?"

I was ecstatic. "Excellent. I'll get the airplane out here this weekend if I can."

"Sure, bring it in. Let me give you a key. We try to go fishing on the weekends."

Friday after work Gus and I loaded the fuselage onto the trailer and nestled the wings on moving blankets alongside it. At the airport we pulled up to Dave's hangar and began unloading. We nestled the Pulsar, looking very small and strange without the wings on, next to the Waco.

"This is perfect," said Gus.

"Tomorrow can you help me slide the wings on?" I asked.

"Absolutely."

Saturday I was at the hangar at 7 am. Knowing Gus would not be arriving until later in the morning, I went through my checklists. Andy, one of Dave's mechanics, drove up with a boat trailered behind his truck.

"Look at that! Dave said you would be out here this weekend. When will you taxi test?" asked Andy.

"As soon as I get the wings on and the systems checked out."

"Do you need help getting the wings on?"

"Actually, yes, I am waiting for Gus."

"It should only take a minute. I'll give you a hand if you want."

"All we need to do is slide the spars in and I'll install the pins."

"Do it."

I unwrapped the wings and picked up the spar end. Andy got the wing tip, and we tilted it up. I walked it over to the pilot side and slid it into the spar slot.

"It's captured in the structure, you can let go," I said.

We installed the right-side wing, and I pinned them both.

"That's easy," said Andy. "You could trailer this plane anywhere and then fly."

"True, but then you'd have some work hooking up the fuel and the electrical every time, which is what I'm going to do now."

"Ok, have a blast, I'm off to catch some Marlin."

I spent the rest of the morning on hookups and system checkouts. Gus showed up at 9 am, which I anticipated.

"You already got the wings on!"

"Yep. No worries. I think I'm actually ready to start the engine and test the brakes."

"Are you mad I wasn't here?" Gus looked concerned. He came over to me and put his hand on my shoulder.

"Oh, no, I knew you'd sleep in. You work hard cutting lawns all week, all I do is sit at a desk."

Gus shook his head and grimaced. "My other girlfriends get mad when I say I'll show up at a certain time and don't, and then I have to buy them something to make up for it."

I laughed. "Hey, my mother didn't tell me about that ploy. I know your habits. Why get upset over something you don't have control over?"

"Want to get married?" said Gus.

"No!" We both said it at the same time and then hugged, laughing, almost falling down.

"Lese, you're a blast," Gus couldn't stop laughing.

I finished the hookups and went through my lists. I grabbed the wood prop at the root and pulled the airplane out onto the ramp in front of the hangar. At 635 pounds empty, the airplane was easy to move. The prop was geared to the engine so there was little danger of damage when it was off.

Can't do that with a Cessna 152.

I looked into the cockpit. Checklists covered the passenger seat. I stepped up onto the wing and swung my legs over into the cockpit, sliding down into the seat.

A sports car of the sky.

During the building process I'd spent hours sitting in the cockpit imagining flights. Now I was in the pilot seat for real. My pulse quickened. I looked around to make sure the area was clear.

"Ok here we go. Stand back, Gus. Clear prop!" I shouted. I held my breath and turned the ignition key.

The engine sprang to life in an uneven loping beat and began to speed up and smooth out as I pushed the choke in. I let it warm up at 1,800 rpm and watched the temperatures and pressures. The engine monitor showed an array with EGTs, CHTs, oil pressure, and fuel pressure and flow.

I closed the canopy part way and put on my headset. I could still hear the throaty beat of the Rotax engine as it warmed up to operating temperature.

I applied some power and took my toes off the brakes and put them onto the rudder pedals. The toe brake setup I designed seemed to be working well, giving me more braking leverage. The Pulsar began to move. I applied a little more power and watched the engine monitor for signs of trouble.

Onlookers had gathered at Dave's hangar, watching.

I leaned back in the Temper Foam® cushions, which were body hugging and firm. I had the sensation for a brief moment that the craft was simply an extension of my own body. A flow of cool air blew through the cockpit. I closed the canopy to see how the air vents worked. Lots of air. I was pleased.

I applied more power, getting the airplane to taxi across the ramp. Applying some brake, I noticed that they were mushy. Deciding to stop completely, I applied pressure to the brake stems. The airplane kept going.

Uh oh.

I pulled the power to idle, and reapplied brake, pushing hard. All I got was mush, but the airplane came to a stop on its own. I turned the ignition off and allowed the excitement to ebb. Except that it didn't. I opened the canopy and jumped out.

Gus helped me pull the airplane back to the hangar.

"Brakes."

"Air?"

"Yep."

We looked at the lines, the reservoir, and the fittings.

"No leaks."

"I'll get a bleeder from home. I need to finish all my hookups properly and go through the checklists this afternoon before more testing."

■ ⟶ ■

The next morning I gulped down my coffee and eggs and was at the hangar just as the sun came up. Morning burst upon the small airport with vivid rays of light shredding the remaining clouds on the horizon. A cool breeze moved across the ramp in the stillness. Soon the airport would be bustling with weekend flying activities. A perfect day for taxi testing.

I rolled the giant hangar doors back on their rails, startled by the loudness of the rumbling. I looked at the Pulsar sitting in front of the YMF-5. It was sleek and graceful. The beauty of the craft took my breath away. What a contrast; a beautiful biplane from the forties, and a beautiful low-wing airplane from the 90s.

I pinched myself.

Brakes. You need brakes. I shook off my reverie and pulled out the toolkit. I began examining the lines. Like the day before, Andy pulled up with his boat to retrieve his tackle boxes and cooler.

"Brakes? I've got a really nice brake bleeder. It will be easier than the one you have. Let me get it."

"You're too much, Andy. Put it on my tab."

"Ok. I will," he laughed, handling me the bleeder. "See ya."

I got the air out of the system and I was ready to test again. I pulled the airplane out, hopped in, and started the engine. After the temperatures came up, I got the airplane rolling with some power and tried the brakes. They felt firm. I started to taxi, applying more power and then stopping. Good.

I spent the day taxiing about the airport and writing down what I was seeing on the monitor. Then I ran through tests of all the systems. I would spend several days ground testing before thinking about a first flight.

The boring part that's not boring, I thought.

"Happiness is a butterfly, which when pursued, is always just beyond your grasp, but which, if you will sit down quietly, may alight upon you."

~ Nathaniel Hawthorne

34

FIRST FLIGHT

DECEMBER 6, 1997. THE MORNING began just like the morning I'd soloed 22 years earlier-with quiet anticipation. Like that morning, I didn't know how things would unfold, but I sensed a buildup of excitement, of positive energy filling my body like water filling a glass.

I turned the radio off as I drove to the airport. If I had a helicopter, I thought, I'd shoot straight for the field from my house. A jet pack would be better. Roads are so inconvenient. They were dark and quiet at 6 am, the air still. Rolling down the window, I caught a whiff of palm and saw grass, mixed with salt and sand. The ocean was two miles to the east. Today would be a good day for boating, with seas flat as a mirror. If all went well, I'd get a look at that ocean from the air.

There's that flutter thrill again. The same one you get when you miss a step. I felt the tingle move up from my feet to my chest and back down.

I'd told only Gus and Steve of my plans to make my first flight today. A crowd and the pressure it brings are not a good recipe for safety, I thought, as I pulled through the airport gate. It would only add to my nerves.

In a few hours the airport would begin its early morning bustle. Students would begin their preflights, flight-seers would claim their bench spots on the porch of the quaint FBO, and cars would be parked at tie-downs.

The air was silent and still, with not even a stirring of dust.

Perfect.

I unlocked the side door to the hangar and flipped on the lights. There was my Pulsar, dwarfed in the corner. I walked over and rolled the canopy forward, retrieving my tool kit from behind the seats. Check everything twice. Last night I'd checked everything twice, and it was time to do it again. Removing the engine cowl, I began going through my checklist.

"Hey," said Gus, startling me.

"Yikes! You're early!"

"I didn't want to miss anything," said Gus. "And, I wanted to surprise you."

"You did. What did you do, stay up all night?"

"Almost. Does everything check out?"

"Yes, so far so good. I'll taxi around a bit and only go if I feel ready."

"What can I help with?"

"Stay tuned to the radio. If I have a problem, you'll know it. I'll stay in the pattern for the first flight and if there's an engine issue, I should be able to glide in to land."

"That's the nice thing about having three runways," said Gus. "And not being too busy."

Nestled into a cutout in Palm Beach Class C airspace, Lantana was a thriving non-towered general aviation airport. With six runway choices, pilots of all types loved the field. Weekends were busy.

I rolled back the hangar door on the south side and pulled the Pulsar out onto the ramp. The sun presented itself as an orange quarter slice orb peeking through the low-level white mist of the lake to the east. The filtered light glinted off the Pulsar canopy, and the shiny white wings glistened.

A car drove up and parked at the side of the hangar. Steve, a close friend spanning my multiple business career tracks, walked over.

"Thanks for coming out, Steve. Are you up for some photography?"

"Yes indeed, and quite honored." Steve displayed a beaming smile, and I gave him a hug. Steve spoke with clarity and the perfect diction that only a former radio broadcaster would have.

"The plan is for me to do a little bit of taxiing and decide if it's the right time to get into the air. If it doesn't feel right, then I won't."

"A safe plan," Steve nodded and reached into his camera bag.

It was now 7:30 am, and the sun had fully cleared the lake marsh. The windsock hung limp in the center of the field. In spite of temperatures in the 60s I had on a light cotton polo shirt and a pair of jeans.

The rest of the world retreated as I focused on my readiness. With the preflight checklist completed, I hopped up on to the left wing and stepped into the pilot seat. I slid down the tall seatback cushion, locating my legs under the instrument panel and settling into the seat. I buckled up the five-point harness, feeling like an astronaut, with a one buckle lever across my hips for an easy out if I needed it.

I looked around the airplane. Several onlookers had joined Steve and Gus by the hangar.

Where did they come from?

"Clear prop!" I pulled out the choke and turned the key. The engine jumped to life and smoothed out as I pushed the choke back in slowly. I set the speed at 1,400 rpm.

I focused on temperatures and pressures for several minutes, waiting for the oil to warm. I went through another checklist: headset; radio check; controls; fuel flow, and mag check. Altimeter 12 feet. Pitch trim neutral. Fuel pump on.

I finished the checks and took my toes off the brakes and applied power, taxiing just as I had done numerous times in the preceding week. Engine monitor data were good and the brakes were firm.

I waved to the bystanders and closed and latched the canopy. It was much quieter in the sealed cockpit. I took a deep breath. Airplane ready. Pilot ready?

Suddenly I was lifting off from my backyard, arms out, carried on a platform of cool breeze, higher, higher, weaving left and right, seeing the landscape flow underneath me as the homes became tiny and melted away.

I lined up on Runway 27. Lantana's longest runway at 3,500 feet, fields and open spaces would be ahead of me. "Lantana Traffic, Pulsar Experimental Four Five Six Lima Tango taking off, two-seven, Lantana, will stay in the pattern." I was the first flight of the day.

My breathing quickened as I gripped the stick, applying power with my left hand. Throttle all the way in. Feet on rudder pedals.

Be ready to abort.

The Pulsar accelerated with so much power it caught me off guard. In all my dreams I had not felt this strength. I felt like I'd been shot out of a rocket.

Stay light on controls.

At 500 feet the little airplane leapt into the air in spite of my plan to build more speed before taking off. Air rushed through the vents as the runway disappeared beneath me. The sky filled the bubble canopy.

With the throttle all the way in the aircraft continued to build speed, with 1,200 fpm showing on the VSI (vertical speed indicator). I resisted pulling power back, knowing I needed to get to a safer altitude. I was at 500 feet before I knew it. Adrenaline coursed my veins, and every sense was tuned to the heartbeat of the small airplane.

I turned crosswind and attempted to slow the steepness of the climb. I felt I was strapped into a runaway jet. I thought about my flight with Bob Kromer, when I was feeling as if the airplane would never slow. I turned downwind, continuing to gain altitude. I pulled the throttle back to 4,200 rpm and checked the climb at 1,200 feet. I was 200 feet too high. It had happened so fast.

Settle down.

My logical brain was holding the exhilaration of leaving the runway captive. I knew that I had to gain control of the craft before celebrating leaving the ground. I didn't want to return to the ground in a heap.

"Lantana Traffic, Pulsar Six Lima Tango, downwind for two-seven, landing."

"You go girl!" someone shouted over the Unicom.

"You have the airport to yourself, no traffic," said Rick in the FBO office. "Good going."

Don't celebrate yet guys.

115 mph. Way too fast. I was totally outside my test plan speeds.

Settle down.

How am I going to land this thing? A sudden chunk of fear hit me. What was I thinking? I don't have enough experience. I remembered a friend at work who used to say, "Get a grip," whenever someone got nervous.

Get a grip.

"I can't slow enough for flaps," I said aloud to myself. "I can't slow at all!"

That's ok, pull more power.

I turned base at 800 feet and 95 mph.

Nope, this isn't working.

I turned to final and lined up on 27. 90 mph. I took a gulp of air.

Nope. Get a grip.

"Lantana Traffic, Pulsar Six Lima Tango on final for two-seven is going around, Lantana."

With the pressure off at 200 feet, I maintained my speed as I overflew the field. The small gathering at Dave's hangar looked up and waved. Later they said that they thought my flyover was on purpose and thought it was cool. If they only knew.

I've got to see if I can land this thing.

Flying over the end of the runway, I applied power and accelerated once again, rising at 1400 fps. This time I pulled out some power as I transitioned to the crosswind leg.

Not supposed to pull power so early but this thing is so fast.

Turning downwind, I pulled more power and settled in at 1,000 feet and 100 mph. I took a deep breath and looked out the canopy. My shirt was wet. I felt my hands tremble.

Your own airplane.

With the speed and altitude where I wanted them, I glanced out the wide canopy. The Palm Beach coastline stretched north for miles, and boats dotted a glassy ocean surface, sparkling under the rising sun.

I looked back at my panel and felt myself taking control. The Pulsar was now the airplane in my dream. All the nights I had fallen asleep imagining how the airplane would wrap itself around me and I would know exactly how much input to provide on the controls, a perfectly matched connection. Practicing takeoffs and landings over and over.

As I imagined that sensory experience now, I realized that all I had to do was adjust for the amazing increase in power. I'd never anticipated such a fast machine. Stick inputs were quick and required a light, smooth touch. Adjust.

I put in half flaps across from the numbers at 80 mph and turned base. Full flaps. Slow to 75. Sight picture.

You can always go around again.

"Lantana Traffic Pulsar Six Lima Tango turning final for two-seven, landing, Lantana." I now noticed a Cessna 152 waiting for takeoff.

Waiting on me.

I crossed the runway threshold at 70 mph and let a little more speed bleed off as I attempted to stay a few inches off the runway with the nose wheel slightly up. Deep breath. The mains rolled on to the surface together with a muted chirp and I held the nose off as long as I could. It came down to the pavement quietly, and I gently applied brake and was able to turn at the first turnoff, barely a third down the runway.

I stopped at the taxiway and unclipped the canopy, rolling it forward half way. I closed my eyes and drank in a gulp of the cool air coming through the cockpit. The adrenaline continued to course through my body as a tonic sense of relief washed over me.

It's real. The dream is real.

I looked around the small airport. The world was carrying on, as if nothing unusual had happened. But to me, everything had changed.

A blissful relief engulfed me as I applied power and taxied over to the hangar. I turned the ignition off and the engine shuddered to a quick stop. I pushed the canopy forward and wiggled up out of the seat and sat on the seat back, my arms outstretched in the air. Then I jumped down from the plane's wing and did a forward somersault on the pavement, coating my damp shirt in shiny Florida sand. I lay there for a few seconds and then got up, dusting myself off.

Gus and Steve came over to the airplane and we hugged. I shook my head from side to side. "I can't believe it."

"I believe I snapped some representative photographs," said Steve in his broadcaster voice. "I'll take them to the Delray Photo Shop for developing straightaway." We hugged again.

The rest of the day was a euphoric blur. After removing the cowling and checking all the systems in the airplane, I sat down on the bench just outside the hangar door. I gazed at the Pulsar, noticing for the thousandth time the clean lines and simple grace of the small craft.

Calm down and go again.

"Expect problems and eat them for breakfast."

~ Alfred A. Montapert

35

THE ROCKET

L UCK STUCK WITH ME on weather as the next day dawned identically to the one before it. The anticipation I felt driving out in the dark to the airport was every bit as strong as the day before. But today there was a new assuredness I had never felt before. I hadn't mastered the airplane yet, but I felt as if I could.

Arriving at the hangar, I was pleased that no one was around, not even early morning fishermen hooking up the boats they stored in the hangars on the east side of the field.

Glad that I'd brought a jacket, I shivered slightly as I removed the cowling in the 57-degree hangar. I ran through my checklists diligently and rolled back the rumbling hangar door. Like the morning before, the sun threw golden petals of light across the lake to the east. The mist moved slowly across the water surface as it evaporated into the cool morning air. I took a deep breath as my heartbeat quickened.

I'm more excited than yesterday. How can that be. Yesterday went so fast.

I pulled the plane outside and continued my inspections. *While it's early and not busy, you should practice pattern work.* I stepped up on to the left wing and entered the cockpit, sliding in.

Astronaut in a space capsule.

The warmth of the sun hit my jacket. A gentle breeze moved over the ramp, bringing with it a moisture-laden grass and salt smell from the marsh. It was clean and refreshing. I looked around. With no one in sight, I shouted out "Clear!" and started the engine.

The Rotax settled into a mid-frequency beat as I removed the rest of the richness from the fuel. This engine did not need a mixture control, as the twin Bing carburetors were self-compensating up to the service ceiling of 15,000 feet. Many Pulsar pilots did not use an auxiliary fuel pump for takeoff and landing, but I'd made the decision to install one. Little did I know that a time would come when I was thankful for that pump.

Scanning the engine monitor, I made notes on temperatures and pressures at idle as I waited for the oil to warm. I finished my checks and taxied over to 27. Might as well be the first flight of the day again and pick the runway.

"Lantana Traffic, Pulsar Six Lima Tango taking off on two-seven, Lantana, staying in the pattern."

Pushing the throttle forward, I felt the thrill of the surprising acceleration once again. The craft left the pavement quickly, and I let the speed build at 10 feet over the runway before I pulled into a climb.

I glanced down at the little airport. Nothing was stirring. I had it all to myself. I knew that an hour later the place would be buzzing with students and sightseers.

I turned downwind and adjusted my speed. I was getting the hang of it. This airplane was just so slick. I made my radio calls and put in half flaps. I turned to base leg and put in full flaps. The flap handle was mechanical and right by my left hand. Full up brought flaps down 40 degrees. It felt natural, dropping the nose to improve the already great sight picture.

I turned to final conscious of my shallow bank angle. Not knowing how the airplane would react in turns, I wanted to be as safe as possible. I lined up with 27. I was prepared for a case of nerves, but they didn't come. I was comfortable, and no one was watching.

I was a little fast at 75 mph over the fence, but it felt fine as speed bled off to 64 as I touched down with the left side first. I waited for the nose wheel and tried to keep the stick still. *Don't bounce.* For some reason, in spite of my complete inexperience, the landing was good, and I was delighted.

Go again!

Only 1,000 feet down the runway with 2,500 left, I took out the flaps and pushed in full power. I was off again in 200 feet and began another trip around the pattern.

Lining up on final, I decided to slow the Pulsar down a little more and see if I could get more of a stall on landing. Full flaps, 65 mph. Over the numbers I was going 56 mph, and suddenly the aircraft seemed to waver. Something didn't feel right. A stall in the Pulsar is listed at 45 mph. My speed was now 52 and I hadn't landed yet; I felt the Pulsar drop under me. The raw edge of fear hit me as I realized I was in trouble. Add power! Too late. I'm falling.

Just before the aircraft fell onto the runway, I added power. Flaps. Raise the flaps! *No, don't fool with it now.* I felt a simultaneous tire busting bounce on the left wheel and then the aircraft jumped back into the air. With the throttle all the way in, the Pulsar surged straight up into the air.

Now I was a rocket.

Get control! You're going to stall! A voice was shouting in my head. Panic raced through my body and my field of view shrank down to the small space I was in.

I'm in big trouble.

The airplane was pointed toward the sky. Don't panic, get it, come on, get it. *Stick forward, don't jerk it, smooth, do it.* I pushed the stick forward quickly but smoothly. For another moment I envisioned the mess I was going to make on the runway falling out of the sky. I was now at 50 feet, this was not going to be survivable. It would be fast. I wouldn't even know. Alarms were going off in my head as fear expanded in my lungs. Get level. Reduce power.

Your own airplane.

My vision broadened as the little craft recovered and began to level out at 200 feet. A palpable relief filled me and I began breathing again in big gulps. My chest was pounding.

I heard a loud voice through my headset. "What the hell was that?"

I realized they were talking about me.

"Six Lima Tango, are you alright? That was some almost landing you made."

I pushed the radio button. "Yeah, I'm fine, I'm fine."

"We weren't expecting aerobatics so close to the field and so early in the morning."

"Right. Right. I wasn't either," I replied. My voice was trembling and my hands were shaking. I was still shocked at my screw up. I realized the voice was Rick in the FBO. *Oh damn. I thought no one was out here yet.*

I reached pattern altitude and wondered how much damage I'd done to the left wheel and tire. I guess I would find out. Although I'd planned to leave the field for testing, I decided I'd better land and check the systems.

"Lantana Unicom, Six Lima Tango."

"Lantana Unicom," said Rick.

"Can you send someone out to look at the gear as I come in for landing? If it looks ok give me a thumbs up? If not I'll do my best."

"Already done. Mike is out there."

On short final I saw Mike on a golf cart with his thumb up in the air.

Over the numbers I kept power up for a speed of 65 instead of the previous landing's 52. This time the airplane behaved predictably, and the gear rolled on smoothly in spite of my still shaking hands. My shirt was wet under my nylon jacket. I pushed the canopy forward for more air as I taxied, more than embarrassed, off the runway.

The airplane seemed fine. I got to the hangar and shut the engine down. After a few deep-breathing exercises I lifted myself out of the cockpit and onto the wing. I jumped down and sat on the pavement to look at the gear. I couldn't see any damage. But that didn't mean anything. I needed to do a complete check.

I pulled the Pulsar into the hangar, hoping that no one would come ask me what had happened. My heart was still racing, and the adrenaline was still surging. I sat on the bench and opened a bottle of water. I drank thirstily. I looked at the Pulsar with a big sigh. *You are one lucky pilot, idiot.*

"Hey!" Gus came around the corner of the hangar. "You didn't tell me you were going to do tricks in the airplane so soon."

"Gus! Hey. Oh jeez, I feel awful." I closed my eyes and looked down, shaking my head.

"I thought you might be out here. I had to go to Home Depot for some plumbing supplies, I saw your car."

"Was it as bad as I felt it was?"

"No. I have seen worse from new students. But it did look like the plane was falling out of the sky for a minute. You would have taken out the gear completely."

"What about when it almost flipped on its back though?"

"You may have felt that, but all I saw was you jumping back into the air and zooming off for Mars."

I laughed. "You're making me feel better, Gus, thank you."

"No, really, it wasn't that bad." He gave me a bear hug.

"Well even if you're lying to me, I feel better."

"Are you going back out today?"

"Actually, after a detailed airplane inspection and lunch, I'd like to. Give me a hand and I'll take you to lunch?"

"Deal."

"Don't Let Yesterday Take Up Too Much of Today."

~ Will Rogers

36

THE HOBBS

W E SPENT SEVERAL HOURS checking and rechecking the Pulsar and could not find a single thing amiss except for a wobbly nose wheel.

"This friction deal on the swivel joint is prone to loosening. You'll need to keep an eye on it. I'm surprised it wasn't shimmying on taxi."

"It was."

"One tough little airplane," stated Gus, as he finished putting the cowling back on.

"But just wait. It's only the second day, and I have all afternoon to screw up."

Gus laughed. "Stop that. Let's eat."

We walked over to the hamburger stand near the breezeway of the FBO. A line had already formed.

"Popular place," said Gus.

"In south Florida, in winter, on a sunny day in the low 70s with lots of airplanes and hangar parties—you betcha."

We sat down at a table where we could watch the flight activity.

"Maybe I'll see a landing worse than the one I made earlier," I said.

"Couldn't happen," Gus said, looking at me with a straight face and then an impish grin.

"No fair!" I replied, giving Gus a scowl.

"So, really, what do you think so far of the airplane? Is it what you expected?"

"Wonderful and yes. I've got a total of 114 flight hours as a pilot. Most of them are in a Cessna 152. When you're flying a 152, you feel like you are flying inside a little box. It's not particularly easy to get a wide, expansive view; you always know you're looking out windows. The Pulsar, on the other hand, makes you feel like YOU are flying. You forget you're looking through a canopy. The controls feel like putting your arms out and flying. Don't get me wrong – 152s are fine, but the Pulsar is the difference between the Hardy Boys and Tom Swift."

"Who?"

"Gus, you young thing. The difference between ordinary and advanced, how's that."

Just when I thought that no one else besides the FBO office manager had seen my landing mishap, Andy came up to the table, smiling.

"That looked like fun this morning."

I shook my head from side to side.

"That Pulsar can move. You must have a hidden jet engine on it."

"I came in too slow and didn't get the power in soon enough."

"No one's a pilot if that hasn't happened to them," said Andy. "May I join you?"

"Sure. Were there a lot of people watching?"

"No, there was just me, Mike, and Rick in the office when I saw you come in the second time. That is one gorgeous airplane, Lisa.

So, I saw you sink and overcorrect. I closed my eyes and gritted my teeth expecting something really bad, but you pulled it out. Then I told Rick he was going to get in trouble for swearing over the Unicom."

"I hope my instructor, Ellen, didn't see it. It was embarrassing enough without onlookers."

"It was too early."

"Good. All right, I'm going to go flying. I wish I didn't have to go to work tomorrow, I need to make the most of today."

"I've got to get over to Home Depot sometime today. I'll see you later," said Gus. "Be careful, Lese!"

"I will, I will."

I headed back to the hangar, hoping I wouldn't keep getting ribbed about my ugly go-around.

My near accident shock had faded and hadn't dampened my enthusiasm for getting in the air again. But I wasn't going to forget the lesson. I ran my checks and jumped up on the wing and slid into the cockpit.

The engine fired up immediately, still warm from the morning's exercise. I looked out over the airport, seeing a line of aircraft waiting to do run-ups for Runway 27. The slight breeze out of the west wasn't even enough to lift the windsock. The air was warm and light across my arms as I taxied with the canopy open over to the line.

No rush.

I left the pattern and headed west, just beyond the student training area, climbing to 2,500 feet. While I was looking at instruments and getting the data log out of the passenger seat, I was also scanning the air for traffic. I didn't want to go too far west, which would take me over even more remote land – the Everglades. An unplanned landing there would introduce me to alligators up close.

I tried to settle down and fill out my test log, but I was completely immersed in the flight experience. Here I was in an airplane I'd built in my garage, going 145 mph over farmland on a stunningly beautiful day. The sky was a vivid blue with a few wispy clouds much higher in the sky. All by myself. I thought back several weeks ago when the FAA Designated Airworthiness Representative, Walt, had inspected the airplane and given me my airworthiness certificate.

"You're going to hate this," said Walt. "You'll have to fly off 40 hours in this test area." He pointed to the chart where he'd drawn out the exact boundaries for my testing. It stretched from Lantana all the way out to Lake Okeechobee in a triangle shape.

"What's wrong with that?" I asked.

"That's a long time to be flying over fields."

"I won't mind that."

"Just wait."

Experimental airplanes without a certified engine and prop combination were required to spend 40 hours in testing, and the certified combination required 25. I didn't see why 40 hours would be a problem. I loved it. I reached for my log and began recording time, date, hours, speed, and the data in my engine monitor. Oil pressure, temperature; cylinder head temps, left and right; exhaust gas temps, left and right; fuel flow, and rpm.

Since I was left handed, I expected I'd write in the log on my lap with my left hand and fly the airplane control stick with my right. But I quickly discovered that with a little fiddling, the electric stabilizer trim gave me hands off stability.

The test plan called for flying the aircraft across a range of parameters, from climbs, turns, and descents at different airspeeds to stalls, and finally to maneuvers at gross weight. The Pulsar was rated at +6 and -4 *g*'s (units of gravity) so I'd need to load it up later in the testing. Right now with me in the airplane and 75 percent fuel I could handle another 275 pounds.

That's a lot of sand bags.

As I re-focused on my data recording, I realized that at 140 mph I was using about 3.4 gallons of gas per hour. At that rate I had a range of more than 600 miles, leaving a healthy reserve. The airplane had more endurance than my bladder did.

I flew for two hours and covered dozens of test items. I headed back to Lantana. It was turning into a long day and I was beginning to feel a pleasant but still energy-laden exhaustion. I made my approach calls and noticed that there was a lull in the traffic.

On final approach, with the painful memory of the slow landing still smarting, I made sure to stay above 65 over the threshold. I landed a little hard at 68 mph, still learning, but it was not a bad one. I turned in at the first turnoff and taxied to Dave's hangar. All was quiet on this late Sunday afternoon.

I nestled the Pulsar next to the Waco in the corner. Forty hours of testing? Maybe Walt was right. I longed to fly over the beach.

34 hours to go.

"Adventure is worthwhile in itself."

~ Amelia Earhart

37

IMPETUOSITY

"CONGRATULATIONS ON YOUR first flight!" Carl came into my office on Monday morning and plopped down in front of my desk.

"You're here to see the pictures, right?" I said, laughing. Over the last 20 months I'd gotten ribbing after ribbing about the photo album on the corner of my desk showing the progress on the airplane.

"Oh no! Not more pictures! Do I have to?" said Carl in an aggravated tone, holding up his hands as if to shield the sun from his face. "No! Torture!"

"Come on, you sound like Martha," I said.

Martha, the lobby receptionist, gave me the worst time about the pictures. She would stare at me sternly and say, "Lisa Turner, you are even more rabidly excited about your airplane pictures than a mother is about her *baby* pictures! It's awful! Stop it!" Then she would start giggling and ask me where they were and why I hadn't shared the latest with her.

"No," said Carl, "I could never be as bad as Martha. Close, though. Ok really, do you have pictures of your flight? What was it like? Were you nervous? The word is all around this morning that you almost crashed it. Is that true?"

I handed Carl the stack of 4-x-6 photos that I hadn't had a chance to put in the album yet. "No, I didn't almost crash it! Well, maybe, sort of."

"Aha, it is true. What happened?"

"Let's not talk about it and say we did."

"Come on, Lese, tell me?"

"I was practicing landings, and I got too slow. My instructor Greg warned me about that and the Operating Handbook says the same thing -- don't get too slow. It's a slick airplane. I was trying to get slower for a gentler landing and inexperience just got hold of me. But I found if you keep just a tiny bit of power in and stay over 60 mph, it's really straightforward. Hell, it was only my third landing."

Greg was poring over the pictures. "Is that you doing a somersault? Greg held up the picture of me getting out of the airplane after the first flight on Saturday.

"Uh, yeah, I went wild."

"Ha! I love it. A 46-year-old woman somersaulting on concrete! You could have split your head open."

I pursed my lips together in a mischievous smile. "Yeah."

■ ⎯⎯ ■

Just before leaving work, Heather gave me a call.

"Lisa, I got your message; that's amazing you made you first flight. Feel like coming over for dinner? We'd love to hear about it."

"Sure, I'll see you at 6:30 pm?"

"Perfect."

What got into Heather? Maybe she's coming around.

I entered the house to find Perky in the living room fiddling with one of his grandfather clocks. "These things are so temperamental. One second, move the minute hand...ok, Lese, congratulations! What a milestone! How was it?"

"It was just like the dream! The airplane behaved just the way I thought it would." I didn't bring up my near crash landing on Sunday.

"I wish I'd been there. I know you didn't know exactly when you would be ready, so I understand why you'd want to be low key about it. I would have done the same thing. Smart."

Heather came out of the kitchen and we hugged.

"You got into the air? Was everything fine? Were there any problems?"

"Everything was great."

"I worry about you, Lisa."

"I know. Really, it's safe. And I'm being conservative."

"Well, you being conservative would be new. Come on in the dining room and get yourself a drink."

Heather went back to the kitchen. Before I followed, Perky touched my arm. "She's coming around," he said.

During dinner I told them about the preparations and the early morning flight. I left out Sunday's mishap. I knew it wouldn't help me sell the idea of flying a homebuilt airplane.

"When can you take passengers?" asked Perky.

"As soon as the testing is done – a minimum of 40 hours on the Hobbs. I've got a set test area that the designated airworthiness examiner gave me – it's all west of the airport over fields and swamp. I hope I don't have to land there."

"No, I guess not!"

Heather listened attentively. She had an uncanny ability to become interested in anything a person said, even if she didn't agree with it. She was an attentive listener and remembered what people told her.

I wish I could be like that.

"Sis, I have a question for you."

"Yes?"

"I know you're going to Northeast Harbor again this summer. Can I invite myself for a visit?"

Heather dropped her look of concern and smiled. "Of course you can – we'd be delighted to have you visit. I know it's tough with your work schedule, they don't give you a lot of vacation, but I was thinking that we could put together a family reunion. Dad and Pauline talked about something like that earlier this year, and even Jeffrey and Elisabeth said they might be able to make it. Wouldn't that be great?"

"Yes! I can't remember the last time we were all together," I said, "It's been years, and even then, it doesn't seem like we had enough time to catch up."

"So you'd drive to Maine, like the last time, and visit your friends along the way?" Heather asked.

"Ah, no, actually I was thinking about flying."

"Fly into Bangor? You might want to make your reservations now, the summer is a busy time."

"No, actually, I would fly the Pulsar."

At first I wasn't sure that Heather heard me.

"The Pulsar, I'd fly the Pulsar."

"That's what I thought you said," answered Heather. "Lisa, do you think that really makes sense? Florida to Maine? In a tiny plane you built in your garage? With all the things that could go wrong?"

"I'll have four months of flight time on it."

"But Lisa, you only got your pilot's license last year. You're inexperienced. What if something happened that you couldn't handle? Your impetuosity could get you in trouble. I don't think it's a smart idea so soon."

I didn't know what to say. I looked away in disappointment.

"Lese, why don't you finish the test hours on your airplane and make the decision later?" said Perky. "It's not as if you have to make reservations for Pulsar airlines! We won't be going up until May, and Jeff and your Dad wouldn't be coming until the end of May."

I looked at my sister. I knew her reaction was out of concern, but I didn't feel I was connecting with her.

"Sis, I appreciate your advice. I like Perky's idea. But if I decide to fly my own airplane, I hope you will understand why it means so much to me."

Heather got up from the table. "Ok. Let's drop it for now. But please think carefully about not taking the risk."

"Ok."

Perky and I cleared the dishes, and I started washing up the pots and pans. Heather was in the dining room, straightening up. Perky placed a hand on my back.

"Lese, Heather loves you dearly. I know you are disappointed." Perky looked at me intently. "Get your testing done, and then I want a ride. Let's see what happens."

My dejection lifted for a moment as I saw Perky's eyes radiate warmth. "Everything will work out," he whispered.

"Difficulties mastered are opportunities won."

~ Winston Churchill

38

FIRST PASSENGER

THE SATURDAY DAWNED CLEAR and cool. After breakfast I jumped in the car and drove to the airport in anticipation. I felt I couldn't get there fast enough.

I pushed the hangar door open in the morning stillness. I pulled the Pulsar out and filled the two wing tanks with premium filtered auto gas. I threw the notebook and test log in the passenger seat and went back to the car for bottles of water.

A feeling of disappointment cut into my anticipation as I remembered the discussion with Heather. *I was trying to forget that. How will I convince her it's ok? I so much wanted everyone to be as excited and happy as I was.* What a Pollyanna I am, I thought. I'm too sensitive. I pushed the concern out of my mind and slid into the cockpit, letting the excitement displace my worry.

I taxied off to Runway 9 as the sun broke through the low-lying clouds. The wind was picking up earlier than usual, out of the east. Good conditions for more testing. Once again I had the airport to myself so early. I took off and headed west to the test area, climbing to 3,000 feet.

I stuck to my FAA designated area. I worked through the test tasks, finding myself at hour 22 as I signed off my flight characteristics at gross weight.

Oh, to fly down the beach! Walt was right.

Back at the hangar one day, I saw Andy tinkering with his motorcycle and walked over after putting the Pulsar in the corner.

"Andy, I'm getting stir crazy to fly the beach."

"Yep, I figured that. You can hook up a battery to your Hobbs meter and the hours will be there after a day," said Andy.

"That would be illegal!" I exclaimed, surprised that an A&P mechanic would say such a thing. "You're kidding."

"I sure wouldn't do it, but I have seen it done. The fact is, by 20 hours you know everything about the aircraft, so it's not particularly dangerous. It's just unethical. It's a tested design with a tested prop and a tested engine."

"I'll be patient."

On a bright warm day in late January, as I flew along the edge of Lake Okeechobee, I watched the Hobbs meter turn over 39.7 hours.

Yes!

As I returned to the Lantana airport, I got an idea. I landed and taxied to the hangar. I pulled out my cell phone, a Motorola StarTAC. In the just the last two years, a cellular telephone had become almost commonplace. To me, it was magic.

I dialed Heather and Perky's number. Perky answered.

"Perky, it's Lese. What are you doing today? I know you usually run errands on Saturday. Can you come out to the airport? It's a beautiful day and I want you to see the latest mod to the Pulsar."

"I do need to run some errands in Boynton. I'll be there within the hour."

I went to work checking the Pulsar from end to end and left it chocked on the ramp in front of the hangar. Then I officially signed my Operating Limitations, making it legal to carry a passenger.

I watched Perky drive up in his BMW convertible and park. Perfect timing.

"You extricate yourself from that sports car the way I slide out of the Pulsar."

"Lese, that is really a gorgeous airplane. I can't get over it. Look how the sun produces a star on the canopy." Perky pointed to the sparkle emanating from the canopy screen. "Picture perfect."

"I'm biased. I think it's gorgeous too," I replied. "Why don't you get into the cockpit, I'd like to see what it's like with two people in this thing."

I gave him instructions, and soon he was in the passenger seat. Well over six feet tall with a medium build, Perky took up all the passenger real estate.

"What do you think?" I asked.

"It's good, it's cozy."

"It's tight, isn't it?"

"No, really it's fine, it reminds me of the BMW."

I slid into the pilot's side and looked at Perky.

"Would you like to taxi a little?"

"Yes, I'd love it," he said.

I looked around. "Clear prop!" I turned the key and the Pulsar sprang to life, still warm from the morning flying. I pulled the canopy closed and latched it. "Here, headset."

Perky put on his headset and grinned.

"I know what you did now!" He looked at me excitedly and pointed to the Hobbs meter. "40.2 hours!"

I smiled broadly. "What do you say we take a flight down the beach?"

"I would love that Lese, I would love that."

"Let's go."

I taxied to Runway 9. I focused on my checklist, realizing I was suddenly nervous with Perky in the airplane.

Would Heather be upset? What if something happened?

"I'm your first passenger?"

"Yep!"

Perky grinned again. "This is great!"

With another 200 pounds in the airplane, I knew performance would be different. During testing I'd loaded the plane right up to gross weight and it handled the extra pounds well. But this was a person.

"Lantana Traffic, Pulsar Six Lima Tango taking off Runway niner, Lantana, will exit straight out to the east."

I applied full power, and the airplane surged ahead. We had plenty of acceleration as we left the pattern at 500 feet, climbing at 1200 fpm.

"Wow," said Perky. "This is just amazing. I can't believe the power, and the visibility is stunning. It's as if you didn't have anything around you. A bird."

I nodded. "That's what I think, too."

I was feeling a little uneasy, thinking about what I would do if there was a problem. Looking down, we were over subdivisions of homes arranged on small lakes and canals. Taught to consider every conceivable emergency, I suddenly reconsidered my idea to take off over a populated area with my first passenger.

Impetuous. I should have asked Heather if this was ok.

"Lese, this is incredible! Can we fly over the house?"

"Sure, let me get my bearings. Keep your eyes open for traffic."

"I am."

I looked ahead and saw the Boynton Beach inlet. Dozens of boats dotted the Intracoastal and beach area south of the inlet. At the beach line I turned south. At least now I have a place to land, I thought. My unease started to drain.

"There it is." Perky exclaimed, pointing to the right. "There's the house."

The sprawling single-story house with the white tiled roof came into view. The Intracoastal canal and vacant lot next to the home were easy to spot.

We flew down the beach, slightly offshore, our eyes searching out other traffic. I knew that a Saturday afternoon would be busy, including sightseeing flights, banner tows, and sightseers.

"I'm speechless. This is marvelous, Lese."

The beach was teeming with swimmers and sunbathers. The water was so clear that the reefs looked like they were floating on the surface, like looking into an aquarium. The ocean was a light emerald color, the sun playing in diamonds across its surface. Dive boats were anchored in a line offshore over shipwrecks located 100 feet down and in favorite fishing holes nearby.

A cool salt sweet, sun-drenched breeze came through the vents as we flew south. Off to our right the mansions of Gulfstream came into view along with sporadic areas of residential construction.

"Look at the manta rays," I said, looking down into the clear water.

"Stunning! You'd never see that from the beach."

The excitement and beauty of the flight was overpowering. Yet my heartbeat hadn't slowed. First passenger. Although I might have sounded calm, I was acutely tuned to every sight and sound in the airplane, and every conceivable misfortune filling the edges of my awareness.

"I could spend all day flying!" Perky remarked, oblivious to my fear of a mishap.

"I'm so glad you enjoy it! I wouldn't be a pilot without your gift 20 years ago, Perk." I glanced over to see a special smile on his face. That look was everything to me.

I looked to my left and made a shallow 180-degree turn to head back up the beach. Perky carried on in an excited chatter as I started thinking about an uneventful return and landing at the airport. At the inlet I turned in toward the airport and made my radio calls, entering the pattern on the downwind leg for nine.

Perky went quiet, understanding my need to concentrate on the landing. As I turned to final and lined up on the runway centerline ahead, I was careful to maintain airspeed.

"You've got it," said Perky quietly as we crossed the runway threshold. Keeping a little of throttle in, and leveling out over the pavement, the Pulsar rolled on the mains with a tiny squeak. I held the nose off as long as I could. My intense excitement had not screwed up the landing.

"Outstanding!" exclaimed Perky.

As we taxied to the hangar, my remaining anxiety drained away like emptying a bucket of water, leaving me effervescent and exhausted at the same time.

The second phase of my dream had come true.

Boynton Beach Inlet

"Jobs fill your pockets, but adventures fill your soul."

~ Jaime Lyn Beatty

39

FLORIDA KEYS

"THE LAST WEEK IN MAY would be a good time," said my sister Heather over the phone from Northeast Harbor, Maine.

"Are you sure?" Weather could change the date since I could get socked in somewhere along the way.

"We'll be flexible."

Since the Florida to Maine trip discussion, Heather had not brought it up again, and I stayed away from the topic. But I knew Perky had been working behind the scenes.

"That's great. Jeffrey and Dad are coming?" I asked.

"Yes, plus Jeff's family, and Pauline, are coming."

"That's a house-full! We'll all buy you lobster."

"Some help around the house would be good."

"I'd be happy to, Sis, I'd be happy to."

"Lisa."

"Yes?"

"Be careful."

"Yes, I'll be careful."

Every time I thought about the trip from Florida to Maine in the Pulsar I got that lightning flutter bolt, like the days I had a crush on Larry and would chance encounter him coming up or down the school hallway.

Since finishing the tests on the airplane, I decided to make a day trip to the Florida Keys to see how a cross-country felt in the plane. Landing at Marathon Airport in the Florida Keys, I taxied up to the little FBO.

"It's tiny!" said a man coming out of the FBO. "Can you really fit another person in there?"

"Sure, get in!"

"No, just wondering."

My stepmother's sister owned a home in Islamorada, and they all pulled up in a sedan as I was post-flighting the Pulsar.

Hugs and greetings ensued while the airport personnel continued to ask questions about the little airplane.

"This is amazing, Lisa," said Sue, in her lilting, matter-of-fact voice. Bob Turner and Sue's sister Jean and husband Tommy gathered close around the airplane and looked into the cockpit as the FBO manager and mechanic pored over the engine compartment.

Sue said, "Lese, you know when you leave for Maine, we will still be here in the Keys. I'm sorry we'll miss seeing you land in Hornell on your way."

"That's ok; the Shinebargers will meet me at the airport, and I'll stay a few days with them."

"Good, I'm glad. But at least we get a chance to see you and the airplane right now. After seeing all the pictures and reports, we really wanted to see it up close. It's smaller than we thought it would be."

"That's the best part about it; it's small and cozy," I replied.

We went to a leisurely lunch at the Green Turtle Inn and then cruised the flats and mangroves in a pontoon boat. The gulf-side waters were crystal clear and flat as a sheet of glass. But I could feel a change in the air as we returned to the small basin at the house and tied up.

"The wind is picking up, I should get going on my trip back to Lantana," I said to Tommy.

"Well, come on in for an iced tea before you go and then I'll run you over to the airport." Tommy smiled and placed his hand on my shoulder. "It's great to have you here, you need to stay longer next time."

"I will."

We climbed the stairs to the vacation home on stilts. The elevated view of the Gulf from the porch was a postcard. The sun shimmered on the flat waters stretching as far as the eye could see. We sat around on the porch, enjoying the view and the calm.

Jean handed me an iced tea. "Here's the fun part for you, Lisa. Typically when relatives and friends visit from south Florida, they leave early because they know they will encounter stop-and-go traffic Sunday afternoon, stretching what should be a three- or four-hour drive into a six-hour drive. You can just get in your airplane and wave as you fly over that mess."

"Right," I replied, "In the airplane it's less than an hour and a half."

"I've often wished for something like that," exclaimed Sue, with a chuckle. "A magical levitation device."

Everyone laughed in delight.

"Well, I better not stay too late, and not because of traffic. I don't want to be caught in one of those early evening thunder-boomers we get regularly."

"Let's get you back to the airport," said Tommy.

The whole crew piled into the car and we drove the 15 minutes to Marathon. I was surprised that everyone wanted to see me off. I was pleased.

"Hey, winds are coming up, good timing," said Roy the FBO guy as I removed the cover from the Pulsar and untied the ropes. "Don't you need fuel?"

"No, I fueled up in Lantana before I left, so I have another two-and-a-half hours of flight plus a half hour reserve."

"You're kidding." Roy shook his head. "That's less than 4.5 gallons per hour fuel burn."

"And over 34 miles per gallon, if you put it into car terms," I replied.

"I love it."

After hugs and goodbyes all around I finished my preflight and slipped into the cockpit. I waved to everyone standing at the FBO and taxied off to Marathon's Runway 7.

As I did my run-up, concern about the weather and the timing jumped to the forefront of my mind and consumed my attention.

"Marathon Traffic, Pulsar Six Lima Tango taking off Runway 7, will exit to the northeast."

The 5,000-foot runway was so long I could have taken off and landed five times. I applied full power, and the airplane was quickly airborne. I rocked wings to family below and was soon out over the coastline. I punched in the ATIS frequency to get another weather briefing from Miami.

Still shy about controlled airspace, I decided to fly just outside the Miami Class B area, traveling north off the coastline. On the way down, the seas had been calm and inviting. Now they were turning dark and angry looking. I was surprised at how quickly the weather was deteriorating. Looking to the west, I could see dark cloud lines forming.

Get home. Get home.

The warm Florida air began to turn cool as it came through the vents, and the little aircraft began to bump and rock as winds gusted to 20 knots. The seas below me had developed whitecaps. I slowed my speed from 150 mph to 135 in the buffeting winds. It would take longer to get home, but I was more comfortable.

If my timing held, I would get to Lantana ahead of the storms moving west to east, but the margin of planning had evaporated.

I made a mistake leaving so late.

As my uneasiness grew, I hoped that there wasn't anything else that I'd done wrong in the planning or the building that would cumulatively bite me. As I looked down at the ocean growing more and more angry and dark, I thought about an engine failure.

My second mistake was not talking to Miami and flying closer to the coast.

I looked out to the left and spotted the Miami Beach coastline three miles away. It was awash in a fading glow of pinks and blues as the sun dropped lower in the horizon.

I wouldn't want to ditch an airplane out here.

Impetuous.

Was Heather right?

A voice spoke up in the back of my brain. *"You don't know what you don't know."*

Fear and uncertainty added to my unease as I thought of the things that could go wrong. Foundering in my dark thoughts I knew I had to regain confidence and logic. I took a deep breath and looked again at the sectional chart.

Forty minutes to home. You're fine.

As I looked back up from the map, the sky to the northeast was clearing and brightening, but the darkness to the west continued to march eastward.

I can beat it.

The waters below me continued to churn and lurch, but the wind gusts had lessened, and the airplane reached smoother air. I increased speed to 150 mph.

As I turned in from the coast and lined up on Runway 9 at Lantana, I felt the apprehension drain. Large raindrops reached the canopy just as I rolled out and braked. I taxied to the hangar as rain beat loudly on the airplane. Pulling up to the hangar, I stopped and let the engine idle for a moment before shutting down. I leaned back in the seat, taking deep breaths of the moist cool air.

Another lesson.

Miami

*"The only Zen you find at the top of the mountain is
the Zen you bring with you."*

- Proverb

40

PHYSICS

THE CELLPHONE RANG, startling me. I reached over to the
passenger seat and picked up the phone, flipping it open.

"Lisa, this is Tommy. We just wanted to make sure you got
home ok. You were going to call us at 4 pm."

"Yes, Tommy, thanks, I'm home, I just got in. I had to reduce
speed a little on the way back with the wind gusting."

"How was the trip? We saw some kind of disturbance over
Miami that seemed to come out of nowhere."

"It was a little bumpy, but fine. A great airplane."

"Hope we see you again soon."

"Thanks Tommy. Say hi to everyone and thanks so much for the
visit."

By the time I got off the phone, the downpour had ended. Florida
rainstorms act like a shower faucet: on full, off full 15 minutes later.

The bright Florida sun was now beating down on the concrete,
causing steam to dance in moist swirls and wisps. Sweat dripped
down my face and arms as I unlocked the canopy and slid it forward.

Rainwater dripped down my shirt from the back of the canopy as I hiked myself up on to the back of the seat.

"Nice; no leaks except when I open the canopy," I said aloud.

"Well that was good timing." Gus came around the corner of the hangar.

"I'll say it was. It hit just as I landed."

"How was the trip?"

"Bumpy on the way back. But a terrific visit with family. I got a free lunch and a pontoon boat ride. I just waited too long to leave."

"Well, your favorite saying is, 'All's well that ends well'."

"Yes."

But I was stupid to fly so far offshore. What if something had happened?

"I'm learning, Gus. I'm learning."

"How many flight hours do you have now?"

"Ah, let's see…here's my logbook. I reached into my headset case and withdrew the log. 195."

"How many in the Pulsar?"

"Probably about 100 of those."

"Sounds like a lot."

"It's not a lot. I need to be careful and detailed, and plan well to make up for my inexperience. Believe me, I really don't know much. I think that's why I get so nervous at the first sign of a problem. Do you think I'm too sensitive?"

"Yes."

"Gus! Come on, you're a risk taker."

"You won't get anything done if you don't take some risks. You might as well wrap yourself in a mattress to leave the house."

I laughed. "You're a kick, Gus. I love you."

Gus came over and gave me a big hug. "I love you, too. Banish the nerves and be confident."

"Easy for you to say. I'm trying."

"When are you going to give me my ride?" asked Gus.

"I thought you said you'd need to drink a six pack before you got in the airplane?"

"Well, maybe just a few."

"C'mon, let's go now. The sun is back out, and it's beautiful."

"Really?"

"Yes, really."

I was surprised that Gus wanted to fly, and I was pleased. I gave him the briefing, and we took off to the East. I kept looking over to see if he was ok with it.

"What do you think?" I asked.

"Incredible! I'm scared to death, but I love it. I'm glad I didn't drink a six. I can't believe I'm doing this."

We looked down at the clear ocean reefs and the sailboats. I made it a short flight, and we landed smoothly and taxied up to the hangar.

"Ok that's enough for today! 320 miles."

Gus took his headset off and looked like he'd just gotten off an amusement ride.

"Well?" I said.

Gus shook his head. "That was definitely ok! But I have to tell you something."

"Yes?"

"That was the first time I've ever been in an airplane."

"You're kidding me."

"No, I'm serious."

"No wonder you wanted a six pack," I said as we clambered back out of the cockpit.

"Ok, change of topics. I have a personal matter to discuss." I added.

"Uh oh. I don't like those."

"No, no, it's not what you think. I love being able to talk to you about anything."

"I thought you were going to criticize me."

"No! Of course not! Why would I do that?"

"My other girlfriends do that."

"Do?"

"Uh oh. Did."

"Ha! Gotcha. No, don't worry. That's not how I operate. Earthlings have enough troubles without making more of them by manipulating each other," I waved at the air and laughed. I was still feeling the relief of escaping the thunderstorm.

"I really do like you. You're easy to be around," Gus said.

"We're friends before anything else, right? That's how that works. We care about each other."

Gus nodded and smiled. "Ok, what was the personal question?"

"You know on this trip to Maine the airplane can easily outlast my bladder capacity. I'd like to drink plenty of water on the trip. There's just one problem. I'd like to, ok, well I'm aware of some anatomy differences between you and me."

"Wonderful differences."

I smiled. "I'm just wondering if I could figure out a way to, uh, funnel it to under the seat into a container, or a tube that went overboard."

Gus smiled and shook his head. "You're right, it's pretty easy for us guys. I wouldn't channel it overboard. You might end up with positive pressure and then...."

"Oh!"

"Right. Well, before your trip you might want to experiment a little. I'm really of little help, unless you want me to watch and evaluate."

"Ha! I don't think so. I'll just sneak in here super early one morning and try it out."

"Good luck. Sure you don't need help?"

I shook my head and laughed. Gus placed his hand on my shoulder and squeezed.

"There are always diapers."

"Doesn't that sound exciting? No, I don't think so."

The next morning I was in the hangar at 6 am. It was Sunday. There wasn't a soul around. If my plan worked, I'd place a narrow plastic funnel through a hole in the seat cushion which drained into a container under the composite seat panel. There was a large cutout at the front of the seat, so the container could be removed easily. I still wasn't exactly sure how it would work, but that was what experiments were all about.

For the test, I removed the cushion and placed a shallow container under the seat. If it worked, I could use something with a narrow top and even something with a screw-on lid with a tube coming out the top.

Then I placed the funnel into that from the top of the seat. I'd be able to raise and lower it.

I climbed into the cockpit and started to slide down in the seat. I'd forgotten that the seatback was on a 30-degree angle, and the seat was also canted back at least 20 degrees. I realized immediately that staying fully belted in with the five-point harness and having gravity work in my favor was not in the realm of possibility.

I shook my head from side to side in disappointment. You can't ignore basic physics.

Oh shoot. Lucky guys.

What did Amelia do, I wondered.

PART THREE

FLY

"The soul can split the sky in two and let the face of God shine through."

~Edna St Vincent Millay

41

THE SWAMP

MAY, 1998.
"Wow, that airplane is packed!"

Gus and Andy looked at the cockpit. A suitcase and backpack in the baggage area behind the seats with an extensive toolkit and a box of food, a cooler in the passenger seat footwell, and maps, sunglasses, towels, and an assortment of flight plan logs in the passenger seat.

"Even with all this, I am nowhere near gross weight."

"With you in it, how much?"

"925 pounds."

"When are you leaving?"

"Tomorrow morning at 6 am."

"Maybe I'll come see you off," said Gus.

"6 am? Are you kidding me?" I smiled gently.

"Well, maybe not." Gus grinned and gave me a big hug. "If I'm not here, hey, you take care. I love you." He held me out at arm's length and smiled, his eyes intense as he gazed at me.

"Love you, too. Go, I'm going to get weepy."

■   ✈   ■

That night I was a child waiting for Christmas morning. I lay on my back and went over my lists one more time.

I'd just as soon get back out of bed right now and go to the airport.

Sleep finally engulfed me and I was thrown into dreams of tumultuous ocean waves and emergency landings. Then I was on the sandy shore of the river, with the gentle eddies passing around smooth black rocks next to glistening white sand. My raft was close by.

"Lese." It was my mother's voice.

I looked to my left and my mother was right there, sitting next to me. Since losing her I'd had dream after dream filled with her voice and words, but not a physical presence. Solace and tranquility washed over us in a gentle wave of light.

We hugged tightly.

■   ✈   ■

The alarm went off at 4 am. For a second or two I wasn't sure where I was. Then I sat straight up, realizing that today was the day. I threw the covers off and sat up, the lightning flutter shooting head to toe.

Today is the day. The day I've been waiting for.

I ate a quick breakfast of scrambled eggs and buttered toast and was into the car and off. As I drove through the airport gate I tried to think of what I'd missed on my checklist. I'd kissed the two cats goodbye. "Don't you two get into any trouble," I'd admonished, knowing the sitter would spoil them more than I did. I smiled.

The airport was quiet as I pushed the rumbling hangar door open and pulled the packed Pulsar out into the night air. I closed and locked the doors on the hangar. I'd preflighted the airplane the night before, but now did a walkaround to double-check everything. The 24-hour spotlight at the corner of the hangar pushed out a yellow splay of light.

I could feel my heart beating quickly. I needed to settle down. I took a deep breath. I transferred the two bags and the cooler that I'd left until last from the car and slipped into the cockpit. The air was heavy with moisture and smelling of saw grass.

Great. No one is here.

I went through my checklist and started the engine. The oil temperature up, I closed the canopy in the chilly air. I thought I heard a horn. I looked over at the hangar. There was Gus, standing next to his truck under the spotlight. Late morning Gus. It was 6:30 am. I flipped open the canopy latch and pushed the screen forward, waving excitedly. Gus waved and gave a thumbs up with a big grin.

Gus waited on the ramp as I taxied to Runway 33 and then took off to the west. I rocked my wings. I saw him wave once again as I disappeared into the night air, my single halogen landing light punching through the mist.

The dull glow from the east provided just enough light to afford ground visibility. My plan was to skirt the Palm Beach airspace by going around the west side.

All swamp.

I scanned my instruments and took a look at my flight plan and charts. My plan was to climb to 1,500 feet but as I looked up and ahead, I saw shifting dark shapes. The lights of the town faded behind me as I flew over marsh and forest. I maintained 1,000 feet and hoped the mist would clear.

Was the day starting out all wrong?

The sun's corona, still below the horizon, glowed a luminous yellow through a thick veil to the east. The forest canopy below my craft seemed alive as clouds parted and then reattached themselves to the treetops. Damp air snaked through the air vents as I held the control stick in a tight grip.

The instruments glowed in muted reds and greens on the panel, a measure of reassurance that would not last long.

I looked down at a pockmarked expanse of pine forest and glimmering pools. With alligators cruising through the ragged islands of tall grass and stagnant water, this would not be a comforting place for an emergency landing.

Tendrils of mist elongated and began to obscure the landscape below. Islands of dark cloud reached down from above. What had been a kernel of doubt now blossomed into a jagged chunk of fear as I observed the fast-moving darkness close in.

Trapped.

I took a deep breath and willed calm into my growing panic. I pushed the control stick forward, descending to 500 feet, trying to find a channel of visibility.

The sun materialized slowly in the east, a multicolor aura circling a bright yellow core. Fingers of peach-colored light reached out and touched the shiny white wings of the Pulsar.

What should I do?

The ground haze continued to grow, moving in patches, as the upper masses of cloud stood their ground. Technically I was still VFR (Visual Flight Rules), having the ground in sight, one mile of visibility, and clear of clouds. Barely. I took in another gulping breath, feeling the sharp edges of failure.

In flight training they tell you that multiple small mistakes in judgment add up until you have a serious set of problems. In training I always vowed to not get myself into a dangerous situation.

Climb.

I pointed the nose of the little airplane up into a narrow channel of clear sky and applied power. I leveled off at 1,000 feet. I could no longer see the ground, except for holes scattered in the clouds. The silver sheen of the swamp pools reached up to my airplane in dancing beams, as if to draw me down and in.

Disappointment joined the knot of fear. The day I've dreamt about my whole life.

What am I going to do?

I banked my little craft to the right, changing course 180 degrees, heading back the way I had come, threading my way down through the gaps in the dark twisting cloud banks as rain began to splatter loudly on the canopy.

I'd just return to Lantana and wait for the weather to clear.

As my breathing began to steady the sun burst out onto the landscape to my right, illuminating steaming mists rolling off the mosses and silver pools of the wetlands. The rain stopped as quickly as it had begun. The brightness re-colored the cloudbanks above in pastel tones as they evaporated before my eyes.

It's going to be ok.

As I came out of the cloudbank and into clearer weather, my mood lightened. I will call Palm Beach and transition over to the coastline. My plan to fly over the Loxahatchee Preserve so early in the morning was a mistake. I was avoiding Palm Beach's Class C airspace. I needed to get over my radio fright.

I gulped in air and then exhaled deeply. Looking at my flight plan, I verified I had the right frequencies in the radios. I keyed the mike.

"Palm Beach Approach, this is Pulsar Experimental November Four Five Six Lima Tango, VFR four miles to the south eastbound at one thousand en route to Daytona, would like to transition your airspace to the northeast."

"Pulsar Six Lima Tango squawk three four zero two."

"Squawk three four zero two, Pulsar Six Lima Tango."

I entered the squawk code into my transponder and waited.

"We have you Six Lima Tango. Follow heading four five at one thousand and report coastline."

I followed the instructions and soon I was back out over the ocean coastline northbound on my solitary way.

That wasn't so bad.

"Every day is an adventure. "

~ Joseph B. Wirthlin

42

NORTH CAROLINA

I LEANED BACK IN THE SEAT and began breathing normally. I hadn't realized that I'd been hunched forward and breathing in little spurts as I extricated myself from the swamp. I let out a loud sigh of relief and loosened my grip on the stick. With the sun coming up full force, I turned off the cockpit heat. Not seeing any abnormalities on the instruments, I took a good look outside the airplane.

The Florida coastline was visible below off my left side as a narrow strip of beige-colored sand dotted with dunes. Hobe Sound mansions stood prominently behind the dune line. Looking north I could see the tiny strip of land with the A1A highway and the Sebastian inlet; farther to the north lay Cape Canaveral. I would have to thread myself carefully between Orlando airspace and Titusville airspace; there was a lot of flight traffic in this area, and I would have to keep a sharp lookout on my way to my first stop, St. Simons's Island.

There was a VFR corridor I'd take at 7,500 feet. I had about 10 more minutes of beach sightseeing before I'd begin my climb. I began to relax a bit more, but my senses were finely tuned.

I took a moment to review the flight plan and sectional chart. Although the Garmin 250XL navcomm had a GPS moving map, I wanted to check that against landmarks to get confidence in its accuracy. I reflected on the advances made in avionics in the last few years. The performance I had in my IFR-rated panel was advanced compared to what I had trained in.

In addition to the traditional altimeter, attitude, airspeed, turn and bank, directional gyro (DG), compass, hour meter, vertical speed indicator, and tachometer, the panel had a G-meter (accelerometer), an engine analyzer (temperatures, pressures, and flow rates), fuel levels, voltmeter, ammeter, transponder, backup radios, clock, VOR/Glideslope, and audio panel. I'd also installed a remote control for the stereo radio behind the seats. I marveled at all the information available right here in front of me.

Time to climb. I added power and left the coastline, turning left. At 800 feet per minute I was at 7,500 feet in less than 10 minutes.

350 miles and 2.5 hours later I arrived at St. Simon's Island, my first stop. Forest-covered islands dotted the Atlantic Ocean. I made my calls for the small non-towered airport and turned to final. At nearly 5,500 feet long and 150 feet wide, Runway 34 surprised me with its size. Finding myself going fast, I eased the stick back slightly, and the Pulsar slowed to 65 over the numbers. In 100 feet the mains contacted the pavement firmly and I held the nose off before braking.

For the first time on the trip I experienced a flush of confidence. First trip leg complete and I didn't screw up the landing! The feeling was welcome but temporary as I realized this was a fraction of the trip.

I made the first turnoff and taxied up to a modern FBO. A linesman directed me to a parking spot on the ramp. I let the engine idle for a moment and then turned off the ignition.

I was full of excitement as I slid out of the cockpit and jumped to the ground. The fuel truck pulled up, and I watched the fuel hose nozzle quickly filling each of my 10-gallon tanks as onlookers gathered.

"Be careful on the fill. I expect they will only take six gallons each," I said to the young man wielding the fuel hose.

"Yep, no problem," the lineman said as we watched the tank overflow. "Oops!" He was aghast at his mistake and quickly placed the hose aside and got his water and soap bucket out.

"Sorry!" he exclaimed, cleaning the blue 100LL fuel from the wing.

"It's not like filling a Cessna." I reached for a cotton towel behind the seats and finished cleaning the wing. Then I reached into the baggage compartment for a small plastic dispenser of fuel additive.

To counteract the high lead content of the 100LL aviation fuel standard at airports, I carried small 1-oz bottles of TCP (TriCresyl Phosphate) that I added to the fuel at each fill-up. This chemical scavenged the lead from the 100LL. Although the LL stands for "low lead," it is anything but. The Rotax engine was designed to run on automotive fuel, but it was hard to find auto gas at airports. Running the Rotax engine on a steady diet of aviation fuel without the additive would shorten the time between overhauls. I added a half-ounce to each tank and returned the dispenser to the plastic bucket in the baggage compartment.

"What kind of airplane is this?" the fueler asked.

"A Pulsar XP, it's experimental."

"Experimental? What does that mean?"

"It means you build it yourself."

"You built this?"

"Yes."

"You're kidding."

"No, really."

The lineman didn't look like he believed me. I was used to that.

By now six people had gathered around the Pulsar and asked questions while I did an inspection. After I removed the engine cowling, the onlookers commented on the small engine and then the cockpit.

"Can you really fit two people in there?"

"Yes."

"Why don't you have someone with you?"

"I'm on a solo cross country."

"Did you really come all the way from West Palm Beach just today?"

"Yes."

"How many cylinders?"

"Four."

"Only four?"

"Yes."

I found myself not minding all the questions. In fact, I was enjoying the interest in the airplane.

I went into the FBO to wash up and check weather. I was pleased to see a clear forecast on my route to my next stop, Lumberton, North Carolina. I reviewed my flight plan and recorded the fuel in the log. Twelve gallons – 4.8 gallons per hour at 140 mph. That exactly matched my engine analyzer fuel flow, giving me a better predictor of fuel burn than the analog fuel pickups. I was pleased.

I said goodbye to the friendly FBO folks, and I was on my way. I took off to the northeast and added power for a climb. As I fed in the throttle, the aircraft surged forward with surprising energy. I still hadn't gotten used to the powerful acceleration.

I felt my breathing become deeper as I climbed through 8,000 feet. I had never gone this high before as a pilot, much less in something I'd built in my garage. A tinge of apprehension followed my ascent, reminding me of the first time I had gone wreck diving. I remember having a surge of anxiety passing the 85-foot-deep mark as we explored the Mercedes shipwreck, a 200-foot freighter off Fort Lauderdale Beach. Looking up, the barnacle-encrusted ship loomed as a massive black hulk above me. A healthy amount of fear was mixed in with the adrenaline and excitement.

At 9,500 feet I leveled off and trimmed the airplane for level flight at 4,200 rpm. The radio was eerily quiet. As the engine settled into a steady beat, I scanned the panel. Oil temperature within range; cylinder head temperatures and coolant in range; no alarms.

Warm air flowed through the side vents, and the air had a clean smell to it. There wasn't a cloud or other airplane anywhere in sight. The bright blue sky appeared boundless as I looked through the clear canopy bubble, across the engine cowling and past the prop turning so fast it was invisible.

The nervous energy of the morning drained, leaving me limp. With a deep breath all the way into my lower ribcage, I pushed back against the seat and stretched my legs out under the panel. I exhaled.

Straight and level at 9,500 feet, hands off.

The tension fell away tangibly, like a wind blowing cobwebs from my face and hair. The sun's bright rays penetrated the cockpit with unwavering warmth and danced on the white wings of the craft. I closed my eyes for a moment and reopened them.

I looked down at the tiny patchwork quilt of fields, roads, and rural towns. A spring bouquet of color stretched out below, shimmering in the anticipation of summer. Beyond a stratum populated by butterflies and the machinations of men, I had entered another dimension of the Universe. I felt the thrill of awe in its breadth and splendor as my field of vision took in the vast horizon. I felt the magic between earthbound beings and the sky.

You can't explain it in words.

I allowed the moment to linger. Happiness filled my consciousness and took up permanent space in a corner as I bathed in the delight of flight.

Just like the dream. Only better.

*"More than anything else the sensation is one of
perfect peace mingled with an excitement that strains
every nerve to the utmost, if you can conceive
of such a combination."*

~ Wilbur Wright

43

FBO FRIENDS

NOW I UNDERSTAND.
It was as if my mind had gone blank, freed of the concerns
and baggage of ground living, and was now a reflective showcase
for a sleek and agile machine, smooth running. An engine purring,
a propeller turning, a warm sun cradling the day amidst light blue
breezes in a grand vista continuing to spread out in detail before
my eyes. I shook my head and closed my eyes, reopening them to
see if I was dreaming.

*Is this real? You're almost 10,000 feet in the air in a collection of
mechanical and electrical parts that you assembled in your garage.*

A sliver of fear stabbed at my reverie, catching me by
surprise.

Anything could go wrong.

As the interlude lingered, my logical mind interceded. I reached
for my flight plan. Why was the radio silent? Had it stopped

working? I thumbed the mike. "Flight Service, Pulsar Experimental Four Five Six Lima Tango with a Pirep."

"Flight Service, Pulsar Six Lima Tango, go ahead with your pilot report."

"Flight Service, Pulsar Six Lima Tango nine miles south of Florence Regional, nine thousand five hundred feet, reporting clear and smooth."

"Six Lima Tango, we don't usually get those kinds of reports; we like good news, have a great day."

Ok good. The radio is working.

My stomach began to complain. I hadn't even thought of food all morning in the continuing excitement, but now the thought of it made my mouth water. I reached into the passenger foot well and popped the top off the cooler, removing a tuna sandwich in a zip-lock bag and a bottle of water.

I spread a few paper towels out on my lap and laid out the sandwich, a granola bar, and my drink in front of me.

"Can't do this in a car," I said to myself out loud. I smiled. I did notice that the airplane left its flight track – both altitude and path – when I reached behind the seats, or into the foot well. The airplane was so small that minor weight shifts made a difference.

I should have installed an autopilot.

I adjusted the flight track and then dug into the sandwich. It tasted extraordinarily good as I looked out on the panoramic scenery of towns, roads, and fields stretching for miles below me. Once again, the ecstatic excitement of riding in the sky in a relatively tiny conveyance rang its note.

I finished my lunch and looked at the sectional chart and the GPS. The trip was going fast with a nice tailwind. The flight from Brunswick to Lumberton was less than two hours.

I landed at the small, uncontrolled airport at noon with almost no traffic. The experience was similar to Brunswick – the fueler was in front of my airplane immediately, and at least five onlookers gathered around to ask questions.

"It's just you?"

"Yes."

"What kind of airplane is this?"

"A Pulsar XP, experimental."

"Where did you buy it?"

"I built it."

"Yeah, right. Of course you did," said a sandy-haired man in his 50s, laughing.

It didn't bother me at all anymore. The only thing that mattered was that I was flying it.

"Are you married?"

"No."

"That's good; your husband wouldn't let you make a trip like this by yourself."

"Well then, I'm lucky to be single, right?" I said, smiling.

The sandy-haired man looked at me curiously, frowning. "Hmm," he said, flummoxed.

A visit to the FBO, a careful preflight, and I was on my way. The sun was high in the sky and the air was warm. The musky smell of freshly plowed fields floated through the vents as I climbed out of the pattern. I climbed to 7,500 feet and leveled off. My time to

Frederick would be under three hours, and I planned to stay there with a friend if the weather didn't hold or if I was delayed. But the weather continued to be glorious, and I hoped that I'd be able to reach western New York by 7 pm.

To get into Frederick, I'd need to follow a narrow VFR channel around Washington, D.C., with the Blue Ridge Mountains to my left and Washington to my right. Air traffic would be heavy. Although I'd done detailed flight planning, I grew apprehensive at the thought of threading my little airplane through the corridor. I would need to keep a sharp look outside for traffic, as well as monitor my position between mountains and Washington D.C. airspace.

As I approached Washington, I began to hear a lot of radio reports and chatter. I began an intense scan for other airplanes outside, and inside at my navigation units and the GPS moving map as my nervousness rose.

I probably had too much electronics in the panel, but I loved it. Not just for redundancy, but because I imagined that this would be what Tom Swift would have in his airplane. For a moment I remembered a Honda Accord I had bought in 1975. The Japanese being typically minimalist when it came to instrument panel gauges and other accouterments, I decided to scour the JC Whitney automotive catalog for every instrument I could think of to mount in the small car. I installed an overhead panel and a center console panel. I installed switches that lit up and did nothing so that my niece and nephews could flip them on and off. My sister's kids thought this was a blast. We'd be at a light and I'd say, "Ok, get ready for takeoff. Hit switch 2." The child in the passenger seat would flip switch 2 up and the light would come on. It was endless fun.

I respected my brother's opinions as they related to car and gadget matters. He sat in the car one day and looked at everything.

His comment was, "Intergalactic." Then he shook his head. I could tell that he thought it was silly, but he was kind enough to play along.

The radio crackled with a pilot position report. I snapped back to my scans. I looked at the VFR flyways mapped on the GPS. The backup Garmin Pilot III mounted above the Garmin 250XL showed the Beltway around the capital and the rivers and lakes, while the 250XL showed the larger picture of ATC airspace in monochrome yellow. Along with the sectional charts and my flight plan log, I would have a lot of explaining to do if I wandered into the wrong airspace or flew into a mountain.

As the Appalachian foothills appeared on my left, I concentrated on sighting and listening for traffic. I thought I'd actually see other aircraft, given the remarkable visibility, but I heard, rather than saw, the other airplanes.

Before leaving on the trip I had tried to imagine the sight picture coming into each airport in my mind. Frederick was one I couldn't figure out. I would be coming through rolling hills, and I couldn't imagine the flight path. Depending on the wind direction I could be landing on a 3,600-foot runway or a 5,300-foot runway.

I made my approach calls. The Unicom was reporting Runway 30 with light northwest winds.

As I made my calls and entered downwind, I noted the apparent shortness of Runway 30 and the fact that there was a large hill on final approach. I knew about this hill from the chart, but seeing it on a chart and seeing it in front of me were two different things.

As I made my base turn the ground loomed up at me, and the Pulsar appeared to lose altitude. A bead of sweat ran down my neck, and my grip tightened on the stick. The sight picture was all-wrong. I was going to fly into the ground. In panic, I added power and removed flaps. The Pulsar leapt forward, climbing.

"Frederick Traffic, Pulsar Experimental Four Five Six Lima Tango on base for three-zero and going around."

Should I just break off and go calm down? I thought. I decided against it because of the traffic density surrounding Frederick. Now was my chance. I had to get it right.

I turned crosswind and then downwind, taking a very careful look at the hill that had surprised me.

That's not a hill. That's a mountain.

I turned to base.

Concentrate on your instruments.

This time I ignored the feeling that the hill was going to reach up and smash me to bits. I could make out the minute detail of the trees and paths on the ground. I could feel my heart racing as put in the rest of the flaps.

Watch your speed.

Still too high and too fast.

Sideslip.

I put in left rudder and right aileron, keeping my track on the runway. Good, let the speed bleed off. I crossed the runway threshold at 70 mph and straightened out the airplane. Hold it off, hold it off, pretend you're flying five inches above the ground . . .

The mains met the ground smoothly, and I held the nose off until it came down on its own. I braked and made the first turnoff. Heat from the summer day simmered inside the little cockpit as I unlatched the canopy and slid it forward.

A line boy greeted me at the FBO and directed me to a tie down. I let the engine idle a moment as I always did and then turned the ignition off. I took a deep breath in relief, leaning back against the seat and rested a moment before unbuckling the harness and getting out of the cockpit.

I have a lot to learn.

"The Heavenly Spheres make music for us, The Holy Twelve dance with us, All things join in the dance! Ye who dance not, know not what we are knowing."

~ Gustav Holst

44

REAL MOUNTAINS

"HEY," SAID THE LINE BOY. "This is nice. What is it?" He looked the Pulsar over from front to back. "And nice landing."

"Thanks. I bet you say that to all the pilots." I hopped to the ground and stretched. I felt a little stiff.

"Yeah. I get bigger tips that way. Fuel?"

"Yes, please. But be careful, each tank will only take 6.2 gallons."

"That sounds super accurate, what do you have a flow meter or something?"

"Yes. It appears to be about 99 percent accurate."

"Maybe you will be one of the pilots who doesn't run out of fuel." I looked at the line boy quizzically.

"In this area it seems like twice a week you hear about someone having an emergency landing because they ran out of fuel."

"I'll try not to be one of those."

I looked at my watch. 4:30 pm. I opened my cell phone and dialed.

"This is Dick."

"Dick, it's Lese. I'm at Frederick. I'm going to press on and catch you on the return in 10 days. Is that ok?"

"So glad your trip's going well Lese," said Dick. "Would love to see you on the return."

Then I called Larry in Hornell, New York.

"I can't believe you're in Frederick. What time did you leave this morning?"

"Seven." I didn't mention spending from 6 am to 7 am almost alligator petting in a swamp.

"I can't believe it."

"I'll see you around 6:45 p.m."

"Really? Tonight? Are you sure?"

After all these years I still got a big thrill talking to Larry. I'd gotten to know his family and visited them every chance I got. My crush had never ended. The sound of his voice still sent an adrenaline rush through my veins as I thought about completing this leg of my trip, returning to my home and my friends. I felt completely overwhelmed for a moment.

"I'm sure," I replied.

"Ok, we'll be at the airport waiting for you. I can't believe it."

"I can't believe it either."

"Please be safe, Lee. Bye bye," said Larry.

"I will. Bye."

After a trip into the FBO with its attendant curious questions about the Pulsar, I checked flight service for weather and did a thorough preflight. I checked my log and noted that I'd spent $70 for 970 miles of flight.

I handed the line boy a five-dollar bill. "Thanks for the landing compliment."

"Oh, no, you don't have to do that. I was kidding."

"I know. Keep it."

"Hey, my name is Marty if you come back."

The runway in use had changed to 5, and a Learjet, a Cessna 210, and a King Air were in line.

Wow, this is new. Traffic.

I did my run-up and got in line. As I looked into the cockpit of the Learjet ahead of me, the copilot was smiling and pointing me out to the pilot. I smiled. He nodded and made a thumbs up gesture.

My nerves returned, realizing I was entering a sky full of other airplanes. Every bit of my attention needed to be on following procedures, spacing, making radio calls, and watching the sky like my life depended on it. Because it did.

My nervousness moderated as I left Frederick and started my climb to 7,500 feet, flying away from the very busy corridor. On a heading of 05 degrees, this portion of the trip would take me over the Appalachian mountain chain and Cumberland Valley in Pennsylvania, and then to the Allegheny Plateau stretching into western New York. Rising to 3,700 feet in spots, crossing mountains would be another new experience for me.

I reached my cruising altitude and leveled off. The hills and valleys of Maryland gave way to the foothills of the Blue Ridge Mountains. A watercolor vista below me shone in deep blues and bright greens mixed with rose and yellow pastels. On the horizon orange and cream layers mixed with the platinum and cobalt-colored hilltops, foretelling a stunning sunset to come.

You can't see this from the ground.

The stunning landscape brought my flying dreams flooding into my consciousness. Tension drained from my body and I was free and floating like a bird on the gentle airwaves, drinking in an infinite panorama of texture and color as the engine purred in reassurance. The air through the vents was crisp.

As I left the foothills and entered the mountain chain signs of civilization started to vanish. The mountains looked more like hills from the air, rounded off on the tops and fully forested, bright green with new spring growth. Looking out the front of the canopy, the mountains presented themselves as a vast expanse of green and brown in gigantic, glacier carved furrows.

I planned on 50 minutes to traverse the range and re-enter population centers. When flying, all pilots think about emergency landings. If I have a system failure, or an engine out, where will I go? Practice is critical, because a failure may induce panic, which will reduce a pilot's ability to think through a checklist, and land safely.

As I looked out at the rolling mountain scenery, I realized I wouldn't have a lot of options if I had an emergency. But I would do the best I could, including setting up a glide of 70 mph and going through my checklist. Then I would make emergency calls and set up for a landing on a hilltop ridge. A shiver of apprehension went through me thinking about it.

I pulled up the frequency for Allentown, PA on one of the radios just in case I had a problem. I listened to the engine's steady music as the radios maintained their silence. Of course, anything could go wrong – there was so much that had to be right to keep an engine going – but the reliability of this four-stroke was its hallmark.

I took a swig of water and tore open another granola bar. I hadn't gotten used to the apparent desolation of where I was – from an unbounded sky devoid of any living thing to forests rolling by below with no sign of human life anywhere. But with the growing confidence in my little airplane the tension was just under the surface as I continued to feel exhilarated by the flight.

I'd envisioned myself turning on the stereo just as you do in a car when you're on a trip. But I now realized that it would be distracting. A little like going to an IMAX theater and deciding to read a book. I had all the entertainment I needed right here, right now. The time passed quickly.

A measure of relief flooded my thoughts as I looked at the GPS and the chart, realizing I was less than 15 minutes from Hornell. As I descended, small towns and roads became more prominent and I realized I would fly over the family farmhouse. A sentimental happiness filled me a few minutes later as I spotted the house. I looked down at the barn and the long winding road from the air.

Several minutes later I rounded a hill to the west and there was the airport. A single 5000-foot runway in a meadow surrounded by oak, birch trees, and fields of flowers. It was an inviting and comforting sight.

6:42 pm. Perfect. I overflew the runway, looking at the windsock. It was limp. I set up for a landing on 36. There was no traffic anywhere, on the airport or the small road leading to it. I saw five people on the ramp at the FBO, a tiny building next to a row of T-hangars. The Shinebargers had arrived.

I was back in the dream I'd had over and over again – coming home to friends and family in my own airplane. I tried to calm myself as I set up on final, but I could feel the inevitable surge of excitement. I took a deep breath and landed smoothly on the well-maintained runway, bleeding off speed and turning off a third of the way down the long strip.

As I taxied up to the FBO, I saw big grins on the faces of my friends, but none was bigger than the one I had on my face. The smells of sweet spring vegetation cooling from the summer day and the hillside hayfields entered the cockpit as I unbuckled and slid the canopy forward, turning off the ignition.

"Wow, look at that, Lee!" Debs pointed to my left as I jumped to the ground. As my friends came over to greet me, I glanced at the sky. Bright beams of light from invisible prisms splayed in bright blues, pinks, and yellows across the fields, touching the wildflower blossoms in pinpoints of luminescence.

"You should have seen it from the air." I said.

"Wow, I can't believe you're here!" said Debs, giving me a bear hug. Her two small children were enthralled with the little airplane and were speechless.

Larry was shaking his head, grinning, his eyes sparkling in astonishment. "I can't believe it, Lee, I can't believe it."

"Believe it," said Betty. "You can believe it. Look at that airplane!"

"The guy in the FBO left at 6 pm. He said you can put the airplane next to his John Deere tractor in the first building here," Larry said, pointing to the open hangar next to the tiny one-room building. "But the day after tomorrow when you leave at 6 am, you'll have to tie it up outside, because he won't be here to open up for you."

"What do I owe for the overnights?" I asked.

"Nothing. He said, 'Welcome home, Lisa.'"

I led the airplane into the hangar. I soaked one of my towels with clear water and cleaned all the bugs off the leading edges and canopy as my friends walked around the craft.

"Can the kids get in it?" asked Debs.

"Sure. We'll get their picture."

Larry kept shaking his head. "I can't believe it."

My hands were trembling in excitement and amazement at completing the first day of my journey.

"Will you take me flying tomorrow?" asked Debs.

"Absolutely."

"Dad, Mom, you can go after me."

"No, that's ok, you go."

"Let's go home. There's a cold drink waiting in the refrigerator for you," said Betty.

I got my backpack and cooler out of the airplane and kissed the tip of the spinner cone on the way out.

"There is only one corner of the universe you can be certain of improving, and that's your own self."

~ Aldous Huxley

45

BUZZ THE HOUSE

I AWOKE OUT OF A sound and deep sleep populated with colorful horizons and fields of flowers. Muted rays of sunshine danced through the sheer white curtains in the double casement window in my room. For a moment I didn't know where I was.

I sat up in amazement as I realized I'd completed the first leg of my trip. I was in Hornell, New York. And another beautiful day.

"Lee, I can't believe you're here in your own airplane," said Debs as she pushed her long blonde hair back and flipped it over her shoulder at the breakfast table.

"I can't either, pinch me," I said as I held my arm out.

"Your family must be very proud," said Betty.

"Some of them are."

"Well, we certainly are," said Larry, flashing his signature enigmatic smile. "Who's not excited about it?"

I still got the trip-down-the-stairs feeling when Larry spoke in his measured, Socratic way. I got the impression that he knew a lot more than he was indicating, and delighted in leading me, and others, down a path to a kernel of truth.

I was caught off guard. "It's not a matter of excitement; more one of risk taking."

"You're not answering my question."

"My sister and my dad are a little concerned."

"I can understand that, Lee, there's a part of us here, as your surrogate family, that is concerned," said Debs. "But that doesn't mean we're going to tell you not to take the risk. I think together we all trust your decision-making capability." Debs made a broad sweep of her hand at Betty and Larry.

"There's more to it, isn't there." Larry looked straight at me. How did he bring out the deepest of emotions?

"It's hard to know if I've progressed from the wild child to an adult with good judgment," I said.

"Ha!" Larry let out a deep laugh. "Hard for who to know? You just turned 47."

"Larry." Betty shook head. "Let Lee go on."

"I'm not trying to be critical," Larry said, "I'm just pointing out that at 47 you don't need to be concerned about what other people think." Larry's eyes were radiant as his expression got serious. "Listen to others and take what they say into account, but don't let it upset your emotional equilibrium."

Debs smiled and flipped her hair back. "Dad gets right to the heart of things, doesn't he."

"But I do care," I said as I played with the edge of the tablecloth and sighed. There was complete silence for a moment as I collected my thoughts. "I've always been concerned about what people think. Mom asked me to straighten out, and I've been trying ever since."

Larry cleared his throat. "But you did straighten out. You've gone overboard. Your Mom asked you to do well in school; you responded by never stopping school, getting your English, your engineering, your masters, your doctorate. You keep pursuing accomplishments. Lee, you don't need to impress people, you need to be happy inside yourself. Don't worry about your mom, your sister, your dad, or anyone else judging you. Because no matter what you end up doing, there will be someone out there who thinks what you're doing is a bad idea, and be critical."

I took a deep breath and picked up my coffee cup. Rays of warm sunlight floated through the window. I took a long sip and set the cup down. My friends were looking at me, allowing me to think and respond.

"How do you not care?" I said, looking at Larry. "It's good advice but how?"

"You've been trying to prove that you're 'ok' over and over. You are already ok. When you're constantly seeking approval, your happiness is dependent upon other people. Set your compass and go."

"That still doesn't tell me how," I replied.

"I understand. If it was easy, everyone would be enlightened. So many people look for happiness, but forget that life is made up of contrasts. Happiness is accepting all the ups and downs, not just the ups."

"That's Larry for you, the deep philosopher," said Betty.

"I didn't mean to get so deep, but I felt I hit a nerve, right Lee?"

"You did, you are. I associate achievement with approval, and now you say approval is bad, so where are we?"

Larry always did this. He took me from wading on the surf next to the beach all the way out to the depths with sharks, leaving me wondering if I'd be able to get back, swimming against the current.

"Dad, let up," Debs said. "We're going flying!"

I smiled. "Yes, we're going flying."

Larry came around from the other side of the table and put his hand on my shoulder. He looked at me intently. There was a hummingbird in my chest, its delicate wings beating.

"You're a pilot. You decide where you're going. Share your emotions with your family. Accept where you are. Accept that not everyone is going to give you approval. You already have that approval – from your mom, and from the others who love you, from us."

I closed my eyes as tears spilled out.

"Jeez, he always does that. Sorry Lee!" Debs handed me a tissue.

"You can imagine with a dad like that, I got all kinds of advice when I was growing up, and most of it I didn't have a clue what he was talking about," said Debs as we pulled up next to the hangar.

"He wouldn't spend the time if he didn't care deeply."

"You're right," said Debs.

"You know I had a hell of a crush on your dad when he was my English teacher."

"I know. We could tell."

"I hope that was ok."

"Sure it was ok. You were 13. You're part of the family, Lee."

"I'm going to start crying again."

Debs laughed. "Can we fly over our old lake house?"

"Sure."

As the Pulsar came into sight next to the tractor, I felt a flood of happiness and anticipation. "I think you're going to love this, Debs. I guess Larry and Betty don't like small airplanes?"

"No, they don't like ANY airplanes," said Debs.

"Too bad the kids had to go back so soon."

"That's ok, they are pretty tiny, they wouldn't even be able to see out."

It was another brilliant spring day, color and texture bursting from the fields and surrounding forests as we left the pattern and headed east.

"Incredible!" Debs exclaimed, "I can't believe the visibility and the power."

I nodded, looking down at the roads to figure out where the house in Hornell was.

"Buzz Mom and Dad!" Debs exclaimed.

"Ok," I said, knowing that for me, especially with a passenger, a 'buzz' would be a shallow circle at 700 feet and not a wild set of antics that would take us near obstacles.

Debs had her camera out, and we both delighted in flying over the things we'd never seen from the air before. After rocking wings to her parents in the backyard we flew over the Shinebarger's lake house and spent an hour sightseeing.

Returning to the airport, I was surprised to not see any other traffic. "On a day like this I can't believe there aren't a lot of pleasure flights."

"There never is. Beats me."

We landed smoothly and taxied back to the hangar.

"You'll need to leave the airplane outside here next to the FBO if you're leaving early," said the airport manager as he finished topping the tanks.

"No problem, Tim. I have a tarp for it."

"It's going to be cold."

"How cold?"

"Ah, 'bout 15 degrees."

"Whoa. That's cold for May."

"Not in western New York it's not. Might snow."

"We'll see what happens in the morning."

With Debs' help I placed the blue tarp over the Pulsar with bungees, and we drove back to the house.

"What an exquisite day," said Debs to Larry and Betty as we walked in. "I got plenty of pictures, and Lee's airplane is incredible. Never have had such a bird's-eye view, ever."

"Lee, I hope I didn't upset you this morning. I didn't mean to," remarked Larry.

"No, no, actually I feel better after your fault-finding therapy." I walked over to Larry as he was shaking his head and about to say something else, and gave him a big hug. "That's how you are, always trying to fix us with a Zen kind of question game."

"You can see how far he got with me," said Debs, screwing up her face and flailing her arms.

We all laughed.

"Flying is learning how to throw yourself at the ground and miss."

~ Douglas Adams

46

NEW YORK TO MAINE

I AWOKE TO A PIERCING ALARM in the dark. Instantly I knew where I was. If all went well, today would be the day I arrived in Northeast Harbor, Maine. I figured on four hours to make the 445-mile trip, with a stop in Massachusetts for fueling.

I hopped out of bed, pulse quickening. I looked out the window to see a dusting of snow on the green ground. The room was cold, and I shivered as I went down the hall to the bath.

Debs had agreed to get up at this early hour and drive me to the airport so I could get off to an early start. But seeing how cold it was, I wondered if it was such a good idea.

I brewed a pot of coffee and poured out some cereal. Debs and I sat at the breakfast nook and sipped our coffee, steam pouring off the tops of the cups.

"Yeah, it's a little chilly. You can fly in this?" Debs pointed to the thermometer mounted outside reading 18 degrees.

"Sure, I think, well, I don't know – if the airplane starts and there isn't ice on the runway, I should be fine."

"You're brave."

"No, not really. I just have never flown in the cold before. I will need to stay at a lower altitude to make sure I don't pick up any icing on the wings."

"What would that do, Lee?"

"It would make the airplane heavy and it would remove the airfoil characteristics that make it fly. I'd fall out of the sky like a rock."

Debs screwed up her face and then threw her long hair over her shoulder. "Why don't you stay here another day?"

"I doubt it will be much warmer tomorrow. And I really want to get to Maine."

"Right, your family is all there, isn't that great, a dream come true, right?"

"I've looked forward to this day for a long time."

"An adventure, Lee!"

"I hope it's sort of a boring trip without any real adventure, if you know what I mean," I replied.

I grabbed my bags, and we got in the car. I had checked weather the night before. It would be less than two hours to Orange, Massachusetts, where I'd refuel and check the weather again. The high was continuing to hold, and I knew how fortunate I was to be able to fly in such clear, calm conditions.

I realized this would be a test of the battery when I turned the ignition key. I also wondered if I had covered enough of the oil cooler. On the Pulsar XP, the cooler was on the large side and had to be partially taped off to achieve the necessary temperatures to boil off any moisture in the system.

I'll find out.

As we rounded the corner to the airport, I strained to pick out the Pulsar. The first time sitting outside, I was concerned that something might have happened to it. I felt as if the airplane was a live companion, my bond with it had become so strong.

We came up to the small FBO shack and there it was, undisturbed. The blue tarp was covered in a layer of frost. Debs helped me knock the rime off the top portion, and we lifted the whole frozen thing off the airplane and on to the tarmac.

"Jeez, this is freezing! My hands are going numb," I remarked as I rubbed my ungloved hands together.

"May in New York for ya!"

"Yup, I remember. Unpredictable."

"Lee, I don't see how we are going to get this tarp folded."

"I think it's just a thin layer." I worked off most of the coating, and finally we were able to fold it. Wet and stiff, it would not reduce much in size. I toweled off what I could and placed it, still crackling, behind the seats.

"Here, take these." Debs had retrieved a pair of gloves from the car. "You can bring them back next time you're here."

"Thank you! My fingers are about to fall off, and I still have the preflight to do."

Fifteen minutes later we both paused to watch the sun break out above the horizon.

"Ok, gotta go. I'll call when I get to Maine."

Debs gave me a big hug. "Take care. Love you."

"Love you, Debs. Don't drive off until I see if the engine will turn over."

I was chilled to the bone as I clambered into the cockpit. I felt some tension as I wondered if the airplane would start. I'd had my share of troubles with batteries in the cold.

I turned on the master switch and welcomed the hum and low whine of the gyros coming up to speed. I looked across the hills and saw the rays of the fast-rising sun splay across the fields and treeline onto the runway. The ice in the grass turned into dancing diamonds, sparkling and glinting across the large field.

Ok, here we go.

I pulled out the choke and turned the key, hoping. The starter turned briskly and the engine sprang to life. I breathed a sigh of relief. There were so many unknowns on this trip – threading the delicate balance between exhilaration and worry. I let the engine temperatures come up and slowly pushed the choke in. I scanned the instruments and read through my checklist. I reached over and pulled on the heat knob. Surprisingly warm air came flooding into the foot well, and I shivered again involuntarily as I realized how cold I was. The warmth removed the last bit of tension I'd had wondering how everything would work in this freezing air.

This clear and cold morning was one of the most beautiful I had ever seen. Visibility appeared without limit, there wasn't a cloud in the pale morning sky, the windsock hung flat. The rising sun began to melt the white frost, which continued to sparkle in rainbow colors under the growing brilliance of the day. With the entire airport and surrounding hills devoid of planes or people, I waved to Debs and latched the canopy. Everything looked fine on the run-up, and I lined up on the mile-and-a-half-long runway. In 400 feet I was in the air and waving goodbye again to Debs.

My flight plan called for a cruising altitude of 9,500 feet, more than enough to carry me over the tallest terrain on my route to Maine – the Catskill Mountains at 4,200 feet. As the airplane climbed with ease in the chilled air, I reached over and pushed the cabin heat back in half way. A tingling feeling had come back into my cold fingers. I thought about carburetor heat. The Pulsar did not have a carb heat control, as it was deemed unnecessary with the engine configuration. Both self-compensating Bing carbs were located at the top rear of the engine where heat was plentiful, even with icy outside air. Or so I hoped. The temperature gauge inside the cockpit indicated an ambient engine compartment temperature of 85 degrees F; outside air at 2, and cockpit air at 68. Oil temps were sitting at 182 - low, but nothing to worry about. As long as I could periodically get the oil up to 212 degrees for short stretches to boil off condensation, it would be ok. I made a mental note to cover a little more of the oil cooler.

I reached altitude and leveled off. I decided to kick up the cruise to 5400 rpm. I settled in at 152 mph airspeed, which gave me a 168-mph groundspeed with a following wind. I'd burn more fuel, but with a flight of under two hours I was only using half my tanks. The oil temperature came up, too. Good.

I felt euphoric in the tiny space at almost 10,000 feet, zipping along above ice-filled valleys covered in colorful variegated mist. Above me in a cloudless panorama the sky stretched to a horizon still painted in morning pastels. The radios remained quiet. I realized that I was unable to describe what I was feeling; I could only drink it in, overwhelmed by my awareness.

You only have right now.

Once again I considered what an emergency landing would consist of in this remote and rugged environment. Even a personal parachute or a ballistic parachute in this territory would not guarantee a safe descent. I was ready to glide this sleek airplane to the best possible spot, and, in fact, was more comfortable with this thought than the thought of giving up control to another mechanism.

I was jolted out of my reverie as the radio came to life. I realized that at the speed I was traveling, I needed to change frequencies faster. I picked up my flight plan and entered Albany in the comm.

I was still frightened to talk on the radio, but if I didn't practice, I'd never get comfortable. At least with a noise-canceling headset and a quiet airplane I could hear what they were saying.

My flight plan called for a stop at Orange, Mass, but I was making such good time I decided to fly another 12 minutes and stop in Fitchburg. At 10 miles out I made my position calls. The traffic was light, and I landed without incident.

After taking on less than 12 gallons of fuel, I went into the FBO office for a weather briefing. The forecast was excellent, with one big exception: wind. I wrote down in my flight planner what wind speeds were being recorded at what altitudes. There was no guarantee that I'd be able to avoid turbulence, but having the forecast might help.

Back outside, I noticed the breezes picking up as I did my preflight. I didn't realize at the time just how much they would pick up in the coming hours.

"The engine is the heart of an airplane,
but the pilot is its soul."

~ Walter Raleigh

47

EJECTION SEAT

I LEFT THE AIRPORT to the east, climbing to 7,500 feet. Just outside Boston Class B airspace, I turned north to avoid the busy, high-traffic area. Not that this corridor wasn't busy itself; the radio chatter was non-stop. I'd need to be very attentive.

My visual scans out the panoramic canopy didn't show any other aircraft, but I could hear them. I was thankful that the airplane was equipped with a Class C transponder. This meant that air traffic controllers would be able to see me on their radar screens.

I could also look at my charts and dial in the frequency of ATIS or ASOS (weather) broadcasts from nearby airports as I flew over them. I dialed in the ATIS for Manchester, New Hampshire, to the left of my flight path. The high-pressure area was holding throughout the northeast.

I reflected on how lucky I was to be flying in such ideal weather. In one of the busiest corridors in the United States, I didn't want to think about bad weather adding to the load. I knew that in poor weather I would need to land and stay put until things got better. I was prepared for this possibility, so my jubilance at the wondrously gorgeous day today was especially high.

I had a twinge of nervousness as I thought about landing in Bar Harbor, Maine. I recalled my difficulty in the foothills of Maryland, and decided that if I had any concerns in Bar Harbor, I'd circle the airport until I was comfortable with the approach. So many unknowns. I felt like a nervous rabbit sometimes. I was also hoping my family would be there to greet me, though that thought just increased my nerves.

I hope I don't screw up.

The sound of the engine was soothing in its unwavering harmony, and the readouts from the engine monitor maintained a steady rotation. Although my airspeed was 148 mph, groundspeed was 165 mph. I was being propelled by the winds from the west. With this speed I would have less than an hour to Trenton.

The airport's name is Bar Harbor (BHB) on the chart. But it was actually in Trenton, Maine. The town of Bar Harbor is 20 miles to the southeast by car. If you want someone to pick you up at the airport, make sure they don't drive to Bar Harbor looking for it. For the folks who live in Maine, the airport is often called "Trenton," or "Hancock County."

I looked at my flight plan and decided to call up Portland. Since I wanted to let down to 3,500 feet, I'd need to get permission to traverse their airspace. "Portland Approach, Pulsar Experimental One Four Five Six Lima tango."

"Pulsar Experimental Six Lima Tango, Portland Approach, go ahead."

"Pulsar Experimental Six Lima Tango, 20 miles to the southwest at 7,500 en route to Bar Harbor, VFR, requests transition at 3,500."

"Pulsar Six Lima Tango, squawk 6242 and ident, altimeter two-niner-niner-zero, Portland."

"Pulsar Six Lima Tango squawk 6242 and ident," I repeated, entering the code with a push on the ident button.

"Pulsar Six Lima Tango negative contact, ident," said Approach.

"Pulsar Six Lima Tango, ident."

"Pulsar Six Lima Tango please recycle. Not reading."

I was rattled. What the controller was saying was that I was not showing up on their radar screen. I turned off the transponder, turned it back on, and entered the code again. My hands were trembling. I wondered why it wasn't working. What was I doing wrong?

"Pulsar Six Lima Tango, recycled, squawking 6242," I said again.

"Pulsar Six Lima Tango, your transponder is not working. Maintain current heading and altitude over Portland and get that checked when you arrive at your destination. Maintain VFR, good day."

"Pulsar Six Lima Tango maintaining heading and altitude, VFR, thank you."

Oh great.

A bad transponder. Would I be able to get it fixed in Trenton? I'd have to stay out of controlled airspace on the way home if I couldn't get it fixed on my trip.

Nothing you can do about it now.

Past Portland airspace, I began a slow descent from 7,500 feet. The Maine coastline began to take shape off to the right in an intricate arrangement of speckled islands, harbors, and inlets. Long, thin clouds stretched out on the light blue horizon to the northeast.

The ocean was a medium teal color, turning dark blue as the depths increased, to almost black miles offshore. I saw frothy waves crashing on the rock outcroppings on the jagged coastline. The air through the vents grew noticeably colder, and I closed them down a bit. The smooth ride was turning choppy.

Before I could consider whether to descend further, the airplane took a surprise lurch sideways and down as if an invisible hand had grabbed it, right out of thin air. My body was thrown upward towards the canopy, stopping an inch from the Lexan, straining against the five-point harness holding me in the seat. If the canopy unlatched and departed, I would be in almost fatal trouble. Just as I thought the airplane couldn't fall any faster, another invisible wave hit the craft from below, tossing it skyward. I sank back down into the seat, and grabbed the center harness strap and tightened it. In a panic I reached for the throttle, pulling it out to slow the airplane. Up, up, and up we went as my stomach sank and I bored down into the seat. I was beginning to get vertigo.

As the aircraft slowed, I tried to regain control. Nothing worked to slow the roller coaster ride. I continued to be at the mercy of the violent wind.

The charts and clipboard were lodged above the panel at the front of the canopy and now flew back towards the passenger seat as the aircraft slowed. I ducked as they flew at me and landed in the passenger seat. Another wave of turbulence hit sideways and then down. My seatbelt harness held me again as my body flew up towards the canopy as the airplane tilted to the left in a 60-degree turn.

I saw the ground moving under me, green pine trees, a boiling sea, the islands and inlets in a jumble and tumble of vision as I fought to right the airplane. I was on a wild mouse ride in one of the curves, gravity pulling, pulling, then releasing in the stretch. I scanned the airspeed and altimeter as they jumped about in a blur, showing 95 mph and 3,800 feet.

I haven't crashed yet.

As suddenly as it at appeared, the most violent of the waves stopped. The airplane rocked slightly and then began turning to the right. With stick pressure and rudder I brought the wings to level, and I added power.

Up and down, right and left, I continued to be pushed and bumped. If training is good enough, you do the things you are taught even through a veil of terror. I knew the maneuvering speed in turbulence for this airplane was 110. I saw 110 now on the airspeed indicator. Severe turbulence could do damage at any speed. Structural failure. I thought about that now.

Even though the air through the vents was cold, I was drenched in perspiration. My entire world had contracted to this tiny space around me and the degree to which I could control it and decipher it. It was a ride that refused to show me what kind of curve or dip was coming next.

As I kept the wings level, I descended to 3,500 feet. The ride began to smooth out, the frequency and violence of the bumps becoming more manageable.

All the parts look like they're still attached and working.

I lightened my death grip on the stick and looked around the cockpit. Thank God I had made a practice of strapping in the luggage and the cooler. If not, they would have exited upwards, through the bubble screen, taking the canopy along with them. Without a canopy for protection at any speed I would not have been able to see.

Next time put goggles in the airplane.

I continued to scan every section and component of the airplane that I could see or operate – ailerons, rudder, control stick, trim – nothing was missing, the craft was steady and not pulling in either direction.

Stop worrying and navigate.

I smoothed out the crumpled sectional on my clipboard and reviewed my position. My encounter with turbulence had only lasted a few minutes but felt like my whole life had been encapsulated into that one excursion.

With logic and some measure of confidence returning, I dialed in the nearest ATIS broadcast. Sure enough, winds were increasing by the minute. I looked out on the horizon at striated clouds being driven horizontally from the northwest – winds in the vicinity were 22 to 25 knots and growing in strength.

I was now about 20 minutes from Trenton. I flipped open the StarTAC that had stayed holstered in my belt and autodialed the house in Northeast Harbor.

"Hello."

"Perky?"

"Lese?"

"Twenty minutes."

"We'll be there. How's the trip?"

"Just fine."

"See you soon."

I closed the phone and thought about how amazing it was. I wasn't going to tell my family about the turbulence. I took a deep breath, trying to reassemble my nerves for the next phase – approach and landing.

I studied the sectional and the close-up detail for Bar Harbor that I'd made for the trip. The good news was that my landing would be directly into the 25-knot wind. My Pulsar was capable of landing in crosswinds of up to 15 knots with me as the pilot. Someone more experienced might do better, but I knew my own limitations. Landing straight in with that high a wind would still challenge me, but I had enough runway – 3,300 feet – to take up the slack in speed estimates. And Runway 35 was not used for commercial flights because it was relatively short.

I concentrated on the scan for traffic as I made a gradual descent to 1,500 feet over the coastline. The airplane handled well, the engine kept up its reliable beat, and all engine parameters looked good. I could feel the tension in my body subsiding slightly as I began to feel more in control.

The sweeping view was one of pastel blues streaked with white. Black, jagged cliffs, with a crashing foamy sea, surrounded islands green with heavy forest. Dark blue open water was streaked with wind-whipped furrows aligned with the wind from the northwest. Stunningly beautiful, but dangerous to boats and emergency landings.

"Bar Harbor Traffic, Pulsar Experimental Four Five Six Lima Tango, 10 miles to the south inbound, will enter the pattern on a left downwind for landing 35."

I heard but did not see two other aircraft – a King Air and a Cessna – ahead of me.

The coarse and cold wind continued to buffet the airplane as I worked on getting my bearings straight. I would be flying over water for most of the approach and would need to be wary of the water/land boundary where the plane could lose altitude and throw off slope and speed.

"Bar Harbor Traffic, Pulsar Six Lima Tango is entering the downwind midfield for landing 35, Bar Harbor."

Now I could see the Cessna 172 on a taxiway, and the King Air on final. There wasn't any traffic behind me, so I could take my time and, if need be, abort the landing.

The winds were fierce but steady, pushing me from behind on downwind as I tried to slow the airplane and stay focused on staying stable.

"Bar Harbor Traffic, Pulsar Six Lima Tango turning base for landing 35, Bar Harbor."

I decided not to use any flaps. The wind was pushing me away from the airport and I compensated by crabbing into the wind slightly as I turned to final. I decided to keep 80 mph all the way down. The last thing I wanted was to drop it in.

I turned to final and a 30-knot blast seemed to stop the airplane in its tracks. I added power to slow and smooth out my descent. Right rudder – a little more power - I was at 300 feet and the descent continued to replicate some kind of ride at Disney World. I didn't have much longer to decide if I was going to land, or go around.

Land. Going around will just double the time to get beat up.

As I transitioned from water to land the airplane made one more dip and jump motion, and then as I crossed the runway threshold at 20 feet the air suddenly went still. With plenty of runway, I let the excess speed bleed off and slowly descended, landing about a third of the way down. The Pulsar landed firmly and squarely on the pavement. I stayed off the brakes and let the nose wheel lower with a chirp.

Within 100 feet I was at the second of three turnoffs, braking and then powering up as I taxied, overwhelmingly relieved, down the long taxiway to the terminal building. The tension drained from my body in waves as I took long, deep breaths.

I unclipped the canopy and pushed it forward. A slicing cold wind swirled around in the cockpit. The air was tangy with the smell of sea salt and pine. Memories of summer visits cascaded into consciousness with the fragrant Maine signature.

I taxied up to the terminal building. Behind the chain-link fence stood family and children. I shut down the Pulsar engine and pushed the canopy all the way forward. I slid up out of the cockpit and sat on the back of the seat, throwing my arms up in the air in jubilation. I felt the bite of the wind on my face and didn't care as I jumped down and walked over to the fence. I went through the gate and was quickly embraced by everyone.

A lineman ran over and asked me to follow him in the airplane. He pointed to a large hangar. I motioned to my family to make their way there.

The wind was howling about the taxiways and buildings as I powered the plane over to the hangars. Once again shutting down and then jumping out of the little plane, I pulled it into the large and clean hangar. I was especially glad now that I'd called well in advance to reserve a hangar spot for my visit.

Family members swarmed in and engulfed me and the plane, hugs all around once again. "Where's Heather?" I asked Jeff.

"A roast is in the oven, and making pies."

"Right. Well, let me check in with the FBO and do a post-flight check, and I'll be ready to go," I said as I continued to walk on air around the Pulsar.

"No rush. What an amazing tiny airplane this is," said Jeff. An outstanding photographer, he began snapping pictures as family lined up next to the airplane.

Even the FBO personnel were shaking their heads. "That's a wicked stiff breeze out theha, I haven't seen anything this small come in heah in this kinda of weathah." said the lineman. "Turbulent?" He looked at me with wide brown eyes.

I pursed my lips and nodded my head. "Very. I thought I was on a Wild Mouse ride."

"Ayuh, for shuah, for shuah," said the man in a downeast Maine accent that was a delight to hear.

"Home is the place where, when you have to go there, they have to take you in."

~Robert Frost

48

THE REUNION

WE PILED OUT OF THE CARS at the house in Northeast Harbor, 20 minutes south of the airport. Formally known as Mt. Desert Island, the area is best known as the home of Acadia National Park. The 1879 home we walked into now on Manchester Road had been Perky's mother's summer home. Graciously, Heather and Perky had been inviting family to visit since the early 1970s. Before that, we were all Maine summer campers on Sebago Lake. The summer tradition had made Maine a home away from home steeped in memories.

I drank in the sights and sounds in happiness, noting the smells of freshly cut grass and the sea breeze floating in from across the street, with notes of pine.

Heather came up to me as I entered the front door. I dropped my bags, and we hugged. I smelled baked apple pie mixed with roast beef gravy. Suddenly I felt ravenous.

"I can't believe you flew your plane here!"

"I can't either!" I replied.

"Any problems? Were you scared?"

"No problems, no scares," I lied.

"Thank goodness. I thought about you the whole time. Go put your things upstairs, cocktails in 30 minutes in the front room."

I made my way up the back stairs to my favorite corner room. Prim lace curtains hung in the old windows that still used rope and a counterweight to raise and lower them. A vase of fresh flowers stood on the dresser. I opened the window halfway. It would make for cozy sleeping.

I came back down the narrow stairs to the kitchen where Elisabeth and Jeffery were assembling trays of cheese and crackers and other hors d'oeuvres I couldn't identify, but knew would be delicious.

"You guys go out to the front room, I'll be along," said Heather.

Heather was the consummate hostess and entertainer. A chef extraordinaire, she was incredibly adept at assembling the right mix of people and food to turn the ordinary into supreme entertainment accompanied by epicurean delights.

Perky was at the bar in the front room.

"Beer?"

"Absolutely," I said, as Perky snapped the top off a Bar Harbor craft brew and poured it into a cold glass mug.

I sat down next to Dad. He wrapped his arm around me and smiled.

"So tell us about the trip," said Jeff.

I took a long drink out of the mug and set it beside me.

"It was excellent. I definitely had a combination of tension and excitement together, though. So much of it was new to me, like landing in Frederick." I told them about the hill on the approach to landing, and going around for another try. Knowing how my Dad and my sister felt about the airplane, thinking I was crazy to even think about building it, I wasn't going to share the more serious encounter with the turbulence.

"Lisa," said Dad, as he tightened his grip on my shoulder, "I have to apologize to you."

The room went quiet.

"I made a snap judgment. I assumed that your decision to build the airplane was not rational, not sensible, and that you hadn't thought it through. You know you've always had an impulsive streak."

Dad's been talking to Heather.

"No, Dad," I replied, with a wry smile, "Impetuous."

Everyone laughed, and it broke the awkward moment.

"But I want you to know," Dad went on, "that I'm very proud of you."

"Maybe wait until I make it back home before deciding," I said, raising my beer. More good-hearted laughter. Dad squeezed me tight.

That night I fell into a long and deep sleep, flying the Wild Mouse.

I awoke to the aroma of bacon and buttered toast. There's nothing else in the world like the olfactory richness of cooking bacon and toasting bread. Heather had started breakfast. Time to get up.

"What are you planning to do today?" Heather asked me as I arrived in the kitchen. She gave me a hug. "Flying?"

"Well, I do need to go to the airport and see if I can get the transponder fixed. It failed outside of Portland."

"I'm not going to pretend I know what that is."

"It's the piece of electronics that tells the air traffic controllers where you are on their radar screen. It's important if you're flying into controlled airspace. In my case, I don't have to have it, as long as I stay out of controlled airspace, which I can do." I didn't mention that it was a big added safety factor.

Family started to wander into the kitchen. In this house, the kitchen was the center of the social network. I helped Heather take food trays out to the dining room. She always put on a feast, no matter what meal it was.

Around the table we talked about the day.

"Lese, the weather forecast for the next four days is excellent. It's been raining until now, I'm glad you brought the sunshine with you," said Perky. "I expect you'll want to fly around?"

"Absolutely. I'll head out there after breakfast."

I thought about offering rides to the kids, but they didn't speak up, and I felt uncomfortable with the idea. I needed to get some experience with mountain flying. I knew it could be bumpy and unpredictable.

After clearing the table and doing the dishes everyone dispersed. Dad came up to me.

"Need a ride to the airport?" asked Dad.

"That would be great! You can see the airplane up close."

"Let's go."

The ride to Trenton was a drive of 18 minutes through postcard beauty. Passing Somes Sound on Sargent Drive, and then riding through forests and vistas, the drive was a delight all by itself.

"So the trip was really ok?" Dad asked.

"It was really ok, Dad. I'm not saying I didn't have some scares; I would have had some scares if I had been flying a Cessna 152. The airplane is reliable."

"I know you have low flight hours, so I was concerned about your depth of experience as well as it being a homebuilt airplane."

"True. I have about 215 total pilot hours."

"When you came out to San Antonio to fly the plane I was conflicted because I wanted to renew our relationship, but at the same time I didn't think the idea of an airplane built in a garage was smart, not to mention the financial commitment."

"Right."

"So, I had time to think about it, and I realized that I'm just trying to keep you safe. But life is full of risk. My feelings are complicated by the remorse I still feel for not seeing you more after I left your mother."

"That's ok, Dad."

I remembered all the times when Dad asked to see me and I'd told Mom no.

"When your Mom died, I really wanted to take you in, but your Mom wanted you with your aunt and uncle, and I also didn't think it would be a good idea for you to be brought up by Alexandra."

"Oh God," I laughed, "Not Alexandra! Remember the time I came to visit you and the dog tried to bite me? I think I was about 10 years old. I was terrified. Then Alexandra told me I was a ragamuffin. I didn't know what that was at the time. Good thing. I'm glad you left Alexandra for Pauline. Pauline is sweet."

Dad laughed.

"And then remember the time you took me into Boston," I went on, "to F.A.O Schwartz, and said I could pick something out? I think I was 9. I picked out a Superman costume. A little girl wanting to be Superman. You took me back to your apartment, and I put on the suit and loved it. You told me to just not jump out the window flying. Ha! See. You knew I could fly."

"That's a wonderful story, I'd forgotten that," said Dad, with a loud guttural laugh.

"Dad, listen. I'm the one who told Mom I wouldn't see you. It wasn't her fault, it was mine. It worked out fine with Bob and Sue. I needed some discipline. What matters now is that we established a relationship. Carrying around extra baggage from the past doesn't make sense. Right?"

We pulled up to the FBO parking lot. Dad turned off the car and turned to look at me. He reached over and took my hand in his.

"Lisa. I want you to know that I'm proud of you building and flying the airplane, and that I love you very much. I will support whatever you want to do."

"I love you, Dad." I squeezed his hand, and he smiled.

"Come on in and look at the plane."

We got out of the car and made our way into the hangar. In the corner was the Pulsar with a flat right tire.

"Oh, geez," I said, shaking my head.

A mechanic came up to us and held out his hand.

"I'm Brent, pleased to meet you." He shook hands with us both.

"I'm Lisa, the Pulsar owner, this is my dad, Jim."

"I didn't want to touch it without you here."

"No problem, I wonder why it went flat."

"Nail."

"Nail? Ok, well I'll have to stop driving this airplane on construction sites."

"Want me to fix it?" said Brent.

"No, no, that's ok, I've got a spare tube. But I was going to ask you yesterday, I've got a faulty transponder. Have you got someone on the field who could check it out?"

"Hmm." Brent walked over and looked in at the panel. "We'd have to pull it and send it off. A couple weeks turnaround."

"Ok, never mind. I'll need to stay out of controlled airspace is all." I tried to act nonchalant with Dad there, but I was concerned. I didn't like the thought of all the controllers in the northeast corridor not being able to see my airplane if I had to go into their airspace.

Dad didn't hear me, he was walking around the Bonanza parked nearby.

I spent about 20 minutes going over every item on my checklist, and paid particular attention to areas that could have been stressed by the encounter with turbulence. I shook my head as I realized everything looked perfect.

"What are you seeing?" asked Dad.

"Everything's great on it, it's amazing."

"That's a very good thing," said Dad, smiling. "A very good thing."

I changed the tube in the tire as Dad handed me tools. Then I pulled out a bicycle pump and pumped in 32 pounds.

"What time do you want me to return for you?"

"Three o'clock?"

"See you then."

"Far clouds of feathery gold, Shaded with deepest purple, gleam Like islands on a dark blue sea."

~Percy Bysshe Shelley

49

THE TALK

I PULLED THE AIRPLANE outside, not being able to stop thinking about the talk with Dad. It was more than I could have hoped for. The rollercoaster my emotions had been on in the last few days smoothed out onto a calm straightaway.

The wind was starting to come up as I finished my preflight and got into the cockpit. I took off to the north and doubled back to fly over Southwest Harbor. It looked so different from the air; dozens of harbors and inlets lined the islands, making it difficult to figure out what was where. For a time I simply flew southeast and looked in awe at the numbers of islands populating the Atlantic with emeralds sparkling across the waves in the afternoon sun.

The air was full of small bumps and dips, but they were consistent. I left 1,000 feet once I'd located my position, and flew over Northeast Harbor at 500 feet, following the coast around to the town of Bar Harbor. After the 20-plus years I'd been visiting the island, this astonishing view of the islands, trails, ponds, beaches, and other landmarks was thrilling.

I forgot about the bumps as I swooped down and around the cairn, the hills, the bald rocks at the top of the mountains, the streams. I was flying again in my childhood dream, enraptured by the passing landscape, buoyant and fearless.

■ ⸺ ■

The next day arrived with temperatures in the 40s accompanied by a silver-gray fog. It wasn't quite raining, but it wasn't flying weather. After breakfast most of us scattered about the house or went into the front room to read the paper or relax at the thousand-piece jigsaw puzzle spread out on a card table.

"I would never think to do this at home when I'm not on vacation," I remarked as I searched for green and white puzzle pieces to match a forest glen area.

"Right, we're working. Probably not the best use of our time at home," replied Jeff.

"You're so logical."

"Have to be. There's only so much time you know."

Jeff had a refreshing knack for stating the obvious in an interesting way, almost as if you were learning something for the first time even though you already knew it.

"And actually, the only time you have is right now," he said.

"And I'm wasting it on a puzzle."

"Only if you think you are. If you're enjoying it, then it's not a waste."

"I like your thinking," I replied.

"That's what it's all about. Your thinking."

Heather got up from her side desk. "Are you still going on a hike? It looks like the fog is clearing."

"Yes, let's go. I'll go upstairs and see who's coming," said Jeff.

Heather came over to the puzzle and immediately found the piece I was looking for and set it in front of me.

"How did you do that?" I said.

She shook her head. "It popped out. Are you hiking?"

"Are you?"

"No, I'll stay here, you guys go off. I have some calls to make, and I have some special desserts I want to make for dinner. Just bring me back some heavy cream for toppings."

Jeff came back downstairs and leaned in the doorway, "Come on! Lisa, are you coming?"

"No, I'm going to stay and work on some things."

"Ok, see you later."

Heather sat down at the puzzle. "I'll put two pieces in and then off to the kitchen."

I watched in amazement as Heather found three pieces for the sky area and put them in, in the space of 45 seconds.

"How do you do that?"

"I think I've done this one before."

"No, you're smart. Do you need some help in the kitchen?"

"I always need help in the kitchen. That's not your favorite thing, though Lisa, you just relax."

"No, let me help," I said as I followed her into the pantry.

"Ok, I'll welcome the company."

Heather went to the side room and brought back a bag of potatoes. Then she opened up a dog=eared book of recipes. Going to the refrigerator, she picked out a half dozen ingredients in various forms. I was awed. I didn't have a clue what she was doing. Heather could cook for 16 people and make it look like she had a staff of 25.

I made a concerted effort to not do anything creative in a kitchen. I figured if I knew what to do, people would expect me to do it. Thinking back to Jeff's comment about time, I thought cooking was a waste of time. But it's only a waste of time if you think it is. Obviously, Heather did not think it was a waste of time.

"Here, Lisa, will you peel these potatoes for me? Wash them first, and then you can sit here and put the scraps in this dish and the potatoes in this other dish. We'll have a choice of mashed potato or potato fries."

Amazing.

Peeling potatoes. I never figured out why people peeled potatoes when you could buy it already done. I finished washing them, I went back to the table and sat down with the assigned bowls and the peeler.

Heather sat down across from me and began to line a pie plate with a thin layer of crust. She had more to mix, and more plates. How many pies was she making?

Get brave.

"Heather. Can I talk with you about something?"

"Of course."

"It's sort of personal. Like, sister to sister?"

Heather stopped and looked at me with a concerned expression. "What's wrong?"

"You didn't come out with everyone to see me fly in."

"I was getting dinner ready."

"I know you were, but it was early enough that you could have come out."

"I didn't think buying and building an airplane was a good idea, Lisa. You're always putting yourself into financial risk, and with a kit plane, I don't know what other kinds of risk. I wish you'd be more conservative, save your money, and not always be pushing some kind of envelope." She went back to mixing piecrust.

I sighed. "I don't feel like I can please you. I'm not sure why I care so much, it might be because you're 10 years older than me, and you took care of me when I was a baby. So when I was growing up after Mom died, I substituted you for Mom. But the things I am drawn to and the things that I enjoy are different from what you enjoy. Can you accept that difference?"

Heather stopped mixing ingredients and looked at me. "Lisa, I'm sorry I'm critical. You may be right about the parent displacement, I did feel some resentment when I took care of you when Mom should have been doing it. That may be in the background psychology, but then as you grew up I was very concerned. The people around Mom at the time of her passing said that you would have difficulties navigating the social world and learning. You were so withdrawn. When I returned that Christmas when Mom was ill, I was shocked at the living conditions."

"Mom spoiled me."

"Yes, she did, but that wasn't your fault. But when I left you there, I felt guilty. I felt that I should have done more. So now I overcompensate by trying to direct your life. It comes out as criticism. Lisa, I am sorry." Heather started to lay the crust out in the bottom of a pie plate.

"But I should have listened to you when you said not to marry Randy." I looked up from the potatoes. "That was a three-year rolling disaster."

"I think you were trying to be conventional and please everyone," said Heather.

I put down the potato peeler, no longer able to focus. "I haven't helped things, though, jumping into projects without thinking them through. I'm lucky the bike shop turned out ok. I've tried different things and haven't found a passion until now. I loved building the airplane and even though learning to fly was not smooth or easy, I'm finding that it's the one thing that has given me confidence."

Heather got up from the other side of the table and came around to sit next to me. Her eyes glistened. "Lisa, families carry around lots of baggage, and I have plenty of it. I'm glad that we're having this talk, because I know I have upset you. I love you very much, I care for you very much, and my children can tell you that I can be difficult with them, too, when I don't think they should do something. I know I am critical."

I set the peeler down next to the bowl with the potatoes. "Do you realize this is the first time we'd had a heart-to-heart discussion? All the times we've been together and haven't made the time to communicate? Can we change that?" A tear spilled out of my eyes and rolled down my cheek.

Heather reached for the Kleenex box and passed me a tissue. A tear ran down her face. We looked at each other and began laughing.

"You're crying over the potatoes!" she said in a cry, and reached over to hug me. We both wept uncontrollably for several minutes.

I took a deep breath. "Whew, that was something," I said finally getting control of my voice.

"Yes, you're right, this is the first real talk we've had, Lese – Lese – I know that is your nickname, I've never gotten used to it but you like it, so I will like it."

"Look at the time, we've spent an hour talking. A great hour, Heather – I know I like to call you Sis, and you hate that."

"Jeffrey says Sis. I feel like he's teasing me."

"It's amazing how automatic our reactions are," I said. "You're always so busy, with so many people around, I never had the chance to get this kind of talk in. Last year when I was here – I kept hoping we could go sit on a rock by the water and talk – sister stuff – we never got the time,; you were so busy entertaining."

"I retreat into entertaining because it makes me feel like I'm making a contribution. I get lots of positive stroking, feedback, happiness from it," said Heather.

"I wish I had your ability to bring people together," I replied. "It's amazing to me, and your ability to talk about politics and history and be so informed."

"We are very different in what we are passionate about, we shouldn't let that get in our way," Heather replied. "I can't fix a bicycle or fly a plane."

"Heather, you mean so much to me. Can we talk more often, like this, without a million people around?" I dabbed the tissue to my eyes.

"Yes, we will. I'll make the time. I promise."

"I love you Heather, you know that."

"I know that. Lese, sometimes I just feel overwhelmed, and I react protectively. I express my love in a different way." She went back to the mixing bowl, and I looked around for the potato peeler.

"Understand. I wish I wasn't so dependent on everyone approving of what I do. I guess if I wasn't so sensitive then I wouldn't be so emotional," I sighed.

"Yes, but consider this. If you weren't sensitive you wouldn't be hurt, but you also wouldn't have the depth of wonderful emotions that drive our joy of living. We grow up seeking approval. It's normal and natural."

"It's painful," I replied.

"Well, right . . . you can't have approval without disapproval. I just think you took it too much to heart. Look at your concerted effort going back to school while you were working full time."

"I did it for Mom . . . and for you, to try to demonstrate I could navigate the world, and to . . . get approval. You're right, this stuff is complicated."

We laughed again together.

"Don't give up. It's a journey," Heather said.

"I won't give up. It's a journey alright."

"Look at the time! I guess we better get the potatoes ready and these pies in the oven." Heather looked over and smiled at me.

I'd just gotten off another Wild Mouse.

*"In the sweetness of friendship let there be laughter,
for in the dew of little things the heart finds its
morning and is refreshed."*

~ Khalil Gibran

50

PUZZLES

THAT NIGHT I FELL ASLEEP feeling lighter. I thought about the baggage analogy. I had no idea how heavy those bags could be, and how normal it felt to carry them around. My dreams were about flying again, but this time I was carrying baggage – several large trunks – in the Pulsar and I wasn't able to lift off. I stopped at the end of the runway and unloaded them onto the pavement. Then I taxied back to the runway and took off. Gus was in the airplane.

"What are you going to do without your baggage?" Gus asked me as we left the airport.

"I don't need it anymore," I replied.

The next morning when I woke up I relaxed a few moments before getting out of bed. A gentle breeze was streaming in the window, ruffling the curtains. The sun's rays were playing on the side table. The air was warm and smelled of pine and fresh flowers.

And now the smell of bacon and toast floating up the stairs and through the open door.

I threw the covers off and got up with a stretch. Soon I was going down the back stairs, into the kitchen. Heather and I hugged, a long tight hug.

"Good sleep?"

"Great sleep. I had a weird dream," I said as I helped Heather carry breakfast trays into the dining room.

"Tell me," said Heather.

"I was trying to take off in the Pulsar but I had too much weight in it. I had to stop at the end of the runway and drag two gigantic trunks full of stuff out of the back of the plane. They were like the trunks we used to take to summer camp. I left them on the end of the runway and then I took off!"

"Well, I know dreams can be weird, but that one sort of rings true. We did drop off the trunks of stuff."

"I feel lighter."

"I do too."

"Everybody leaves this morning. Won't it be nice, just you and I and Perky with one more day before you leave. Are you going to fly today?"

"I'd like to."

"I have shopping in Ellsworth, I can drop you at the airport and pick you up on the way back?"

"Great."

After goodbyes to the rest of the family, Heather and I drove to Trenton.

I leaned back in the passenger seat and delighted in the passing beauty as we drove on Sargent Drive along Somes Sound. The ocean breeze was cool, and the bright sunshine reflected off the small waves in diamond patterns.

"I'm so glad we had that talk yesterday," said Heather.

"I was just about to say that, you read my mind. I feel so comfortable," I replied.

"Let's not let that happen again – go so long without sister talks."

"You're the one who's surrounded by people, Heather." I was still trying to get used to saying Heather when I wanted to say Sis.

"You're right. I do that. Ok, we'll make plans for talks."

"Ok."

"Lisa, I mean, Lese, there's one thing that has always been a puzzle to me."

"What is that?"

"You had so much trouble in school, and then somehow you straightened out in college. You actually did well in college. Given the dire predictions of the child psychologist, how did you do that?"

I thought back to my college years. Smitten with Larry and his wonderful ability to build my self-esteem, I began to believe that I could actually navigate the school world.

"Two things. The first was Mom—I told you what she said to me before she went into the hospital–the second was Larry taking an interest in me. Then I developed "school rules.""

"School rules?"

"I was so afraid I wouldn't be able to catch up. I was overwhelmed. I told Larry. He said to take small pieces of the learning, and just do those well, even if I ran out of time.

"One night I was working on math problems. I was having trouble. I reframed my perspective by thinking of each problem as a stepping-stone to a flying project, or an electronics project. Since I love working on those, I'd treat the items I didn't like as necessary to get to the result – the airplane, the bike shop, the degree.

"This perspective got me interested. Once I had a few successes, with teachers giving me positive feedback, it was self-propagating."

"So you made it a rule, an approach?"

"Yes. And I added other rules, from observation."

"Tell me the rules, this is interesting."

"Rule One: Break the project into pieces you can handle. Rule two: Sit near the action. Teachers think you're smarter if you sit in front."

Heather started laughing. "You know I've taught history now for 30 years, and I never really thought about it, but the students that are paying attention and sitting near me automatically start out with more standing . . . subconscious reaction I guess."

"Rule three: Listen and speak up but don't be obnoxious. Rule four: Ask for help when you need it – you'd be surprised how many students try to breeze by."

"I'm not surprised."

"Rule five: Don't take detailed notes. Just main points, and record the lecture. You won't go back to them after the class, believe me, unless it's directly related to a project you're working on.

"The last rule is rule six, the most important rule. This rule says you must get really good at time management, and make decisions based on benefit. This means planning out what you'll do with your time instead of frittering it away. If you have a class tomorrow and you're not ready, you need to study first, play later."

"That's how you got through all of your night school classes, too?"

"Yes. It's all a series of hoops to jump through. It's not based on intelligence, it's based on persistence."

"Lese, that explains a lot. I was never able to figure out what was driving you. Now I get it."

"Heather, we've got to talk more, this is great. Thanks for listening."

We pulled up to the airport FBO, and I grabbed my pack and hopped out. "See you in an hour!"

I enjoyed the flight around the island. The weather was gorgeous, and the usual light turbulence no longer frightened me. Heather was standing at the fence as I taxied back in, smiling.

Later that day I was seated at the puzzle table in the front room, amazed at how quiet the house was without 10 other people moving about in it. The windows were open and I could hear the sound of lawn mowers across the street and the occasional whoosh as a car drove by.

Perky came into the room and sat down at the table with me.

"Watch out, Perk, this is one tough puzzle," I said.

"Yes. But your sister doesn't seem to have any trouble with it."

"I know. She's amazing."

"Speaking of your sister, it sounds like you made major progress yesterday."

"Perk, it was a breakthrough. All the tension I used to feel has fallen away. Being so on guard about what I would say, whether she would approve or not, has fallen away. It was the right time and place, I am so glad that it happened. I didn't realize what I was carrying around."

Talking to Perky was like talking to Obi-Wan-Kenobi. He'd really think over what you said before offering a thoughtful answer.

"Lese, it is what this house is about. It seems to bring people together. There's something magical about it. I am so pleased."

"Thank you," I said, placing my hand on his arm. "Do you want me to find you some puzzle pieces?"

"You'd better. I can't find any," said Perky, shaking his head.

We laughed.

"Lese, one more thing."

"Yes?"

"What I have learned in my almost 80 years of life is that our nature drives us to protect ourselves. Our defenses then cause us to imagine the worst. Then we suffer. And it's all because we thought it up and believe it."

"What if we take responsibility and control our thoughts?" I said.

"You can, and should, take responsibility, but control is an illusion. Have you noticed how thoughts and emotions will just pop in to your consciousness?"

"Yes."

"Here's a trick I use. Imagine you are on a raft, and you're in a sea with waves. The wave comes up to you and surrounds you, but you are above it. You are not immersed in it. Soon that wave moves on. Waves are the emotions – good and bad – that surround you every day. You can recognize them, but not let them hit you in the solar plexus."

"I'll try it."

As I looked at Perky, I thought about Larry. And I felt confused just as I did when Larry was giving advice.

"Ok, find me a puzzle piece, please," said Perky.

"Ok. I'll find the puzzle piece if you give me one more Zen answer to something else that's bugging me."

"I'll try."

"I'm 47 years old. Shouldn't I have figured out what life is all about and settled into a life-long career by now?" I handed Perky a puzzle piece.

"Lese, when we're growing up everyone else tells us we should have it all figured out. I'm not a social scientist, but I am going to guess that about five percent of the population ends up in one career and stays there. It's not a matter of how long it takes or who approves it; it's a matter of reflecting on where you are in each moment and acting in line with what's important to you."

"Where'd you learn all this stuff?" I asked as I handed Perky another puzzle piece.

"I told you. Almost 80 years of observing earthlings. Hey, this piece doesn't go to this puzzle!"

We both laughed.

"Thanks, Perk.

Granville Toogood, Heather Frazer, Lisa Turner,
Perky Frazer, Patricia Toogood

*"If ever there is tomorrow when we're not together...
there is something you must always remember. You
are braver than you believe, stronger than you seem,
and smarter than you think. But the most important
thing is, even if we're apart... I'll always be with you."*

~ Winnie the Pooh

51

MAINE TO MARYLAND

THE NEXT DAY HEATHER and Perky took me to the airport.
"Where'd I get all this extra stuff?" I was looking at all the bags
I had.

"Baggage!" exclaimed Heather. "We need to get you a trunk!
Maybe two trunks."

I loaded my duffel bag, backpack, cooler, and equipment bag
into the baggage compartment, a suitcase into the passenger seat,
and water and sandwiches in a smaller cooler into the passenger
side foot well. I strapped everything in firmly and did some final
calculations on weight and balance.

I looked at Heather and Perky.

"Thanks guys. What a great visit with you. I'm feeling
sentimental."

"It was a wonderful visit, Lese, I'm so glad you made the effort to fly up here," said Perky.

"And sister talks. We will continue them," said Heather.

"If your entourage lets us," I laughed.

After a careful preflight and goodbyes, I slipped into the cockpit and started the Pulsar. I waved and closed the canopy. I taxied out to 22 and took off, rocking my wings as I left. I was overcome with emotion as I left the airport, and I tried Perky's advice. Accept and settle down. I took a deep breath and picked up my flight plan.

I was starting to believe that all days were cool, clear, and sunny in the Pulsar. I'd been spoiled. Spoiled rotten, as my mother used to say. The spring growth provided a vivid green backdrop to the range of pastel blues stretching skyward, with a few transparent, fluffy clouds traveling slowly across the higher altitudes.

My trip back to Fitchburg and then to Frederick felt routine, since I'd already been to both airports. By now I figured I'd be able to handle the approach to Frederick. The first leg would be about an hour and a half, and the second about two and a half. If all went well, I'd roll into Frederick by 2 pm. I'd stay the night with my friend, Dick Kline, and launch again the next morning.

Flying at 8,500 feet, I was clear of controlled airspace through the high-traffic areas. I was still uncomfortable with not having a working transponder. But there was nothing I could do about it.

I refueled in Fitchburg, and the FBO personnel recognized me from my trip in the previous week. The airplane took about eight gallons for the 187-mile trip from Trenton. I was pleased. I had a light snack, called Dick with an ETA, and I was on my way to Frederick.

The two and half hours went by in a flash, and I found myself looking at the hill that had appeared as a "mountain" the first time in the pattern. This time I didn't have any trouble with it and was able to land the first time around.

Experience counts.

Marty, my favorite line boy, led me to a hangar for the overnight. I'd made the reservation months ago, not knowing how busy the airport would be. I was glad now, as I looked at the massive hangar, packed with fancy airplanes. We backed the Pulsar into the corner next to a stunning white-and-blue striped Learjet 45.

"This is a picture," I remarked to Marty, looking at the sleek white Pulsar with the blue stripe next to the svelte white Learjet with a blue stripe that was 20 times heavier.

"Want to trade?" Marty said with an impish grin.

"No way."

After a post-flight inspection, I grabbed my duffel and cooler and headed to the FBO where Dick was waiting for me. I'd known Dick since the late 1970s, and we'd struck up a close friendship.

"Good trip?" asked Dick as we hugged each other.

"Excellent. I'm beginning to think that this glorious weather will never end. Which is fine by me."

"A front is coming through tomorrow, though I'm not sure what time. You know you can stay as long as you want."

"Thanks Dick, but one of these days I'll need to return to work, right?"

"It's a thought. Hey, I'd love to see the airplane tomorrow when we come back."

"Sure," I said as we got into Dick's car. "It's parked next to a Learjet. I told the line boy I wouldn't trade."

"Clouds on clouds, in volumes driven, Curtain round the vault of heaven."

~Thomas Love Peacock

52

HAZE MAZE

I WOKE UP WONDERING where I was, still engaged in the tail end of a vivid dream. As consciousness returned, I tried to remember the details of the dream—something about sailing the sea in a raft—but it evaporated as I remembered where I was. Maryland. The first thing I did was pad over to the window and look out. All I saw was a white mist thick over the lake.

The sun will burn it off.

I got dressed and packed up, assuming I'd be able to fly out. I heard Dick downstairs and smelled fresh coffee. I made my bed and straightened everything up, leaving a hand written thank you note on the bedspread. I headed downstairs.

I gave Dick a hug and kiss and inhaled the steam coming out of the coffeemaker. He picked up a mug and filled it, handing it to me.

"Ahh! This will do the trick," I said.

"Doesn't look too good outside, Lese."

"I noticed. But hopefully the sun will burn it off?"

"Do you still want to go to the airport this morning? You know you can stay another day, it's not a problem."

"Thanks Dick, I appreciate your hospitality. I'd love to stay another day, but I've got a timetable to return to work. I probably should have built more leeway into it. This is the first time I've ever taken two weeks off. I could get used to it."

"I'm retired and spoiled," laughed Dick.

After breakfast we drove to the airport. It was socked in. We parked and I led Dick to the hangar where my Pulsar was parked next to the Lear.

"That is a sight! A cute tiny airplane next to a handsome big airplane. Imagine if you could get a cross between the two—an offspring—it would be interesting," Dick said as he looked over the Pulsar. "But I can see why you wouldn't trade."

"A cross would be very curious, especially the engine," I laughed.

"I'll head home, Lese, but if you have to stay here tonight, just call me and I'll come get you."

"Thanks Dick," I said as I gave him a big hug and kiss. "I'll see you in Florida." Dick wintered in Fort Lauderdale.

As Dick was leaving Marty, the line boy, came up to me.

"Need anything?"

"No, I'm good. Looks like the place is socked in though."

"Yeah. It'll burn off. There's a notch in that hill over there," Marty pointed out into the white mist at nothing, "that will show up when the airport is VFR. You could leave IFR?"

"I could leave IFR if I was instrument rated."

"Watch for that notch." He waved out into the nothingness again.

I guessed I would know it when I saw it.

I took 30 minutes to perform a thorough inspection of the airplane. I cleaned the canopy and double-checked the straps on the bags and coolers. As I thought back to my turbulence episode, it was remarkable that everything in the airplane stayed strapped in and that there wasn't any damage. I wanted to keep it that way.

I walked over to the FBO and called Flight Service for the latest weather. If I could get out of this fog, VFR conditions prevailed to the south. I sat down and studied my flight plan and charts. I'd listed all the alternate airports I could go to if there was a problem.

After an hour with no improvement I began to worry. With one stop in Lumberton, the trip time into Hazlehurst from Frederick was five hours. I planned to arrive at 2 pm, and now that had slipped to 3:30 pm. I walked back to the airplane.

Goes with the territory. You need your IFR rating.

I remembered Jeff's words about creating problems by internalizing them. It's a non-problem. Make the best decision and go with it. If you need to stay another night, then stay another night, I thought.

Marty came around the corner of the hangar and startled me out of my reverie. "See? There's the notch!"

I looked up, and sure enough, there was a faint notch in the hill looking straight out from the hangar. It was still, in my estimation, pretty misty. I heard engines starting.

"Get in line!" said Marty.

I jumped up and pulled the airplane out.

A line there was. It looked like everyone else had waited for the notch to appear too and were anxious to go. I enjoyed the looks toward the Pulsar and people waving to me. I guess I looked unusual, the small Pulsar in between Bonanzas, King Airs, and Mooneys all lined up for Runway 23.

I listened carefully to the heavy traffic and was absorbed in the scan for other aircraft as I departed to the south. While the report had said VFR, it seemed to me that it was marginal. I wasn't comfortable with the visibility as I approached 1,000 feet. I wondered whether I should turn back.

I stayed at 700 feet as I observed the layer above me. Concern filled my thoughts as I reduced power slightly, afraid of not seeing something in time. I remembered that radio towers could be higher than I was now, and the foothills would be off to my right. Looking at the chart and peering outside, I realized I couldn't thread the narrow corridor between Washington and the mountains safely and legally without getting above the mist.

Turn around.

Suddenly I saw a blue patch of sky above. And then another.

Let me see.

I moved the throttle forward and powered up quickly through the gap at 1,000 fpm. At 2,000 feet I took a good look at the layer to make sure I could get back down if I needed to. It was spotty, but there were lots of gaps where I could see the ground. I still felt a little trapped and wasn't completely comfortable as I powered up to 6,500 feet. I hoped that this wasn't a portent for the rest of the day.

Little did I know.

I studied the chart and reviewed the GPS track on the Garmin 250XL. I was in the right spot in the VFR corridor, neither impinging upon Washington D.C. Dulles airspace nor wandering over into the Appalachian foothills. But my senses were on high alert, realizing that I did not have a working transponder, and scanning like a hawk above a spotty cloud layer that could close in at any time. The two hours to Lumberton were nerve-wracking.

There was no change in the layer as I descended toward my fuel stop. I let down through a large gap in the clouds at about 1,500 feet and oriented myself. There was no traffic in the pattern, and I felt relieved to land. The FBO personnel were pleased to see me on my return trip and several guests in the FBO lounge came out to have a look at the Pulsar.

After refueling with 12 gallons, I went into the FBO to call Flight Service. The report was surprisingly good, but I now knew that what the report said and what it looked like could be two different things. Then I put in a call to my friends in Hazlehurst to let them know I'd be rolling in around 5 pm. I heard excitement in their voices.

"How's the trip going?"

"Great," I replied. No use trying to explain LEPN, or Low Experience Pilot Nerves.

I left the pattern to the south and climbed back up through a large open area in the lower layer. Before I learned to fly, clouds were clouds, all in the same flat dimension. Now, I see clouds in multilayer 3-D when I view them, noticing texture, color, and formation.

I settled in at 6,500 feet. I could see gaps in the lower layer, but my uneasiness returned. The intensity of my visual scan was exhausting. The weather was technically VFR, but I felt as if I was in a huge white walled room where anything could come around the corner as a surprise requiring fast action. It was very different from my trip up that same coast a week earlier. I looked down at the landscape passing by in the cloud gaps. The rich farmland had given way to rolling fields and Georgia swamp.

Forty-five minutes from my destination the upper cloud layer began to descend towards me, and the sky darkened slightly. I looked at my panel clock, which said 4:20 pm.

It shouldn't be getting dark yet.

I looked down, and the gaps in the lower layer were filling in with mist. I dialed up an ATIS broadcast to see what was happening at nearby airports. To my surprise, the report indicated five miles visibility. I found this hard to believe, given my view out the canopy.

I need to get down out of this.

I slowed the plane to 130 mph and descended through one of the last gaps in the lower cloud layer. It was amazing to me how fast weather could close in. Just when you thought you had everything under control and had plenty of time to take evasive action, you were behind the curve.

I continued to descend to 700 feet, where I thought I'd be able to see obstacles and be a safe distance from the layer I'd just passed through. I looked down at the landscape and saw only swamp and forest, with few signs of civilization. I got a prickly feeling on my skin thinking about a forced landing. Tendrils of mist were sliding across the treetops, reminding me of the everglades on the trip up.

I concentrated all of my attention outside the canopy, trying to see through the dark mist. I scanned the panel and then took a quick look at the chart. The nearest airport was Hazlehurst, my destination, 15 minutes away. I scoured the forest again for any sign of a road. Nothing. I felt my muscles get more and more rigid as the tension rose.

I can't land here.

How was it possible that I was still VFR but felt as if I was in a small dark room that was getting smaller? I alternated looking out into the mist for obstacles and examining the chart for towers and obstructions. As I was focused on the chart for one very brief moment, I thought I heard the engine miss.

My mind is playing tricks on me.

I listened. There it was again, a faint blip in the beat of the engine. Was I imagining it? I scanned the engine monitor and the gauges. I heard it again. The engine missed a beat. Wait. I took off my headset to listen. Now the wind was louder than the engine as I listened. I heard the frequency dip and then return. I put the headset back on. There it was again.

Uh oh.

I looked down at the forest swamp, hoping for a roadway. Nothing. I was 10 minutes out and called the Unicom at Hazlehurst.

"Hazlehurst traffic, Pulsar Experimental Four Five Six Lima Tango five miles out inbound for landing on one-four."

"Hazlehurst Unicom. No traffic here, come on," said a friendly female voice with a southern drawl. It broke through my anxiety, and I had to smile.

Without warning the engine went full rough. It sounded like someone had removed half of the spark plugs. It was on the verge of completely stopping.

Be logical.

I started the emergency checklist that I'd committed to memory. I switched fuel tanks and flipped on the fuel pump. Before I could make an emergency radio call, the engine completely smoothed out and even the little blip in frequencies that had started my panic was gone.

I took a shallow breath and listened carefully. Fine. A bead of sweat dripped off my brow on to the sectional I had in my lap. I was on a base leg for Runway 14 and finally saw roads below me. I took a breath.

"Hazlehurst traffic, Pulsar Six Lima Tango on base for one-four."

"No traffic, come on," said the Unicom lady again in her southern-accented convivial tone. This time I laughed out loud, relieved and amused at the same time.

Without thinking any more about the cause of the engine problem I concentrated on my landing. My hands were still trembling slightly as I descended over expanses of pine trees. I landed squarely on the 4,500-foot runway, which was pockmarked and full of weeds, repairs, and stress cracks.

The landing was rough, and bouncy, but I didn't care. I back taxied down the single runway and turned off at the FBO. FBO? It was a small building with a barking dog and my friends waiting patiently nearby, with the Unicom Lady and the Hazlehurst newspaper photographer.

"Be like the bird who, pausing in her flight awhile on boughs too slight, feels them give way beneath her, and yet sings, knowing she hath wings."

~Victor Hugo

53

THE SANDY BEACH

MY BODY WAS STIFF WITH tension as I pushed myself up on to the back seat of the cockpit.

"You're here!" exclaimed Lori. "This is amazing!"

"I'm sorry about the runway. It's sort of rough," said the all-in-one Unicom lady who was also the FBO airport manager.

"Can I get a picture of you next to your plane?" said the photographer.

I shook my head. "Sure, but what's so exciting? Lori, what have you been telling them?"

Lori laughed. "I called up the newspaper and said you're a celebrity for building your own airplane and flying it to Maine by yourself."

"Well, thanks for that, but it's not that big a deal." I hopped down from the wing and posed for Hazlehurst's *Jeff Davis Ledger*.

"Hi, I'm Sally," said the Unicom lady. "Let me show you your hangar space." We shook hands.

"I'm glad you have some hangar space, because I had a problem on the way in that I'll have to fix before I can leave tomorrow," I said, as I removed my backpack and cooler. Lori picked them up and placed them in the car nearby.

"What is it? Serious?" asked Al, .

"Yes, a fuel problem. I almost lost the engine."

"Goodness. Can we help you?"

"Sure, let's get it into the hangar." I grabbed the prop at the root and led the airplane behind the all-in-one Unicom lady to the open hangar door.

Lori and Al followed. I'd met the approaching-retirement-age couple 10 years previous when they lived in Boca Raton, Florida. We'd spent time boating, fishing, and diving, and had become close friends.

Sally led us into the large building. You could have put 40 cars or 20 airplanes in this space. It was massive. A layer of dust covered the floor. Against the walls were antique aircraft parts, lawn mowers, tractors, a few antique cars, sickles, and tools. The innermost recesses of the hangar were dark with cobwebs and furniture. The air was humid and musky as we entered. You could smell the swamp sulphur of the Georgia wetlands.

"So the engine quit?" asked Lori.

"Almost. I switched tanks, and it smoothed out. I am expecting to find a problem with the left tank, the one I was running on. The visibility was low, and I was concentrating my attention outside, so I didn't see or hear any fuel pressure drop. Usually you get an alarm from the engine monitor when something goes out of range."

I removed the toolkit from behind the back seat and removed the pilot seat cushion. Lori and Al pulled up lawn chairs and sat down.

"Fuel," I mused, "look in tanks; check sumps; check connections, hoses, and filters." I went through the checklist.

"Well, I'm glad you were so close to the airport," said Al.

"Me, too," I affirmed, scrunching my face.

Everything looked fine until I got to the filters. I had fitted three clear glass and metal filters to the fuel system for the Pulsar: one on the exit for each tank and then one after the auxiliary pump. I had a suspicion that the problem would be in the filter exiting the left tank, but I worked my way from the carbs to the tanks methodically, checking everything.

Reaching the left tank, I looked through the glass at a clog that filled the entire capsule. "Look at that!" I exclaimed.

Lori and Al came over to look.

"Looks like cotton," said Al.

"It's fiberglass," I replied.

"What will you do? I wouldn't know where to get one of those filters around here," said Al.

I reached into my parts bag. "You mean one of these?" I held up another glass filter and replacement mesh screen.

"You think of everything."

"Have to." I got out a plastic bag and vinyl gloves and quickly changed the filter. "I'll change the others too, you never know."

Fifteen minutes later the filters were changed and everything was back in the airplane. "Let me just clean the bugs off the canopy and we'll be off. I'll do the testing in the morning."

We drove out of the airport as the sunlight was setting across the surrounding forest, fading yellow rays leaving shadow patterns on the road. I took a deep breath and felt a cloak of comfort surround me as my friends chatted from the front seat. I was back in the airplane, thinking of the trip home. I felt different. I felt stronger.

That night I fell into bed exhausted yet invigorated.

I thought I heard a voice. Where was I? Floating down a stream; the raft with the rope across the middle. The rapids had turned into a slow, gentle current. The water was clear and I could see brightly colored rocks on the bottom of the river. It felt familiar. Where was I?

I looked to the right, and I was being pushed into a cove with a sandy beach, passing shiny black rocks, the sand glistening and shining like tiny diamonds. I got out of the raft and sat on the beach.

I couldn't see Mom, but I heard her voice. I felt the presence of others. The collective consciousness of all the people I loved and had friendships with and who had helped me at each stage of my life seemed to be there somehow.

This has to be a dream.

An instant later Mom was sitting next to me and I looked at her. It was so comforting to see her. She embraced me with her vibrant blue eyes. She looked wonderful.

"Suffering, loss, and the ups and downs are life's very fabric. Instead of struggling, relax. As your shyness tries to protect you from fear, it introduces it. Allow it to fall away, and embrace the full range of experiences, both good and bad."

A light wind rustled through the trees, and the sand was warm and soft under me. I picked up a handful and let it sift through my fingers. Everything seemed to be glowing.

"Accept each moment as it comes to you. The trip – the path – the journey – is not about arriving or getting, it is about right now, right here. Shift from self-consciousness, which is fear based, to conscious awareness where you drink in everything in front of you.

"It's not easy. If it was, humans wouldn't be so caught up in struggle, panic, and fear. Whatever spiritual path you're on, you will realize that each of us is not separate. We are all in this together." My mother touched my hand and smiled.

Rather than feeling the confusion and loneliness I often felt when talking philosophy with Perky, Gus, or Larry, I felt as if I understood what my mother was saying. I felt a warmth, a sense of safety, a sense that I could stop the world and breathe, if for a moment. I felt calm. I felt confident.

"It feels good to be lost in the right direction."

~ Anonymous

54

THE FOG WALL

BACK AT THE AIRPORT the next morning, I went through my checklist. Lori and Al, and the Unicom lady were watching my preparations.

"If you guys have other things you need to do, feel free to do them," I said. "I don't want to suck up all your time, you've been so gracious already."

"Wouldn't think of not being here for your takeoff home," said Lori. "Don't forget, we're retired. We have nothing else to do except hang out, if it's ok with you."

"First thing is I'm going to do some fuel flow testing. I'll take off and do some circuits, come back and check it, then if everything is good, I'll be on my way."

"Why did that filter clog up?" asked Al.

"Because the pilot didn't realize how much junk was in a brand-new fiberglass tank, that's why. Check, check, and re-check. I didn't realize how long it would take to clear out."

Moist warm air flowed through the cathedral-like space of the hangar. The air was still, and a mist hung through the trees. I preflighted and then pulled the Pulsar out on to the rough and cracked pavement in front of the hangar. I got into the plane and started the engine. As the oil temperature came up, I listened carefully as I switched from the right tank to the left. It sounded perfect.

"Ok, I'll be back!" I shouted as I closed the canopy. I taxied out to the pockmarked runway, thinking I really didn't want to take off and land on it again, but there was no choice. I had to test the fuel system before leaving for home.

I took off to the south and stayed in the pattern. There were no airplanes in the vicinity and the radios were quiet. I concentrated on switching tanks and watching fuel flow and pressure. After 20 minutes of not being able to replicate the problem from the day before, I landed to say goodbye to my friends. The landing was rough, like the day before, and I held off the nose wheel as long as I could. I imagined what all of this vibration was doing to the airplane and hoped that everything on the craft continued to be as tough as it appeared to be.

I said my goodbyes, checked weather, and I was on my way. I back taxied to 32 and took off into a pastel blue sky streaked with a beige haze. The visibility was better than the day before, but had a blurry kind of look that I hadn't seen before.

Acutely tuned to the sound of the engine, I scanned the fuel pressure and flow over and over again. In the tension of the flying the day before, my scan had failed to catch the dropping fuel pressure on the left side. I resolved to be more attentive.

With a cloud layer at 4,000 feet, I decided to stay at 2,500 feet. The problem with this altitude was that if I encountered a problem over the thick forest passing below, I would not have much time to find a safe spot to land.

As I looked out the canopy into the cloudiness ahead, I saw a change in coloring and the shape of the air. I couldn't make out what I was looking at. It was almost as if I was looking at a false horizon that stretched from one side of my vision to the other and stretched up into the sky as far as I could see. It felt as if I'd been dropped into a cage where the air was clear but a reflective mirror was shining white light back towards me.

I looked down to see desolate stretches of sand-colored land with scraggy pines. A few straight roads came into view, along with an occasional farmhouse and plowed field.

I looked up again to see the strange reflective object in front of me. It appeared to be a cloudbank – transparent in spots and solid in spots. I was having trouble estimating how close it was, and its size. Should I turn around? Should I climb? Could I exit out the other side? I'd never seen anything like it.

In the moment that I was forming a decision about the mystery, I was suddenly inside it. It wasn't a single cloud with an exit on the other side. It was a massive fog wall. As I realized my mistake, I knew that I would be in very serious trouble if I didn't exit the mass immediately. I needed to turn around, and turn around fast.

Non-pilots remark that they don't understand how a pilot can lose control and crash an airplane just by not being able to see the ground or flying at night. In a flash I recalled a conversation with a friend.

"Why can't you keep the airplane stable in a cloud? Don't you have instruments to look at?" she asked.

"Yes, you have instruments to look at. But a VFR pilot may not have the experience and confidence to realize that the instruments are correct."

"I don't understand that."

"When you don't have a horizon to look at, the brain relies on the inner ear. The problem is that the inner ear recognizes short-term shifts and then resets. Once you *think* you are diving, or turning, without the visual stimulus your brain assumes that is what you are doing and those signals go out to your senses. This is why we call it a 'seat of the pants' sensation – you believe it unless, like an IFR-trained pilot, you know how to stabilize your visual field on the instruments and follow them without question. Any pilot who has experienced spatial disorientation, however brief, can tell you it is terrifying."

Now I was there. I quickly realized I was second-guessing whether I was still going straight. Had I bumped the stick? I needed to turn. I felt panic well up in my chest and my breathing got shallow.

Instruments. Start a low bank turn. Now.

I began a left turn, feeling as if it was getting tighter and steeper than it should be. I glanced outside the cockpit. Mistake. All white, nothing to see. Too fast! I'm turning too fast! Pull up! My heart was beating like a drum.

Lock on the instruments. Don't look out.

I focused my vision on the turn-and-bank indicator and the airspeed again. I saw that I was in a constant rate 30-degree bank and holding altitude. My butt didn't believe it for one minute.

Keep on. Steady.

I felt the airplane steepen its turn and descend. The instruments had to be wrong! I was falling.

No. Don't look outside.

My vision stayed locked on the turn-and-bank indicator, altimeter, and airspeed. I'd made a 180-degree turn and straightened the wings. I popped back out of the cloudbank as quickly as I'd entered it, suddenly in clear air with a bright sky.

I had lost all of 25 feet in the death-grip effort. Relief washed over me as I continued back the way I had come, the airplane seemingly impervious to my machinations.

Thank you, Ellen. All that time you put me under the IFR hood paid off today.

I took a breath and entered "nearest airport" into the GPS comm. I wanted to get on the ground, calm down, and find out what this weird fog wall was all about.

The Baxley Unicom sparkled to life with friendliness, and I looked down incredulously at a runway that had been freshly paved. Was I dreaming? I taxied up to a beautiful little FBO. The inside was nicely appointed with a fully equipped flight service area. Maybe I'd actually perished, and this was my version of airport heaven.

After a call to Flight Service, which indicated continuing IFR conditions below 8,000 feet, I thought about the wall of fog. I had never seen anything like it. I sat down with a cup of coffee, still rattled at my very serious mistake getting too close to the wall.

Another lesson.

I realized that I'd been very lucky to turn around and get out of the cloud bank so fast. It was a tribute to the training I'd received, even though I hadn't gotten my IFR rating yet. Now I fully understood how a pilot could get turned upside down and not know it. As I sat in the lounge in nervous relief, another pilot came in and sat down.

"You see that experimental out there?" said the middle-aged man. He had a shock of dark brown hair that fell across his brow.

"The Pulsar?" I replied.

"Is that what it is? It's gorgeous. I'll ask the owner if they will trade it for my Velocity."

"No, I won't trade it for your Velocity."

"Ha! It's yours. Pleased to meet you, my name is Paul." He reached out and demonstrated a handshake my mother would have been proud of. "Where ya goin'?"

"Palm Beach. Lantana, actually."

"I just came from Palm Beach," said Paul.

"Oh wow, I just bumped right up to that massive fog wall out there, you must be IFR?" I asked.

"No, I'm flying VFR. Just climb up–10 or 11 thousand feet is good."

"But VFR, you have to be able to see the ground."

"You can – there are plenty of gaps," said Paul.

"Really?" My spirits lightened.

"Are you sure you won't trade airplanes with me?" Paul laughed as he pulled charts and paperwork out of his flight bag.

"I'm sure." I smiled. "Thanks for the pilot report!"

"Sure. Take care."

I returned to the Pulsar.

Let's see if I can conquer the Wall.

"Today is the only day. Yesterday is gone."

~ John Wooden

55

THE FLIGHT HOME

I LEFT THE PERFECT AIRPORT called Baxley and took off to the east, turning and climbing. As I flew back to the south, I searched for the wall. Was this a trick? Had it disappeared? But no, as I got closer, continuing to climb through 6,000 feet, I saw the wall. And now I understood how I could have mistaken it for a simple cloud of mist. It didn't reach all the way to the ground, but was clear in spots, with tunnels in other spots, and all the while moving and dancing with the wind currents. Its upper structure was stronger and darker.

I climbed to 7,500 feet, seeing a clear demarcation between the top of the wall of white and the blue iris-colored sky. Puffy round clouds sat on the top of the flat dark mists like abstract museum creations. I'd have at least 1,500 feet of clearance if I stayed at 9,500 feet. I decided to fly over the wall and look down to see if I could actually see to the ground.

Reaching 9,500 feet, I flew over the top of the massive cloudbank. Some sections were so solid they looked like you could walk on them. I peered down and saw the puffs and threads of dark gauze connecting them. Clear zigzag tunnels ran to the ground below. When I looked down, the landscape was visible.

Good.

It was legal for me to fly above the clouds, or "on top" as it is called, as long as I could see enough of the ground to get down. But it's a judgment call. The experience of flying just above a puffy white cloud layer that stretches to the horizon was new to me. I'd seen it in a commercial airliner of course. But being in a 900-pound airplane a little more than three feet across in the cockpit with 12 feet of wing on each side and not even 20 feet of length was a different experience altogether.

I had a sight gauge that I could use to determine the height of anything in front of me. I pulled the gauge up now and sighted over the billowy beds. Ahead it appeared that clouds would bar my way, but the gauge indicated that they were the same height as the clouds under me – 8,000 feet.

Looking forward, I saw wavy multi-shaped cloud masses all the way to the horizon and from side to side as far as I could see. The blue colors of the sky began with pastel at the margin and deepened to cobalt and then to a deep marine streaked with pinks, yellows, and whites. I was in a theater of shape and color.

Without reference to outside objects, the small airplane felt perched atop the cloud layer, stationery, belying the 165-mph groundspeed showing on the GPS.

The air coming through the vents had turned warm, and I squirmed out of my light jacket, placing it in the passenger foot well. I leaned back in the seat and exhaled deeply, taking in several gulps of the fresh air. The tension that had built up from the wall encounter was draining away, leaving a comforting calm. I pushed my shoulders back against the seat and stretched my legs in the foot well.

As I settled down and relaxed, the cockpit seemed to disappear in the expanse of light and color, and I was floating across a field of cloud, untethered and unfettered.

The air smelled like a fresh spring field – how could that be so high up? I felt the mild vibration and beat of the engine and the constancy of the winds flowing over the canopy and wings. The ride was as smooth as skates on clear flat ice. I thought about clear air turbulence and instinctively tightened the seat harness.

I scanned the panel and then the sky, and looked below to make sure I could still see gaps in the clouds. The GPS on the 250XL showed me approaching the airspace gap between Kennedy Space Center and Orlando. This was a busy area. Being at a high attitude was a big safety factor, but not having a working transponder was a wildcard.

As I scanned the sky, my eyes locked onto two dark masses ahead of me. They were moving very fast from left to right. They were so fast that I could only register in my brain that they were military jets. It gave me a start. I grabbed the camera from the right seat. As I pressed the button on the camera, the jets became black dots on the horizon. To this day when I show people the photo they laugh and tell me it's just a couple of bugs that got caught in the film.

Did they know I was here?

Military jets do have onboard radar. But I couldn't imagine how they would see my tiny fiberglass airplane at the speeds they were traveling. I passed through the busy corridor and felt relieved as I watched the Space Center airspace outline retreat in the display, listening to the chatter on the radio.

At almost 10,000 feet above the earth I looked out on the mercurial colors of the sky, a fabric stretched into infinity. The radiance of the midafternoon sun streamed through cloud strata above me in yellows and pinks. The air seemed effervescent.

I thought back to the words in my dream the night before: *The trip – the path – the journey – is not about arriving, it is about right now, right here. Shift from self-consciousness, which is fear based, to conscious awareness where you drink in everything in front of you.*

I thought about my beginnings right here 10 days ago, when I thought my trip would end with a swamp landing. I felt as if I'd grown in the measure of eons since then. I also felt sentimental, thinking about the friends and family who'd helped me along the way. While the proof would be on the ground navigating life, I felt very different returning home now in my special airplane. I was filled with the things I had searched for so long – self-awareness, and self-confidence.

I get it.

I scanned the sky and then the instruments. All was well. I took a long look below me and picked out the biggest gap and headed for it. I spiraled down through the tunnel in the clouds and kept a lookout around the plane. Finally, just when I wondered how much deeper the tunnel would be, I broke out below at 5,000 feet. I continued to descend to 3,500 feet and headed offshore to stay out of Palm Beach airspace.

I looked to the west and saw a thunderstorm forming. I estimated that my timing getting back into Lantana would be good, but close. I kept an eye on the darkening skies.

The air was warm through the vents. The growing currents rocked the little plane slightly, and I reduced speed to 135 mph. As I cruised out over the ocean the dark clouds parted to the south and the sun filtered through in fingers of light stretching across the ocean surface. The sun glinted off the high-rises of Palm Beach, perched on the ocean's edge. A manta ray sped along the white sandy bottom close to the beach. Schools of fish darted away from the shadow of my airplane over the teal-infused water. Brightly colored Hobie-Cats crisscrossed the reefs a mile offshore.

I floated above this in my small white-and-blue Pulsar, coming home. I was filled with happiness as I turned toward Lantana and made my position calls. I felt as if the airplane and I were one single machine as I glided over the runway and landed smoothly.

I taxied over to the hangar. Gus was waving, and the mechanics were scurrying around inside. I let the engine idle for a moment and turned the key off. I turned off the master switch and listened as the gyros wound down. I pushed the canopy forward and slid up in the seat.

"Hey!" The hangar mechanics motioned to me. I looked over and saw them pointing to the west. I hadn't realized it, but the sky was darkening quickly and they were telling me to get my plane into the hangar.

I jumped to the ground. The wind picked up suddenly, a chill ran through the humid air, and large raindrops started to splatter on the hot pavement. Gus ran out and helped me pull the airplane into the hangar as the sky opened up and the rain came down in torrents.

Gus looked at me. We gave each other a long, silent hug.

"Hey, hey, you guys, settle down," said Dave, as he came up to us. "Where's mine?" I grinned and gave Dave a hug.

"So, good trip? Doesn't look like the Pulsar is worse for the wear. She still looks brand new," said Dave.

I smiled. "It was great. You know how people say, 'you don't know what you don't know?'" I asked.

"Yeah."

"I found out there's a lot I didn't know."

"Journeys are like that," said Gus.

"Dave, the transponder failed before I got to Maine."

"Oops, no airspace for you."

"Right. But all's well that ends well," I said.

"We'll pull it today and send it off. Figure two weeks. It's not standard."

The rest of the mechanics finished bringing miscellaneous items in to the hangar as the rain pounded the tarmac and the metal roof. They came over to us.

"Did you ever get here just in time," said Andy. "This frog pounder would have beat your little Pulsar into the ground."

"I saw it from the air. I keep forgetting how fast they move," I said.

I exhaled and sat down on the hangar floor in front of the right Pulsar wing where I could look out. Gus sat down next to me. The floor was cool, and a breeze blew in smelling of ionized rain and hot pavement.

"I missed you Gus. You would have loved the trip. Or, maybe not."

"Are you saying there were 'drink-a-six-pack' moments?"

"Ah, yeah." I thought about the swamp trap, the haze, the near engine out, and the fog wall. "I learned a lot."

"I expect you gained a lot of confidence," said Gus.

"You're a mind reader."

"How did things go with your family?"

"Let me see if I can explain it."

Gus looked at me expectantly. I looked back and realized I was at a loss for words.

"Ah, I guess I can't explain it. But something happened. I think I went from 12 years old to 47 years old in a few days."

"That doesn't sound so great," laughed Gus.

"Ok. Let me try again. If you're on a hike, and you're going up the side of a mountain, you'll travel through valleys and streams and climb rocks. This is all fine, and you think that's all there is. Because it's all you can see.

"But then you get closer to the top. And it may be harder, with more obstacles, and you might get confused because you're not sure where you are. Yet you keep on.

"Suddenly you come out on top. It's a 360-degree view out over the landscape. The sun is out and the valleys are full of color and vibrancy. You can see where you came from down in the valley. And now, you can see where you're going."

Gus kept looking at me, smiling. "Could you make it a little more down to earth? Put it in one sentence."

"Ok. Everything is just fine as it is."

"That's better, even if I don't understand it. But, stay impetuous."

I laughed and put my hand on Gus's shoulder. He put his arm around me.

We gazed out at the rain changing to a light sprinkle falling on the glistening ground. Steam was forming, dancing in swirls, and evaporating off the pavement. The sun began to sift through the clouds. We looked to the sky and watched as a brilliantly colored rainbow formed over the small airfield.

END

"You are exactly where you need to be."

~ Unknown

EPILOGUE

Lisa met her soul mate less than a year after returning from her solo journey. Deciding to build another airplane, she met Jerry who was teaching an EAA SportAir fabric-covering class.

She decided to return to engineering and got her airframe and powerplant mechanics rating (A&P) and her designated airworthiness inspector (DAR) credentials. Along the way she became a home inspector and wrote a book about it. Lisa and Jerry now run an antique aircraft facility in North Carolina.

Glossary

Aeronautical Terms Used in this Book

GENERAL

Airspace classes – Airspace classes are designated around the world to help keep airplanes from running into one another and to help in navigation. They are three-dimensional. For example, Class C space around an airport means that there is a specific space around the airport that you can't enter unless you have permission. The airspace is shown on navigation charts. You need a transponder to enter some types of airspace.

ATC – Air Traffic Control – A service provided by ground-based controllers who direct aircraft on the ground and through controlled airspace and can provide advisory services to aircraft in non-controlled airspace.

ATIS and ASOS - Automated Terminal Information System and Automated Surface Observing System – reports that help the pilot plan for, and avoid poor weather. Can be obtained in the cockpit.

IFR – Instrument flight rules. Means navigating primarily through the use of instruments in the cockpit aided by airport electronic position signals.

VFR – Visual flight rules. Relates to navigation as it relates to visibility and distance from vision limiting conditions like fog or clouds. Ex. "Clear of Clouds."

INSTRUMENTATION

Airspeed Indicator – An instrument that shows speed in knots or miles per hour, in relation to the outside air

Altimeter – An instrument that indicates altitude above sea level

Attitude Indicator – An instrument that shows aircraft in relation to the horizon (level); climbing or descending (pitch), and left or right roll (turns).

CHT – Cylinder head temperature.

Compass – An instrument showing aircraft heading relative to magnetic north

DG – Directional Gyro, or heading indicator. Can also be HSI, a horizontal situation indicator.

EGT – Exhaust Gas Temperature.

Engine Monitor – Varies from simple to sophisticated, a computerized device that measures and monitors engine and sensor parameters and can sound an alarm if a reading is out of range.

***g* Meter** – An instrument showing rate of acceleration, in "*g*s" - in relation to the force of gravity; $1\,g = 32.2$ feet per second per second at sea level.

GPS – Satellite navigation system that shows the airplane in relationship to features on the ground.

Tachometer – Measures revolutions per minute in an engine; a measure of speed, thus power.

Transponder – Radio transmitter that works with ground radar to identify an aircraft's position, altitude, and call sign, generally for air traffic control.

Turn Coordinator – Shows rotation about the longitudinal axis, often with an inclinometer to show slip or skid.

VSI – Vertical Speed Indicator – shows vertical rate of climb or descent (feet per minute in the Pulsar)

AIRPLANE PARTS

Aileron – The ailerons are located at the rear of the wing, typically one on each side. They work opposite to each other, meaning that when one is raised, the other is lowered. Their job is to increase the lift on one wing while reducing the lift on the other. By doing this, they roll the aircraft sideways, causing the aircraft to turn. This is the primary method of steering a fixed-wing aircraft.

Elevator – As the name implies, the elevator helps "elevate" the aircraft. It is located on the tail of the aircraft and directs the nose of the aircraft either upward or downward (pitch) in order to make the airplane climb and descend.

Flaps – Flaps are a "high lift/high drag" device. Not only do they improve the lifting ability of the wing at slower speeds by changing the camber, or curvature of the wing, but when extended fully they also create more drag. This means an aircraft can descend (or lose altitude) faster, without gaining airspeed in the process.

Fuselage – The body of the airplane.

Horizontal Stabilizer – The horizontal stabilizer is quite simply an upside-down wing, designed to provide a downward force (push) on the tail.

Rudder – The rudder is attached to the vertical stabilizer, located on the tail of the aircraft. It works identically to a rudder on a boat, helping to steer the nose of the aircraft left and right; this motion is referred to as yaw.

About The Author

Born in Waltham, Massachusetts, Lisa Turner has had a long and diverse career beginning with owning a bicycle repair shop, serving as the chief training officer for Tyco Fire & Security, working as an airframe-and-powerplant mechanic, and as an aerospace manufacturing engineer.

Lisa and her husband, Jerry Stadtmiller, run an antique airplane restoration facility in North Carolina. Lisa is also a freelance writer for numerous aviation publications, and the home improvement columnist for the local newspaper, the *Clay County Progress*.

Lisa holds an Associate of Science in Engineering, a Bachelor of Arts in English and Philosophy, a Masters in Business, and a Doctor of Science. She has served as adjunct faculty at Nova Southeastern

University, Palm Beach College, and Tri-County Community College.

Lisa has published five books. See them on her Author Page on Amazon: Visit Lisa's Author Page: https://www.amazon.com/Lisa-Turner/e/B018O79HFO and on Facebook: https://www.facebook.com/LisaTurnerBooks.

THE BACK PAGE

Find out more about the story!

For a companion guide and other free self-discovery pdfs, visit my web page:

www.DreamTakeFlight.com